IRAQ: THE CONTEMPORARY STATE

Also published by Croom Helm for the Centre for Arab Gulf Studies, University of Exeter:

Social and Economic Development in the Arab Gulf
Edited by Tim Niblock

State, Society and Economy in Saudi Arabia
Edited by Tim Niblock

Iraq: The Contemporary State

Edited by
Tim Niblock

CROOM HELM
London & Canberra

ST. MARTIN'S PRESS
New York

© 1982 Tim Niblock
Croom Helm Ltd, Provident House, Burrell Row,
Beckenham, Kent BR3 1AT
Croom Helm Australia, PO Box 391,
Manuka, ACT 2603, Australia
Reprinted 1983

British Library Cataloguing in Publication Data

   1. Iraq – History – Congresses
   I. Niblock, Tim
   956.7'043   DS79

   ISBN 0-7099-1810-0

Library of Congress Catalog Card Number: 82-42566

ISBN 0-312-43585-1

Printed and bound in Great Britain by
Biddles Ltd, Guildford and King's Lynn

093458

CONTENTS

Contents

TABLES AND FIGURES

Tables

Figures

PREFACE

Most of the chapters in this book were presented as papers to a symposium entitled 'Iraq: the Contemporary State', which was convened at the University of Exeter in July 1981. The symposium was held under the joint auspices of the Centre for Arab Gulf Studies (University of Exeter) and the Centre for Arab Gulf Studies (University of Basra). The editor wishes to thank the directors of the two Centres, Professor M.A. Shaban (Exeter) and Dr Mustafa al-Najjar (Basra), for having made the symposium possible. Thanks are also due to the members of staff of both Centres—upon whom the burdens of organisation fell.

Iraq is a country which the outside world will need increasingly to understand. The scale of Iraq's oil reserves, the effects which domestic Iraqi political developments may have on the stability of the wider Gulf region and the aspirations of the present Iraqi government towards playing a leading role in the Gulf and the wider Arab world all provide cause for interest and perhaps concern. Unlike most Arab oil-producing states, moreover, Iraq has substantial agricultural resources as well as hydrocarbon resources: the pattern of investment of Iraq's oil revenues could have a significance stretching well beyond the country's borders. This book does not seek to cover the whole range of social, economic and political developments in contemporary Iraq. The object, rather, is to provide some insights into these developments, and in this manner to shed some light on the factors which determine the direction of events.

Mrs Sheila Westcott deserves the editor's thanks for typing the manuscript, as expertly as ever, and Mr H.G. Balfour-Paul for undertaking the chore of proof-reading, without complaint. Acknowledgement is also due to The Middle East Review Co., Ltd for permission to reprint the general map of Iraq.

Tim Niblock

Figure 1.1: General Map of Iraq

Source: The Middle East Review Co., Ltd.

1 INTRODUCTION

Tim Niblock

The historical record shows Iraq (or the area now covered by Iraq) to have been a difficult country to govern. Over the past 150 years there have been few prolonged periods when conditions of internal order and external relations have provided reassurance for those in authority. Since the military *coups* of 17 July and 30 July 1968 formal authority in Iraq has rested with the Revolutionary Command Council, which has seen its role in terms of providing a framework within which the policies of the Arab Ba'th Socialist Party could be implemented. The outbreak of war with Iran in September 1980 seems destined to have significant effects both upon Iraqi domestic politics and upon the country's relations with the outside world; an apposite time would seem to have been reached, therefore, to take stock of Iraq's economy, society and politics.

To conceive of Iraq having a historical record of tortuous domestic politics and frequently disrupted international relationships may, no doubt, give a misleading impression—implying that the causes of disharmony have remained the same throughout. The most critical factors leading to dissension in the domestic and international fields have, in fact, often been specific to one particular incident or period— perhaps stemming from the nature of the class structure at that time, or from the objectives pursued by an outside power in the region. There have, nevertheless, been some continuing sources of dissension and disarray: on the domestic scene, the pattern of ethnic and sectarian division—with the tendency for these divisions to have economic and social dimensions (i.e. involving groups with different modes of economic life, different roles in the class structure and different prospects of access to central government resources); and on the international scene, the country's geographic and strategic position—standing on the fringe of the Arab world, in an area where the cross-cutting interests of prominent non-Arab regional powers (Iran and Turkey), Great Powers and a highly varied collection of Arab states and shaikhdoms have posed inevitable problems.

Up to the outbreak of World War I, the area now constituted by the state of Iraq formed three provinces of the Ottoman Empire, the

1

*vilayet*s of Mosul, Baghdad and Basra. Each *vilayet* was administered by an appointed governor answerable to the Sultan in Istanbul. The power of the Ottoman government to direct affairs in the provinces was, at times, limited, especially in Baghdad from the early eighteenth century through to 1831, when a caste of Georgian *mamluks* arrogated to themselves effective authority. The middle and later parts of the nineteenth century saw a steady strengthening of Ottoman control. The Ottoman government sought at this time, albeit in a haphazard manner, to create modern forms of administration in the area (as elsewhere in the Empire), and to administer policy directly rather than delegating power to semi-independent tribal leaders or feudal chieftains.

Three aspects of the new Ottoman policy were to be of some significance for the state of Iraq as it subsequently emerged. First, some elements of the population (led by tribal leaders or feudal chief-tains whose authority was threatened by the expansion of Ottoman power) came to resist Ottoman intrusion into traditionally locally-controlled affairs. The Ottomans encountered severe resistance from the Kurds in the 1840s (a conflict in which Persia became involved), and sporadically from the *shi'a* tribal confederations of southern Iraq. The growth of incipient Arab nationalist ideas in the towns at the end of the nineteenth century and the beginning of the twentieth century sprang from similar ground. Second, with their strengthened position in Iraq, the Ottomans felt able to assert their influence in the Arab shaikhdoms of the Gulf—thereby establishing an interest and some territorial claims which the independent state of Iraq was to pursue. Third, in 1870 Midhat Pasha (possibly the most effective of the Ottoman governors who held authority in Baghdad) introduced a new system of land registration, intended to make possible a more coherent use of agricultural resources. The land was supposed to be registered in the names of those who were cultivating it, but the realities of social custom and local political power ensured that large tracts were registered in the names of tribal leaders. The role of tribal leaders, therefore, was ultimately strengthened: economic power reinforced a social position which might otherwise have become in-significant. The landowning tribal leaders were to constitute a vital pillar of support for the monarchical regime established in Iraq after World War I, and a barrier to any social or economic reform.

The outbreak of World War I found Britain and the Ottoman Empire—traditional allies in the nineteenth century—on opposite sides. In November 1914 Britain, acting in response to an Ottoman attack upon the sea ports of Russia, declared war on the Ottoman Empire. An Indian Army brigade was despatched on the British government's instructions to capture Mesopotamia (i.e. the Ottoman *vilayets* of Baghdad and Basra). By the end of 1918 almost the whole of today's Iraq was held by the British and in April 1920 Britain was formally given the League of Nations mandate over Iraq. Thus started Britain's involvement in Iraq – an involvement which was to remain even after Iraq became independent in 1932. Britain's role was of crucial importance in setting the parameters within which Iraq's political system moved between 1920 and 1958. On the one hand, it was Britain which installed a Hashimite monarchy in Iraq (choosing Amir Faisal, son of King Husain of the Hijaz, to be king), arranged the pillars of support necessary to maintain the monarchy and determine the regime's character and exerted a continuing influence on the internal and external policies pursued. On the other hand, British involvement constituted a focus around which opposition forces could rally – in the uprising which occurred in 1920, in the movements which came together to oppose the Anglo-Iraqi treaties of 1922 and 1930, in the attempt which Rashid Ali al-Gailani made in 1941 to attract German support and renounce Iraq's obligations to Britain and in the militant anti-regime demonstations of the mid-1950s initiated by Iraq's entry into the Central Treaty Organisation.

The governments which ruled Iraq under the monarchy were not without their achievements. Following the initiation of oil production in 1934, substantial funds were invested in schemes of agricultural development, in expanding social and educational services and in building a communications infrastructure. The coherence of development policy was strengthened by the creation of a Development Board in 1950, which was so structured as to give its technocratic members a relatively independent role in formulating and implementing policy. While there was considerable governmental instability, moreover, the unity of the new state was maintained – largely by ensuring that those with economic power and social influence in the provinces remained well disposed to the central government.

The character of central authority changed considerably (and frequently) between 1920 and 1958: the firm rule of King Faisal I (1921-33) gave way to the rather weak rule of his son Ghazi (1933-9), and that in turn to the somewhat conspiratorial politics of the Regent Abd al-Ilah in the 1940s and early 1950s while King Faisal II (1939-58) was an infant. The military first intervened in politics in 1936, imposing on King Ghazi a government headed by Hikmat Sulaiman, and remained a potent political force — whether or not they formed the government — through to 1941. From the mid-1940s through to 1958 the regime became increasingly identified with the man who held the position of prime minister over the greater part of this period: Nuri al-Said. Whatever changes may have occurred in the character of the central authority, however, the nature of the regime remained largely constant: political power was the prerogative of a relatively small group of individuals who manoeuvred in cliques to attain power. Close links were at all times maintained with the regime's 'pillars of support' in the countryside. With the expansion of the economy and the educational system the political manoeuvring within the regime became increasingly irrelevant to the mass of the population. New social groups were emerging — an expanded proletariat and an educated middle class — with new social demands, to which a narrowly based government, limited by its need to retain the support of large-scale landowners, was unable to respond.

In July 1958 the monarchy was overthrown. The ten years which followed can best be seen as a period in which those who had conspired to overthrow the monarchy vied for control of the republic. Significant social and economic reforms were undertaken: land reform was enacted, thereby striking at the power of the landowners who had kept the monarchy alive, and the state took an increasingly active part in directing and controlling the industrial sector. The links which had joined Iraq to the Western world were disrupted and new relationships were established with the Soviet Union and the countries of Eastern Europe. Yet many of the new programmes and policies were ineffectively pursued, due to the political instabilities following from the struggle for power. The outbreak of the Kurdish rebellion in 1961, moreover, further complicated the task of pursuing coherently the country's economic and social development.

The *coup* of July 1958 brought Abd al-Karim Qasim to power, in alliance at the outset with a loose grouping of Communists, Kurds, Ba'thists, National Democrats and Arab Nationalists. Over the five years which followed Qasim lost the support of each of these groupings. His overthrow in February 1963 was carried out by a combination of Ba'thist and Arab Nationalist military officers. Although the presidency was placed in the hands of Abd al-Salam Aref, a non-Ba'thist army general, the Ba'th Party played the predominant role in the government which succeeded Qasim's overthrow. A campaign of severe repression against the Communist Party was initiated. In November 1963, following attempts by the Ba'th Party to entrench its hold on power, Abd al-Salam Aref ousted the principal Ba'thist leaders from the government and dismissed senior Ba'thist military officers from their posts. To the extent that organised civilian involvement in government continued, it was a loosely organised grouping of Arab nationalists and Nasserists who provided the regime's civilian base. In April 1966 Abd al-Salam Aref was killed in a helicopter crash and was succeeded by his brother, Abd al-Rahman Aref.

The Ba'th Party's take-over of power in July 1968, therefore, came at the end of a period of prolonged instability. Political conditions had not created a favourable environment to ensure the success of such attempts at social and economic reform as had been made. An analysis of the contemporary politics, economics and society of Iraq, therefore, involves an assessment of the extent to which, and the manner in which, the period since 1968 has seen a distinctively different record of practice and achievement than that before 1968. Although the chapters in this book are not directly geared to making such an assessment, their content and conclusions should provide the basis for an assessment to be made.

The chapters cover six broad areas of interest, each of which constitutes an important element in the overall basis for making an assessment of the kind mentioned above. First, in an evaluation of the general character of the regime Joe Stork (Chapter 3: State Power and Economic Structure: Class Determination and State Formation in Contemporary Iraq) examines the class basis of the state, concluding that while there is no large Iraqi bourgeoisie as such whose interests are served by the state, the state itself functions as a bourgeoisie, on behalf of the leading elements in the state apparatus. Peter Mansfield (Chapter 5: Saddam Husain's Political Thinking: the Comparison with Nasser) uses the comparison between Saddam and Nasser to point up an aspect of the Ba'thist regime which, albeit emanating from a very different perspective and approach than Joe Stork's chapter, is not necessarily incompatible with it.

Second, the government's record in working towards a reasonably homogeneous society yet one in which sectional interests are catered for is evaluated in four chapters. Sa'ad Jawad (Chapter 4: Recent Developments in the Kurdish Issue) examines the events which followed the March 1970 Kurdish autonomy agreement. Amal al-Sharqi (Chapter 6: The Emancipation of Iraqi Women) presents an account of the means whereby Iraqi women have achieved liberation in recent years, while Amal Rassam (Chapter 7: Revolution within the Revolution? Women and the State in Iraq) seeks to explain why that liberation remains limited and incomplete. Alya Sousa (Chapter 8: The Eradication of Illiteracy in Iraq) shows how the government has sought to use a campaign against illiteracy as a means to bridge social divisions.

Third, agricultural development is assessed by Robin Theobald and Sa'ad Jawad (Chapter 13: Problems of Rural Development in an Oil-Rich Economy: Iraq 1958-1975). They chronicle the rather disappointing record in this sphere, tracing the causes to failures in planning, the effects of political instability and the nature of peasant society. J.S. Birks and C. Sinclair (Chapter 15: The Challenge of Human Resources Development in Iraq) lay emphasis on a further aspect: the growing proportion of women and children in the agricultural labour force.

Fourth, in evaluating the all-important oil sector Paul Stevens (Chapter 12: Iraqi Oil Policy: 1961-1976) shows that while Iraqi oil policy has failed in its most crucial aim—to raise the capacity of production—this failure has been rendered irrelevant by rising oil prices.

Fifth, in studying development planning and industrial production, John Townsend (Chapter 16: Industrial Development and the Decision-Making Process) identifies the principal constraint on efficient production as lying in the cumbersome decision-making process. While this is of little significance as long as industrial production is geared towards a heavily protected domestic market, it will become important when Iraq seeks to enter highly competitive export markets. Rodney Wilson (Chapter 14: Western, Soviet and Egyptian Influences on Iraq's Development Planning) documents the stages through which Iraq's development planning has passed, tending towards—but never actually reaching—the stage of comprehensive planning.

Sixth, in the international field H.G. Balfour-Paul (Chapter 2: Iraq: the Fertile Crescent Dimension) looks at the objectives which pre-1958 Iraqi governments pursued towards their Arab neighbours to the West, while Tim Niblock (Chapter 10: Iraqi Policies towards the Arab States of the Gulf: 1958-1981) and Barry Rubin (Chapter 9: United States-Iraq Relations: a Spring Thaw?) examine more recent aspects of Iraqi foreign policy in a manner which reflects differing perceptions of the dynamics of Iraq's foreign relations.

2 IRAQ: THE FERTILE CRESCENT DIMENSION

H.G. Balfour-Paul

Perspective

During much of the twentieth century the Fertile Crescent has been a term used to denote both a geographical area and a political concept. This chapter is concerned with the second of these meanings and more particularly with the Fertile Crescent concept as it appeared in Iraqi perspectives between 1920 and the 1958 revolution.

First, however, the term should be defined in its geographical connotation. Although the expression itself does not seem to have been current till well into the period we are considering, the crescent-shaped area concerned has generally been taken to stretch in a semi-circular curve from Basra to Beersheba, embracing Mesopotamia and the whole of Syria (in its Ottoman or 'geographical' sense) or what were once the *vilayet*s of Baghdad, Basra, Mosul, Aleppo, Damascus and Beirut: in effect, that part of Arab Asia over which Ottoman rule was ever seriously exercised. The same area can alternatively be described as consisting of all the territories subjected by the San Remo treaty of 1920 to either British or French mandate: Iraq, Palestine, Transjordan, Lebanon and residual Syria.

Fertile Crescentry as a political project came in several sizes, and several shapes. Before projecting them on the screen something, however superficial, must be offered by way of a prologue. Most people would nowadays agree that, when the Ottoman Empire fell apart in World War I, it did so into pieces which were in one way or another predetermined. To say that is by no means to reject outright the familiar Arab dictum that western imperialism carved up the Arab world (or in this case Arab Asia) to suit its own convenience. A good case can be, indeed has been,[1] made out for the charge that the 1920 share-out of the Arab lands in Ottoman Asia had been agreed by London and Paris as early as 1910, railway concessions being recognised in both those capitals as *jalons posés pour un partage éventuel de la Turquie en Asie*. Be that as it may (along with all other imperialist contrivings of those, and later, days), there is evidence enough that the Arab provinces of Ottoman Asia were edging slowly towards regional

7

autonomy and separatism since the mid-nineteenth century —
conditions envisaged initially within, and latterly outside, the Ottoman
framework.

The extent to which the structure of the Ottoman *vilayets* (or the
mamluk episode in Iraq or the Ma'an/Shihabi experience in the
Lebanese mountains) may have fostered these separatist Arab tendencies, or indeed the extent to which the progressive breakaway of
the Empire's European provinces may have set a chain reaction in
motion in its Asiatic ones[2] — all this lies outside the range of this
chapter. Nor can any fresh assessment be offered here of the degree to
which the various Arab societies set up before World War I in Damascus
and Beirut represented a new sense of unified Arab (as distinct from
Ottoman or Islamic) community. This chapter starts from the date
when the division of the Fertile Crescent had already been determined,
arbitrarily or not, at San Remo. Mesopotamia, Palestine and Transjordan were under British mandate: the rest of Ottoman Syria was under
the French, who proceeded to split it initially into smaller quasi-
autonomous states of Aleppo, Damascus, Latakia, Jebel Druse and, of
course, Greater Lebanon — a process which prompted even British
Foreign Office officials to minute with terse disparagement: '*Divide
et impera*' and 'A curious form of independent government'.[3] Conflicting
war-time promises of Arab independence (at least as the term was
understood by Arabs) showed few signs of implementation and, in
Britain's case, were already complicated by the Balfour Declaration and
its evolving consequences.

What attempts, then, were made in the forty years that followed
San Remo to destroy the frontiers that were there demarcated within
the Fertile Crescent? Who made the various attempts? What were
their differing motivations? Why did they fail?

1920-39: Britain, France and the Unity of the Fertile Crescent

It will be remembered that, as a climax to the wartime collaboration
between mainstream Syrian nationalists and Sherif Husain's family, the
General Syrian Congress in March 1920 took two decisions. The 89
representatives of geographical Syria (they included a fair proportion
from Lebanon, Palestine and Transjordan) conferred the throne of all
Syria on the Amir Faisal, while the 35 representatives[4] from
Mesopotamia nominated his elder brother Abdullah King of Iraq. Both
these resolutions were overturned by the mandatory powers as

pre-empting the outcome of the Peace Conference; but a point of some relevance is that even in the flush of a shared victory over the Turks — shared, that is, by participants from both ends of the Crescent — two separate monarchies were envisaged by those assembled at the Congress, not one single one, though the declared intention was that the two independent states should be federated, politically and economically. The reunification of geographical Syria (not a wider unity) was what the Syrian Congress in July 1919 had urged on the King-Crane Commission; and Faisal himself, in his address to the Peace Conference in January of that year, had looked to the 'formation of such new States (*in the plural*) as are required'.[5] It is also worth observing that Arab nationalists were in those days, and indeed for years to come, still thinking in monarchical terms, as a principle virtually unquestioned: republicanism was a wave of the future.

The Western repudiation of the Syrian Congress's resolutions and the conferment of the throne of Mesopotamia on Faisal (not Abdullah) in 1921 set in train the most conspicuous of the earlier post-war movements towards unification of the Fertile Crescent. King Faisal himself, despite growing awareness that his own pan-Arab vision might not be wholly reconcilable with the particularist instincts of some of his Iraqi subjects, strove throughout his life for the union of Iraq and Syria as a step towards the unification of the Fertile Crescent with other parts of Arab Asia.[6] Although by the time of his death in 1933 he had by no means despaired of achieving his primary aim, Faisal recognised that no political restructuring of the region was feasible without British and French sanction, and he acted with singular loyalty on this understanding.

The responses Faisal received from London and Paris were various and on one occasion unexpected. The Middle East policies of Britain and France, both before, during and after the period of the mandates, were seldom harmonious. Seen from London, the present difficulties arose from two main causes: a difference in the way the two powers interpreted the legitimate exercise of influence in their respective spheres, coupled with continuous and largely misplaced French suspicions that Britain was covertly seeking to undermine France's position, not least by supporting, in her own perfidious interests, moves for the unity of the Fertile Crescent. In fact, British state papers disclose marked British aversion in official circles to the unity project in the 1920s, 1930s and 1940s — and this for several reasons (which we shall come to later), but largely because the Anglo-French *entente* took precedence in London over all other local compulsions. So — and this is

what was meant above by the one unexpected Western response to
Faisal's unity proposals—it must have come as something of a
surprise to London as well as Faisal that, on his visit to Paris in
September 1931, he should have been addressed by his French hosts
as 'King of Iraq and Syria' and even as 'King of all the Arabs'.[7] This,
of course, took place soon after the signing of the Anglo-Iraqi Treaty
of 1930 which, by looking forward to the termination of the Iraq
mandate and giving the Iraqis at least some degree of independence,
had obliged the French to re-examine their own policies in Syria and
Lebanon. But whatever the French motive in 1931 in fostering Faisal's
hopes of kingship over a united area, they surely already knew that,
despite the encouragement Faisal had been receiving from certain
leading Syrians[8] such as Faris al-Khouri and from the Aleppine
People's Party, the general mood in Damascus and in the influential
National bloc had by now turned towards separatist republicanism.
Indeed, the Syrian Assembly's constitutional proposals of 1928
(repudiated by France) were focused by the dominant National bloc
on achieving the political reunification of geographical Syria, not (as
the People's Party had been urging for some years) on the unification
of Syria and Iraq.[9]

For Faisal himself, apart from his pan-Arab aspirations and an
understandable desire to recover for himself the lost throne of Syria,[10]
unification of Syria and Iraq may have had other attractions, internal
to Iraq. He would perhaps have welcomed a reinforcement of Sunni
Arabs amongst his subjects (Iraq on its own having a Shi'ite majority);
and Iraq's ethnic minorities, not least the Kurds, would be more easily
absorbed in a larger whole. It might also, as he certainly hoped, lead to
the ultimate incorporation within a single Iraqi-dominated
confederation of the Hijaz and even Najd[11] and thus reverse the
humiliation of the Hashimites by Abd al-Aziz ibn Saud.

By October 1931 the official but undisclosed British view[12] was
that the best outcome for Syria (in its reduced French shape) lay in a
republic under a Syrian president. If in the event the Syrians preferred
a monarchy, no objection was seen in London to Sherif Husain's
eldest son Ali being offered a throne; but a combined Syrian-Iraqi
monarchy under Faisal was judged unworkable. So British governmental
support for Faisal's proposals, which he recognised as a *sine qua non*,
was never forthcoming. The response he regularly received from London
was that the best thing for the Arabs was that each Arab country
should develop itself first: the prosperity of each would advance the
prosperity of all.

The main potential advantage to Britain of Faisal's ideas, restated from time to time by Nuri al-Said, was that Jewish settlement in Palestine could be painlessly absorbed by the Arabs in a unified Fertile Crescent. Indeed this thought remained a recurrent element in Fertile Crescent thinking for years to come, though only a minority in the British establishment ever endorsed it as a possible solution to the problem Britain had created for herself in 1917. Even the canvassing by Faisal, or by Yasin al-Hashimi on his behalf in November 1932, of his proposals for an Arab Congress in Baghdad met with British discouragement. Moreover, by this time a new element had established itself amongst the unpublished British objections to Faisal's aspirations, namely the rise to a key position in the Arab jigsaw of Abd al-Aziz ibn Saud, whose hostility to all Hashimite plans had increasingly to be taken into account. For this and other reasons, notably consideration for French sensitivities and Zionist pressures, the British, while favouring closer economic and cultural relations between individual Arab states, continued to withhold support for any form of political unification. And when Faisal made what proved to be his last personal bid for British backing, on his state visit to London in July 1933, the Foreign Secretary's promise of a considered reply[13] had not been fulfilled by the time of Faisal's premature death three months later.

The view that was meanwhile being taken of all this by the Iraqi public is less easy to establish. Certainly there was more than one. Many of the intelligentsia[14] were zealous pan-Arabists, some (encouraged by Ataturk's abolition of the Caliphate in 1924) dreaming of an Arab Caliph, some – like the influential Sati al-Husri – canvassing unity in secular terms and on a wider front than the Fertile Crescent.[15] Nor was al-Husri the only thinker of those days to regard the unification of Germany under Bismarck as an inspiring model and Iraq as the Prussia of the Arab world.[16] But the cry for unity, even in Iraq, found no concrete or generally accepted form. And at least one contemporary observer from outside[17] reached the conclusion that the average Iraqi – not just the ethnic minorities – did not view Faisal's project for union with Syria with enthusiasm, reckoning that the more sophisticated Syrians would swarm into Iraq and pick up all the good jobs arising from Iraq's oil discoveries (which had reached commercial proportions in 1927). Indeed the suspicion was already being entertained by British officials that in the event of union between Iraq and Syria Damascus would prove a more attractive capital than Baghdad (a thought that may perhaps explain the French welcome for Faisal in 1931 as 'King of all the Arabs') and that Iraqi loyalties to Faisal would suffer accordingly.

As the 1930s proceeded on their fateful course developments in one area of geographical Syria, that is, in Palestine, were increasingly occupying the minds of the British and of the Arabs throughout the area as a whole. One of the few Arabs who initially welcomed the abortive British partition proposals of 1937 was Amir Abdullah of Transjordan,[18] who was never backward in exploring any prospect of expanding his own small fiefdom. He appeared continuously on the Fertile Crescent stage from 1937 for a whole decade, meeting throughout this period a measure of support from inside Syria but unrelieved opposition to his territorial ambitions from the rival Hashimite court in Baghdad. There, the young King Ghazi was by now enjoying his brief role as the idol of Iraq's junior pan-Arabs and even some of Syria's;[19] but amongst the weightier advocates of Fertile Crescent unity or federation, Nuri al-Said was still dominant. Under his leadership the Iraqis opposed Britain's 1937 proposals for the partition of Palestine and also opposed, at the Palestine Defence Congress in Cairo the following year, a Syrian proposal for the reunion of Palestine and Transjordan with Syria.[20] Both these attitudes are indicative of the motives underlying Nuri's Fertile Crescent thinking.

At the London Round Table Conference on Palestine in February 1939 Weizmann formed the impression that Nuri's posture was primarily motivated by his yearning for a permanent outlet for Iraq on the Mediterranean coast of Syria.[21] Certainly it went beyond that, as we shall see; but in general Nuri still pinned his faith on British sympathies, encouraged so far as concerned the future of Palestine (for which he had constantly demanded independence) by the 1939 White Paper. By the autumn of that year, unfortunately, the outbreak of World War II plunged the Europeans into more desperate preoccupations. *En passant*, it is worth recording that, on the resignation of the Syrian president two months before the war broke out, ideas of a Hashimite monarchy were still entertained by Syrians and rumours abounded that, as a solution to the *impasse* which France continued to face in reaching a constitutional understanding with the Syrian nationalists, the throne would be offered to the Amir Abdullah (or to Faisal or Ali or even the ex-Khedive Abbas Hilmi).[22]

Meanwhile, indeed some years earlier, another and very différent player had emerged on the Fertile Crescent stage, in the remarkable person of Antoun Saadeh, Lebanese-born founder of the Syrian Social Nationalist Party (latterly known, owing to a French mistranslation, as the Parti Populaire Syrien or PPS). The philosophy he canvassed[23] with considerable magnetism on his return home in 1930 after ten years in

South America was based on his conviction that the Syrian nation was a unique regional entity owing its supreme particularity not to Islam or even to the Arabs but to the common evolution of the ethnic mix within the Syrian region's distinctive environment. This region he defined originally as the land lying between the Taurus, the Euphrates, the Suez Canal and the Mediterranean; but his final (1947) definition of natural Syria – and this is what concerns us here – was that it included the whole of the Fertile Crescent. (Indeed it incorporated not just Iraq but part of Iran and, for good measure, Cyprus too.) It was the sacred task of this Syrian nation, with its distinctive sense of identity setting it apart from the rest of the Arab world, to establish and defend its sovereign independence throughout the region described, discarding confessional differences. One would have expected the appeal of a doctrine of this kind, however charismatic its propagator, to be largely limited to the non-Moslem minorities; what is remarkable is the number of influential Syrian Moslems – they included for instance Akram Hourani, Adib Shishakli and Afiz Bizri – who gravitated into Saadeh's orbit. Between 1935 and 1937 the French predictably arrested him on several occasions for inciting disorder, a course of action which, equally predictably, boosted the popularity of his party, whose numbers were later estimated to have reached 50,000.[24] In 1938 he fled to South America. His further contribution to the story after his return to the fray in 1947 will be recounted when we come to it. Meanwhile we must return to mainstream developments.

World War II, the Fertile Crescent and the League of Arab States

A few days before World War II broke out British official views on what was generally referred to as Arab Federation were crystallised in a Foreign Office confidential memorandum.[25] This document recognised the geographical unity of the four components of *bilad ash-Sham* – Palestine, Transjordan, Lebanon and the new Syria – and the growing sense of Arab solidarity in the area (Iraq included) but saw insurmountable obstacles to British promotion of its federal or other unification: divergent interests and personal rivalries in the states concerned, the emergence on the edge of the area of the anti-Hashimite Abd al-Aziz ibn Saud as an outstanding Arab leader, Turkish aspirations to recover parts of the Crescent (Aleppo and Mosul) and the implacable opposition of the French to anything they could interpret as a British ploy to secure predominance throughout the Crescent. (It is also parenthetically of interest that the document expressed the conviction that, in the unlikely event of the countries of Arab Asia forming any sort of union, Egypt – still barely regarded as Arab – would always be likely to remain apart.) The conclusion was that Britain should take no initiative but let natural forces pursue their way.

The first phase of World War II, so disastrous for the Allies, produced a number of relevant developments, not least the arrival in Baghdad of the Mufti of Jerusalem, the emergence of an Iraqi politician to rival Nuri al-Said in the shape of Rashid Ali and, after the fall of France, the transfer from Damascus to Baghdad of the focal centre of Arab nationalist and Fertile Crescent agitation.[26] But in the course of these developments a new and not entirely irrelevant diversion occurred. In July 1940 the Amir Abdullah of Transjordan launched his own Greater Syria plan.[27] For this project – the reunification of geographical Syria under his kingship – he still had a certain backing in the area itself, both among the Druze, the Alawites, the Arab tribes and in the army, as well as from a number of Syrian politicians, not least the independent-minded Shabandar,[28] who shortly paid for it with his life. In Britain, too, there were those – mainly officials retired from Palestine – who had long been highly critical of the break-up of geographical Syria and who, since the 1920s, had been urging its reunification. But they were a spent force; and to Abdullah's plea, British governmental reactions – based on the 1939 memorandum and now the preoccupations of war – were from the first circumspect and unenthusiastic.

Within Iraq itself, though some kind of union or federation was the general demand, the split grew rapidly wider between those like Nuri who thought British support for it essential and those like Rashid Ali (with the exiled Mufti of Jerusalem at his side) who did not. The alienation of Rashid Ali and his supporters from Britain was aggravated by Churchill's turning away from the 1939 White Paper and its expressed concern for Arab Palestine; and, as Hitler's successes echoed around the world, it was in his direction that their thoughts turned. Even Nuri al-Said privately canvassed, on a visit to the Amir Abdullah in August 1940, the idea of the immediate establishment of a Fertile Crescent federation which the Axis powers, once victorious, would accept as a *fait accompli.*[29]

There are various versions in existence of Iraqi involvement with the Axis powers in 1940-1 and of the proposed post-war arrangements proferred by the latter, envisaging the unity and independence of the Crescent under the leadership of Iraq.[30] Nor is it even certain to what extent Nuri himself was privy to the plotting that began when Naji

Shawkat went (in his company) to Ankara in June 1940 and contacted the Germans. Fascinating as the whole subject is, it barely concerns us here. It proved a transient diversion: Rashid Ali would seem to have miscalculated the readiness of the Axis to support him militarily, and his eventual departure in June 1941 left Nuri and the Regent once more in control. Nonetheless, because Rashid Ali had served as a symbol of Arab nationalist opposition to British policy in Palestine as well as in Iraq, the episode left an ugly anti-British taste in many Arab mouths, including those of prominent Syrians[31] who had hastened to Baghdad to support Rashid Ali in his coup. In Syria itself the National bloc had been reported nine months earlier as emphatically collaborating with the Axis powers to create disorder with the ultimate objective of securing, under Axis auspices, Syria's independence.[32]

Britain's main political concern in the area in 1940-1 was to find some posture that would strengthen her position in the Middle East against the Axis powers without, after the fall of France in June 1940, complicating the delicate situation in Syria (recognised, as often throughout history, as the strategic hub). George Antonius, from his position on the staff of the High Commission in Palestine, was urging on the British authorities in October 1940[33] the need to counter Axis successes and political propaganda by a declaration of principles defining the British government's attitude towards Arab national aims, including a readiness to abolish the artificial frontiers imposed after the previous war. But he, too, recommended against premature support for any particular form of political unification. Shortly after, Lampson in Cairo was deploring Britain's failure to get to grips with the same problem;[34] and by mid-May 1941 (the month after Rashid Ali's *coup*) Eden was urging similar considerations for strategic reasons on Churchill. Churchill's response was a trifle idiosyncratic. Apart from declaring Syria (should the Free French fail to get a grip of it) an independent sovereign state, 'we should try to raise Ibn Saud to a general overlordship of Iraq and Transjordan', while 'a Jewish state in West Palestine might form an independent federal unit in an Arab caliphate' (of Saudi Arabia, Iraq and Transjordan). Into such Churchillian realms of fancy Eden did not follow. 'Many people,' he wrote in a memorandum of 27 May 1941, 'have suggested that the only practical solution to the Palestine problem would be a federation of the Middle East states, in which a Jewish state should have a place as one of its component parts. We have never opposed such a federation' (a statement rather less, perhaps, than the truth). He did not, indeed, regard federation as practical politics but, since it was an Arab aspiration, however vague, he now recommended taking every opportunity of publicly expressing support for it. The formula he adopted in his well-known Mansion House speech of 29 May 1941 centred on the declaration of 'full support for any scheme of unity which commands general approval'. Amir Abdullah's scheme of unity, which he continued to press on the British authorities, the Syrians and everyone else every few months for the next seven years, commanded a marked lack of 'general approval' and therefore did not qualify for British support – though the French, as usual, smelt a British rat behind it.

For the next few months the High Commissioner in Palestine (MacMichael) bombarded London with comments on the Fertile Crescent, starting (to his credit) with the admission that the division of Greater Syria had been unnatural and 'against the grain'.[35] By September 1941 the British War Cabinet decided that the idea of federation should receive departmental examination, 'especially as offering a possible solution of the Palestine problem';[36] and Eden called for constructive ideas from his ambassadors in the area – not least on the future structure of the (Syrian) Arab states, their union under a single king or their absorption into Iraq or Saudi Arabia.[37] Most of the ambassadors consulted shared the view that political union was impracticable, though cultural/economic union was desirable and might lead in that direction, while (as Lampson put it) implementation of the 1939 White Paper would do Britain far more good with the Arabs than any other initiative.[38] MacMichael's next contribution was his proposal for a federation of the *disjecta membra* of Syria under a tripartite British/French/American tridominium; the only practical alternative, he argued, was that Britain should remain indefinitely in control of Palestine and 'be honest enough to say so'. The Foreign Office and Eden, despite much debate, were unmoved, and the idea of imposing a foreign tridominium was written off as incompatible with promises of independence (now reaffirmed by the Free French for Syria and the Lebanon).[39]

The next plan for the Fertile Crescent idea reached the British government in November 1942 from an unexpected source (some of us might think) in the person of H.A.R. Gibb. And it was perhaps the most imaginative of all models for the Fertile Crescent.[40] He argued that federation should be pursued not of the existing states in the Crescent (which was impractical) but of the twelve separate provinces into which they should first be broken down again, i.e. Basra, Baghdad, Mosul, the Gezira, Aleppo, Damascus, Latakia, Lebanon, Jebel Druse, Palestine and Transjordan – none of them so much bigger than the others as to enable it to dominate the whole. The dissolved Iraqi monarchy would be compensated by Hashimite emirates in two of the twelve provinces, Baghdad and the Gezira. Even King Abd al-Aziz could not object; and the Jews would be made to accept it by firm handling from the supervising League of Nations. This visionary conception was discarded by British officialdom as academic.

The Amir Abdullah's current version, presented in December 1942 to the British Minister of State in Cairo (Casey) for forwarding to Churchill, added two new elements to his Greater Syria scheme.[41] These were that Greater Syria should, once re-created, establish cultural union with Iraq to bring confederation nearer, and that satisfaction should be secured for Moslem concern about the status of its Holy Land (the Hijaz) where 'a certain religious minority' was 'over-ruling the majority'. The expressed hostility of King Abd al-Aziz to all Hashimite plans for advancement was thus – but with much less effect – repaid in kind.

We now come to the most comprehensive of all attempts by the rival Hashimite court in Baghdad to re-launch the plan for the Iraqi Fertile Crescent, designed by Nuri within the covers of his famous Blue Book,[42] which he posted first to Casey in Cairo in January 1943 and then to three hundred other world leaders. In brief, and starting from the failure of the British government to carry out its declared policy of giving self-government to Palestine with its Arab majority, he proposed the following. The League of Nations should forthwith declare that Syria, Lebanon, Palestine and Transjordan should be reunited in a single state (republican or monarchical, as the people wished), that this state should join with Iraq to form the core of an Arab League (with wide federal powers, including defence and foreign affairs), which other Arab states could join at will. The Jews in Palestine should be granted semi-autonomy, the Maronites in Lebanon a privileged regime and Jerusalem a special commission. The French should be debarred from obstruction, and everything should rest on an International Guarantee.

No comprehensive British reply was ever vouchsafed, partly because the currently gestating cabinet paper on Middle East policy was held up by Weizmann's disruptive announcement of a plan to turn Palestine into a Jewish state, sponsored (so he alleged) by Churchill and to be endorsed by Abd al-Aziz. (Churchill, it must be admitted, was less dismayed by the suggestion than Abd al-Aziz would have been. Abd al-Aziz's name, incidentally, was taken in vain about this time by another visionary schemer in the person of St John Philby, who expounded to Gladwyn Jebb in London a remarkable proposal to solve all Middle East problems.[43] This was that all Palestinian Arabs should be evacuated and a Jewish Palestine be given Commonwealth status. In exchange, Britain should evacuate Iraq and Transjordan and persuade France to evacuate Syria. Abd al-Aziz would then go ahead and form an Arab state from Aleppo to the Gulf of Oman. The Foreign Office officials were left breathless – as indeed would Abd al-Aziz have been.)

But, to return to Nuri and his Blue Book, Abd al-Aziz's own response was to fire two sidelong shots across his bows.[44] First, he complained to Britain that Nuri was scheming to put the Regent Abdullillah on the throne of Syria (which was true) and that the British ambassador in Baghdad was encouraging him (which was false). Second, he reported to Britain the receipt of letters from 'influential people in Syria', opposed to Hashimite influence, inviting him to supply one of his sons as king. For that matter he also drew British attention to the ambitions of another Arab leader, Nahas, to emerge as champion of the Arab world – much as King Farouk and Hassanein had recently also done by disclosing to Lampson Nahas' fury that 'his pet scheme of leading the Arab world had been spiked by Nuri'.[45] The Amir Abdullah, too, resented Nuri's move to trump his own unity card and sought British approval to convene an Arab congress in Amman. Little wonder perhaps that, when Nuri sent Jamil al-Midfa'i round the capitals of the Levant in late February to canvass his Blue Book proposals, the message Nuri received from London was that the British government was averse to any propaganda to support the candidature of the Regent to the throne of Syria, which 'would cause Ibn Saud and the Amir Abdullah to react strongly'.[46]

It was, however, an Egyptian hand that produced the highest trump card in response to Nuri's opener. For Nahas announced in the Senate on 31 March 1943 his intention to consult Arab governments and try to reconcile their ideas on unity by inviting them to a meeting in Cairo.[47] From this well-calculated initiative much was to flow. For despite protests from Abd al-Aziz at not being consulted first and warnings addressed by him to the British government that dissentient
· Arab leaders agitating for Arab congresses were all simply concerned to strengthen their positions in their own countries;[48] despite Nuri's conviction that, in his subsequent discussions with Nahas, the latter had agreed to fall in with his plans for the Fertile Crescent;[49] despite the unexpected assurance given to a British representative by Quwatli (just elected president of Syria in elections sanctioned by the

Free French) that he, too, supported Nuri's plan, as indeed Nuri himself understood;[50] despite frantic efforts by the Amir Abdullah to keep his own unity project on the map;[51] despite British misgivings over the holding of Arab congresses anywhere at all to discuss such explosive subjects while the war still raged; despite all this and much more, Nahas' plan went slowly ahead. The final outcome, as everyone knows, was the establishment a year and a half later of the League of Arab States (embracing initially only Egypt and the independent states of the Mashrek) on Egyptian terms.

In the process both Abdullah's Greater Syria scheme (after much discussion) and Nuri's wider project for the whole Crescent — and indeed the PPS model and all the others — were given what was to prove their death-knell. For, even if Arab responsibility for the future of Palestine was the unifying motif, the basis on which the Arab League was conceived in Cairo and turned to advantage there was that the separate independence of all member states was recognised, accepted and jointly guaranteed and that Egyptian centrality in the Arab world was implicitly acknowledged. There can be little doubt that one of the dominant Egyptian motives in promoting these arrangements was to hinder the aspirations of both Nuri and Abdullah for leadership of a region which excluded both Egypt and Saudi Arabia — and in that respect at least they had Abd al-Aziz's support, as well as that of the Syrian and Lebanese governments.

The Post-war Period: Continuing Schemes for Unity in the Fertile Crescent

But Fertile Crescentry of either Hashimite model, though approaching death, would by no means yet lie down. Even after repeated declarations by the League that such regional groupings were incompatible with its principles, the Amir Abdullah, stimulated at first by the departure of Allied troops from the Levant in April 1946, continued to canvass variants of his cherished scheme for a kingdom of Greater Syria. In 1947 a 'White Paper' on the subject issued from Amman, followed by yet another manifesto. In 1948 he declared himself in favour of the union of Greater Syria with Iraq.[52] Nuri, too, pursued at intervals and for another ten years his dream of Iraqi domination of the area, at very least by an initial merger with the new Syria. In that respect he still received periodical, if guarded, encouragement from old-guard Syrian politicians,[53] from the People's Party and from a series of transient Syrian strong-men — Zaim, Hinnawi and later even Shishakli. But by now it was the army that counted in Syria — and as a whole the army (like most of the prominent civilians) had turned against it. Egypt was in any case too firmly established as the hand on the Arab tiller, and her promotion in April 1950 of the League's Joint Defence Agreement (which prohibited members from making international agreements not sanctioned by a two-thirds majority) was successfully deployed to bar any Syrian/Iraqi union.[54]

By now, too, the Arabs as a whole were so far alienated from the West as a result of developments in Palestine that the Hashimites, still loyal to the British connection, were increasingly isolated; and by a curious twist of fate the plan for the Fertile Crescent, so long resisted by the British, was now identified by many as a British plot.

None of these considerations seems to have mattered to the broodings of Antoun Saadeh in his exile. Returning to the scene from South America in 1947 still bent on his own vision of the Fertile Crescent, he proceeded in July 1949, with the undercover backing of the *arriviste* Syrian president, Zaim, to mount from Syria a *coup* in Lebanon, to make of it a new starting-point for his project. But his *coup* aborted, he was betrayed by Zaim and died before a Lebanese firing-squad. His 'martyrdom' gave a further boost to the zealotry of his partisans; and the party with its philosophy of the Fertile Crescent pursued its course, unrepentant but maladroit, for years to come.[55]

Early in 1954 the Iraqi Prime Minister Fadhil al-Jamali put before the Arab League yet another proposal for Arab federation starting with Iraq, Syria and Jordan, but this was quickly rejected by Shishakli's representatives and other League members as the old Fertile Crescent project in new clothing. After Shishakli's departure (with Iraqi assistance) three months later, Jamali secretly discussed his proposal with members of the new Syrian government of Sabri al-Asali; but the latter's fall from power ended these discussions.[56] Syrian thoughts of union now began to turn away from the Tigris/Euphrates towards the Nile.

Nuri's next endeavour to advance Iraqi centralism in the Crescent, therefore, was to pick up the old 1937 (Turkish-inspired) Sa'adabad Pact for regional security and convert it into the ill-fated Baghdad Pact with British backing. But Nasser's emergence as the hero of Arab resistance to what was seen as Western imperialism put paid to any general Arab acceptance of this line of thought. Indeed the West's growing preoccupation with the Soviet threat to its interests in the Middle East, coupled with Nasser's dauntless aggravation of it, meant, amongst much else, that any moves by Nuri's Iraq to regain the initiative in Syria were diagnosed as Western-inspired. Certainly Nuri kept on prying for openings in Syria. The evidence for Western inspiration or backing for his probings in the mid-1950s, produced in retrospect at the trial of General Daghestani in Baghdad after the 1958 revolution, might not perhaps have satisfied a less partial court.[57] So far as British involvement is concerned, we shall not know the facts until the state papers are released (if then). What worried the Western powers at the time was the leftist switch in Syrian politics: they would have welcomed a change of government in Syria but hardly an Iraqi take-over, which was perhaps, as ever, in Nuri's mind. But Arab suspicions that Fertile Crescentry in its death-throes was a British running-dog will no doubt die hard. On the occasion of the last abortive PPS *coup* in the Lebanon in December 1961, Kemal Joumblatt, the Minister of the Interior, had no scruple in announcing in elaborate detail that it had been organised by the British.[58]

A survey as brief and superficial as this is open to the criticism that it considers only the manoeuvring of leaders of the Fertile Crescent and has paid little or no attention to the views of ordinary people not operating in the corridors of power. Was there ever, one may ask, any serious popular enthusiasm within Iraq or the rest of the Crescent for its unification? Certainly the writings of Arab intellectuals and journalists throughout this period should have received more attention, though a random study of their attitudes to Arab Asian unity leaves an impression of *Quot homines, tot sententiae.* In any case the prime concern of most Arab intellectuals between the two world wars was for Arab independence first: Arab political dispositions could thereafter take care of themselves. And by the time independence was finally vouchsafed, national particularism was, in a sense, too deeply entrenched and was perhaps reinforced, rather than otherwise, by the more vigorous emergence onto a political stage of the common man. In Syria itself, it is fair to say, popular political enthusiasms had been effectively at work much earlier—as the history of the People's Party and of the PPS (*inter alia*) would indicate. There is no clear evidence that the particular Fertile Crescent concepts of Antoun Saadeh ever stirred a chord in comparable sections of the Iraqi public. Whether the Iraqi populace, as distinct from its rulers, was ever greatly interested in merging Iraq's identity with the rest of the Crescent on any other basis is something on which an Iraqi historian would be better equipped to pronounce.

So far as outside powers were concerned, there can be no doubt that

Western governments underestimated throughout the inter-war years, especially in World War II, the groundswell of popular opinion in Arab Asia, out of sympathy with much that its political masters were doing. For Britain – particularly a Britain fighting for her survival – it was on the leaders, rather than on public opinion, in the emergent sovereign states that her government felt constrained to focus its attention. As to this, an observation made by the young Albert Hourani in a confidential report commissioned by the Foreign Office after an eight-months' survey (ending in February 1943) of currents of opinion in the Fertile Crescent is much in point.[59] The feudal governments existing there, he said, though they could not have stayed in power without British approval, were the only kind which could provide the sort of stability a war situation demanded for Britain. (Incidentally, he also recorded the conclusion that everyone in the area was agreed on the necessity of the reunion of Syria, Lebanon, Palestine and Trans-jordan, with nothing more than a political alliance with Iraq.)

The years covered by this survey were a stirring, bewildering and frustrating period for all. It is easy enough to deride the motives of those individual Arab leaders who argued with such passion, forty years and more ago, for the unity of the Fertile Crescent (or against it): indeed they all derided each other's motives at the time. Abd al-Aziz ibn Saud in particular never ceased warning Britain that all the other Arab leaders were simply out for their own personal ends: and he too, of course, had his critics amongst those he criticised. Those who believe, like the writer, that human motives, if never pure, are also never simple, may see things differently. Fertile Crescent unity, as such, was surely a genuine ideal; and those who sought to promote it, whatever personal ambitions may also have prompted them, as surely shared something of this idealism. An impartial study of the relevant policies of Nuri al-Said, the leading protagonist after King Faisal's death, suggests that, even if he was driven on by hopes of securing Iraqi control of the rest of the Crescent, he was also powerfully affected by the fate of Palestine, tried for thirty years to push Britain into carrying out its declared obligations towards it and was convinced that his Blue Book proposals of 1943 offered her the last chance of solving the problem honourably.

In those days one of Britain's dominant concerns was the attitude of Abd al-Aziz. The influence he was able to wield in London (and not just because he was Britain's most loyal supporter during the vicissitudes of war) is a singular tribute to his personality, for he had then no oil to give it material substance – though he did, of course, have Mecca. It is an intriguing speculation what would have happened if Abd al-Aziz had accepted the invitation from those 'influential Syrians' in 1943 to provide a son for the throne of Syria.

It may seem strange today that not only Abd al-Aziz but virtually all Arab leaders in those far-off days were convinced that Britain held the key to the future of the area: and even those not noticeably well-disposed regularly sought prior British approval for their ideas on its political restructuring. The regularly repeated response from London in the critical early 1940s was that, until the war was over and won, the British government was averse to promoting any political innovations to upset the *status quo*. By the time the war *was* over, Britain no longer had the power to engineer them. But if, one wonders, when she still had the necessary standing and despite her other war-time preoccupations, she had grasped the nettle, taken up the suggestion that a scheme for the Fertile Crescent of one kind or another would enable Jewish immigration to be painlessly absorbed within a unified Arab state or federation and pursued a policy of that nature regardless of French, Zionist and sundry Arab objections, would the post-war history of the Middle East have taken a quite different and less painful course?

Notes

1. By R. Khalidi in his *British Policy towards Syria and Lebanon, 1906-1914* (Ithaca Press, London, 1980).

2. A. Hourani, *A Vision of History* (Khayyat, Beirut, 1961), p. 70. See also G. Antonius, *The Arab Awakening*, 2nd edn (Hamish Hamilton, London, 1945), Chs. V and VI.

3. FO371/5040 (E 12976) of 1920.

4. These numbers are taken from reports by the Acting High Commissioner in Cairo, Ernest Scott, at FO 371/5040 (E12137 and 13211) of 1920. Somewhat different numbers are given by Antonius in *The Arab Awakening*, p. 292 and by A. Tibawi in *Anglo-Arab Relations and the Question of Palestine, 1914-1921* (Luzac, London, 1977), pp. 389 and 391. Accounts of the manner in which the members of the Syrian Congress were elected or selected also differ in the various sources, including the accounts of Nuri to Hubert Young at FO 371/5034 (E2524/2/44) and of Faisal to Lloyd George at FO 371/5040 (E11500/2/44), both of 1920. But the main point – though one on which the British government frequently expressed scepticism – is that it would seem to have been reasonably representative, as the King-Crane Commission, which sponsored its recommendations, declared. (The text of the King-Crane report appears in Antonius, *The Arab Awakening*, Appendix H).

5. Antonius, *The Arab Awakening*, pp. 246-7.

6. See, for instance, K. Husri's article 'King Faysal I and Arab Unity, 1923-33' in *Journal of Contemporary History*, vol. 10, no. 2 (1975), pp. 323-40.

7. Ibid., pp. 326 and 332. In fact, the French had consulted Faisal as early as November 1925 on the best way of dealing with Syria. His advice was to grant a re-unified Syria a constitution giving it internal independence, as the British had done in Iraq. See the account of Berthelot's discussion with Faisal at FO 371/10851 (E6771/357/89) of 1925.

8. E. Dawn, 'The Project of Greater Syria', unpublished PhD thesis, Princeton University, 1948, p. 17. Also FO 371/15330 (E6911/6911/31) of 1920.

9. A. Hourani, *Syria and Lebanon* (R.I.I.A., London, 1946), p. 192.

10. FO 371/16041 (E5226/206/89) of 1932. A summary of Faisal's Fertile Crescent aspirations and of relevant reports on them from British representatives in Baghdad is set out in the Foreign Office Research Department's memorandum 'The Greater Syria Movement' of January 1948, at FO 371/61497 (E9137/42/65) of 1948.

11. A suggestion canvassed on Faisal's behalf by Nuri al-Said with his *al-hilf al-arabi* project in 1931 (Dawn, 'The Project of Greater Syria', p. 16).

12. As adopted by the Standing Sub-Committee of the Committee for Imperial Defence and by the Middle East Sub-Committee. FO 371/15364 (E5823/206/89) of 1943.

13. Husri, 'King Faysal I and Arab Unity', p. 337.

14. For a fair cross-section see K. Karpat, *Political and Social Thought in the Contemporary Middle East* (Pall Mall, London, 1968).

15. W. Cleveland, *The Making of an Arab Nationalist: Sati al-Husri* (Princeton University Press, 1971), pp. 47-80.

16. M. Khadduri, *Independent Iraq* (Oxford University Press, London, 1960), p. 64.

17. E. Main in his article 'Iraq: A Note', *Journal of the Royal Central Asian Society*, no. XX (July 1933), p. 434.

18. Dawn, 'The Project of Greater Syria', p. 22.

19. Khadduri, *Independent Iraq*, p. 140; Dawn, 'The Project of Greater Syria', p. 26.

20. Ibid., p. 24.

21. J. Kimche, *The Second Arab Awakening* (Thames and Hudson, London, 1970), p. 147.

22. Hourani, *Syria and Lebanon*, p. 227; Dawn, 'The Project of Greater Syria', p. 29.

23. L. Yamak, *The Syrian Social Nationalist Party: An Ideological Analysis* (Harvard University Press, 1966), pp. 36-88. Also P. Seale, *The Struggle for Syria* (Oxford University Press, London, 1965), pp. 64-72.

24. As reported by Albert Chidiac to High Commissioner Palestine (Mac-Michael), along with comments on German wartime support for the PPS (FO 371/24594 (E2823/2170/89) of 1940). Other estimates of PPS membership are smaller. FO Research Department's 1948 Memorandum 'The Greater Syria Movement' puts its membership as never exceeding 10,000.

25. Text at FO 371/23239 (E6357/6/31) of 1939.

26. Khadduri, *Independent Iraq*, p. 162.

27. Dawn, 'The Project of Greater Syria', p. 37. Abdullah had, of course, nurtured ambitions of reuniting geographical Syria ever since his first arrival in Transjordan in 1921; but the real progenitors of the movement were the Syrian People's Party, set up with that primary purpose in 1925 (FO Research Department memo 'The Greater Syria Movement', para. 16).

28. His discussions with Britain's ME Intelligence Centre in Cairo are recorded at FO 371/24593 (E599G/953/65 and E2422/953/65) of 1940. His alleged Syrian assassins fled significantly to Iraq (FO 371/24594 (E2814/2170/89) of 1940).

29. So Abdullah, perhaps a little maliciously, informed the British represent-ative in Amman (FO 371/24548 (E2418/953/65) of 1940).

30. Kimche, *The Second Arab Awakening*, pp. 148-50, summarises German versions. One alternative version of the alleged secret treaty between Rashid Ali and the Axis is at FO 371/27079 (E4732/1/93) of 1941. For exchanges between the Mufti and Hitler see Khadduri, *Independent Iraq*, pp. 189 and 379-81.

31. Amongst them, Seale, *The Struggle for Syria*, p. 38, cites Akram Hourani, Jamal al-Atasi and Afif Bizri.

32. FO 371/24594 (E2709/2170/89) of 1940.

33. Text of his memorandum at FO 371/24548 (E2418/953/65) of 1940.

34. For this and the Eden/Churchill/Eden quotations which follow see FO 371/27043 (E2191, 2476, 2685 and 2716/53/65) of 1941.

35. FO 371/27045 (E6031/53/65) of 1941.

36. FO 371/27045 (E6189/53/65) of 1941.

37. FO 371/27045 (E6210/53/65) of 1941. It was of the *post-war* structure of the area that Eden and his staff were thinking, there being no time while the war was on to work out a scheme. So Eden said, for example, to the Saudi minister Hafiz Wahba, who asked him in August 1941 for a British lead in plan-ning a federation of Saudi Arabia, Iraq and Syria, observing that the Arabs would be disappointed if it was left till the war was over (FO 371/27044 (E4761/53/65) of 1941).

38. FO 371/27045 (E6636/53/65) of 1941. Stonehewer Bird in Jeddah had been making the same point in September 1940 (FO 371/24548 (E2594/953/65) of 1940).

39. FO 371/31338 (E3121/49/65) of 1941.

40. Text at FO 371/31338 (E7433/49/65) of 1942.

41. FO 371/31338 (E7548/49/65) of 1942.

42. Its full title was 'Arab Independence and Unity. A Note on the Arab Cause with Particular Reference to Palestine and Suggestions for a Permanent Settlement' (Government Press, Baghdad, 1943). Copy at FO 371/34955 (E2315/506/65) of 1943.

43. FO 371/34959 (E3327/506/65) of 1943.

44. FO 371/34955 (E1231, 1234 and 1259/506/65) of 1943.

45. FO 371/35528 (J398/2/16) of 1943.

46. FO 371/34955 (E1227/506/65) of 1943.

47. FO 371/34956 (E1888/506/65) of 1943.

48. FO 371/34957 (E2434/506/65) of 1943.

49. The *procès verbaux* of these discussions, as communicated to Lord Killearn in Cairo, more or less confirm this (FO 371/34961 (E5376/506/65) of 1943).

50. Dawn, 'The Project of Greater Syria', p. 105 and Cornwallis' report from Baghdad at FO 371/39987 (E915/41/65) of 1944.

51. By producing a new manifesto on Greater Syria union and seeking in vain, in the face of British disapproval, to get it broadcast in relevant Arab capitals (FO 371/34960 (E4861/506/65) of 1943).

52. The lengthy White Paper circulated from Amman in May 1947 (reproduced in part as an appendix to FO Research Department Memorandum 'The Greater Syria Movement'), was no more favourably received than the further manifesto issued by Abdullah three months later, in which he argued that either the decisions of the Syrian Congress of 1920 should be regarded as still binding or else a new conference should be held to draft a constitution for a unified Arab State (see the same FO Research Department Memorandum). For his final version of August 1948 which included the union of Greater Syria with Iraq, see Dawn, 'The Project of Greater Syria', p. 86. Throughout all this, British representatives in the

area were under instructions to remain neutral.

53. Khadduri, *Independent Iraq*, p. 271, and Seale, *The Struggle for Syria*, p. 46.

54. Ibid., p. 48.

55. Yamak, *The Syrian Social Nationalist Party*, p. 67, and Seale, *The Struggle for Syria*, p. 64.

56. On Jamali's two initiatives, see Seale, *The Struggle for Syria*, p. 141.

57. Baghdad Radio's extensive treatment of the trials of Daghestani, and others, was reproduced in the BBC's Summary of World Broadcasts Nos 630 to 643 of August/September 1958. For the evidence of British involvement in the apparently continuous Iraqi plotting to overthrow the regime in Syria from 1953 to 1956, see particularly SWB 639 and 640 of 28 and 29 August.

58. A piece of invention to which the present writer, then a member of the British Embassy in Beirut, was witness.

59. Text at FO 371/34958 (E2459/506/65) of 1943.

3 STATE POWER AND ECONOMIC STRUCTURE: CLASS DETERMINATION AND STATE FORMATION IN CONTEMPORARY IRAQ

Joe Stork

Perspective

Iraq presents a considerable challenge to anyone wishing to compre-
hend the intersection of class and state formation in post-colonial
societies. It was the first (and except for Iran in 1978-9, the only)
major oil-producing state to undergo a far-reaching political revolution,
but the legacy of that revolution today appears extremely ambiguous.
Politically, Iraq's escalation against Iran occurs in the context of an
alignment with the more conservative forces in the Gulf region and
with the capitalist industrialised countries internationally. Iraq is
currently the second largest OPEC producer and exporter, with reserves
that most observers agree will ensure its pre-eminence as a producer and
as a market for industrial manufacturers for decades to come. Iraq has
thoroughly nationalised its oil industry, and has used its vast and growing revenues from oil sales to finance an extensive 'socialist sector'.
Nevertheless the economic structure of the country emerging in the
late 1970s shares many features with other oil-producing states.

This chapter represents a preliminary effort to delineate modern
historical aspects of class and state formation in Iraq. The correspondence of these structural features with the changing needs of
international capital forms an underlying theme. A discussion of Iraq's
post-revolutionary economic structure suggests certain interpretations
of the character of the Iraqi state and its relationship to the society's
evolving class forces.

The Iraqi State in History

The modern Iraqi state dates from the British colonial separation of the
former Ottoman *vilayet*s of Baghdad, Basra and Mosul, and their
unification to form the territory of Iraq after World War I. Its
beginnings, though – its apparatus, and its relationship to indigenous

27

social formations—go back well into the nineteenth century, coinciding with the early phase of European penetration and the fitful but persistent process of integration into the world economy.

The formal incarnation of the state following the British occupation in World War I was manifestly dictated by European convenience and the imperative of foreign capital in consolidating and legitimising its rule. The colonial state was built on the existing Ottoman apparatus and personnel and financed by indirect taxes that hit the poorest classes hardest. This hegemony of foreign capital was reflected clearly in the negotiations with Turkey over the inclusion of Mosul, with its oil and its Sunni population, and in the circumstances leading to 'independence' in 1932. In the countryside the large landlord/shaikhs became a main pillar of the 'independent' monarchy. The urban elements with a stake in the prevailing order included bureaucrats, former officers and large merchants who forged close ties with the shaikh/landlords and used their political and military offices to secure large estates and import monopolies.

The entire history of the Iraqi monarchy, up to the revolution of 1958, is bound together as a period in which the state represented a striking condensation of the balance of existing social forces, among which foreign capital was clearly and unambiguously dominant. But World War II and its aftermath substantially altered this prevailing balance and exposed the increasingly tenuous relationship of the state to its rapidly shifting social base. The war brought a halt in imports and large demand for locally produced goods. Productive activities increased. Under the existing social order, though, gains were restricted to the large landlords, merchants and state officials. Inflation and scarcity wrought tremendous hardships on the workers and wage-earners. Trade-union organising and political activity by nationalists and Communists—which had begun in the early 1930s but were largely suppressed through the war years—catalysed the political and economic grievances of the urban masses into impressive strikes and virtual insurrections which came to a head in 1948 and 1952.

This threat to political stability was magnified by simultaneous upheavals elsewhere in the region, such as the nationalisation crisis in Iran and the war in Palestine. This was precisely at a time when the post-war reconstruction of the industrialised capitalist countries required the rapid and assured growth of oil exports. Not incidentally, it corresponded as well to the ascendancy of US political and economic power over that of the British, noticeably in the Middle East. The US oil companies moved to shore up the eroding authority of Iraq and the other oil-producing states by 'sharing' their enormous profits with those regimes. In Iraq, a 1952 agreement between the government and the IPC consortium raised revenues per ton from $1.75 to $5.50. This, and a sharp increase in production, led to a jump in state revenues proportionately as great as that of the mid-1970s. The repressive capacity of the state to secure the maintenance and reproduction of existing social relations was augmented but at the same time altered. The state also acquired the means and the imperative to 'develop' the productive forces of Iraq's economy.

The 1950s were a critical decade of transition and dislocation, following the dialectic of state and class formation that had built up for decades. New social forces, brought into being by the limited integration of Iraq into the world economy and the requisite construction of the modern state, resented foreign control and the privileges of narrow local ruling elements. Their challenges and insurrections precipitated further growth of the state and its services, such as education, in order to pacify and contain the opposition. Such responses added to the numbers of the new forces. The social crisis was heightened by the decomposition of the old order in the countryside and the massive migration of impoverished peasants to the squalid outskirts of Baghdad and Basra. The oil rent, unlike the agricultural surplus monopolised by the landlord class, accrued to the state. Its dispersal from the centre perceptibly accelerated the shift of economic activity to commodity production and services in the urban areas.

The need of international capital for secure and cheap energy supplies to facilitate capital accumulation worldwide increased the share of the oil-producing state in the rent of that commodity. This wealth in the hands of the state, given the continued domination of landlord and mercantile classes, was hoarded and squandered but also circulated and, to a limited extent, appropriated locally as capital. In this manner the Iraqi state, created by foreign capital to maintain its own hegemony, contributed to the development of antagonistic social forces, such as displaced peasants and small producers from provincial towns and wage labour in manufacturing, construction and services.

There was, additionally, some diversification of wealth and property within the existing elite. By the end of the monarchy, investments and profits in manufacturing exceeded those in trade, indicating the formation of a new fraction of the bourgeoisie, linked with the old but with its own agenda, not served by the feudal-like economic and social relations in the countryside. Industrial and transport workers numbered over 150,000 by 1954, more than 43 per cent in

establishments of over 100 workers. The Communist Party enjoyed a
near-political monopoly among these workers, and particularly among
the largest and most strategic concentrations in the state railway, Basra
port and the oil fields. Even more numerous were the traditional and
'new' (wage-earning) petty bourgeoisie: thousands of small shop and
store owners; professionals and semi-professionals employed in services
and the public sector, including the officer corps; thousands of
students looking for scarce jobs. The newer and younger elements of
these groupings were educated and ideologically articulate, and rapidly
increasing in number. Early migrants from provincial towns, or first-
generation city-dwellers, they were concerned with jobs, markets and
social mobility, and were infused with deep hostility towards foreign
capital and the state they saw as its handmaiden. These together are the
social forces that made the revolution of July 1958.

State and Revolution

The first decade after Iraq's revolution witnessed a period of realign-
ment and recomposition of class forces and an open struggle for class
hegemony, focused on control of the state apparatus. The revolution
was implemented by the Free Officers, themselves squarely of the
petty bourgeoisie in their social origins and political inclinations. It was
more than a mere *coup*; in Batatu's words, it was 'the climax of the
struggle of a whole generation of middle, lower-middle and working
classes'.[1] As subsequent decades demonstrated, it brought to power a
diffuse set of bourgeois and petty-bourgeois forces.

The most unambiguous achievement of the revolution, in class terms,
was to break up latifundist social relations in the countryside by
expropriating the largest private landholdings. Though considerable
differentiation in landholdings remained, the political power of the
landlords on the national level was decisively broken. With the disruption of class relations in the countryside, however, there was no
systematic effort to construct new patterns and responsibilities.
Relations of peasants to the land remained ambiguous. The physical
infrastructure – particularly irrigation and drainage facilities – continued
to deteriorate. The means of production – seeds, tools, fertilisers – were
not available in a timely and reliable fashion. Agricultural production
continued to be distressingly vulnerable to rainfall and other natural
conditions, and the overall trend of agricultural productivity continued
to decline. The existing population-shift from countryside to urban

areas accelerated after the revolution.

The propertied classes, urban and rural, played an important role at key political junctures in the decade after the revolution, such as March 1959, February and November 1963 and autumn 1965. But they were clearly without the political or economic weight to act by themselves or to determine the outcome of the struggle among the petty-bourgeois forces. The unity of the urban classes and political factions against the old regime had quickly broken down. The national bourgeoisie (represented by the National Democratic Party) proved to be a marginal force. The working class (represented by the Iraqi Communist Party) was physically crushed. Communists and their allies were systematically eliminated from the trade union and peasant organisations they had built. The impact of the class struggle of this period was imprinted on the ideology of the petty-bourgeois forces, from the Ba'th Party to President Aref: expressly anti-Communist, yet appropriating Marxist vocabulary and categories of thought and, in some cases, Communist organisational tactics.

Although the proper role of the state in Iraqi society was one matter of dispute among the contending petty-bourgeois groupings, there was no denial of the fact that this role would, by its very nature, be considerable. The oil sector in particular – its relation to the state and to foreign capital – quickly became a key issue of contention whose resolution held the promise of restructuring the economy without class confrontation. There were few changes in economic organisation (outside of the agrarian reform) after 1960. While the labour force grew by some 600,000 between 1960 and 1968, for instance, it appears that most of this number were absorbed either into agriculture or the ranks of the unemployed! Changes that did take place were formal, not structural, such as the overnight nationalisation of the largest enterprises in July 1964. The formal economic role of the state was enhanced, and private capital (domestic and foreign) discouraged and restricted. But the political struggle for control of the state among the various petty-bourgeois groupings immobilised any state initiatives. Officers and bureaucrats, backed by one or other faction of the small Iraqi bourgeoisie or foreign capital, squabbled over political conditions as the society deteriorated close to the point of breakdown.

In July 1968, just after the tenth anniversary of the revolution, the Ba'th Party, in alliance with right-wing military officers, seized power in a bloodless *coup*. Its consolidation of power in subsequent years comprises an important chapter in the evolution of the modern Iraqi state and certifies the Ba'th as the most potent political component of the petty-bourgeois forces inspired by Arab nationalism. Its significance lay not in any sharp break with the outlook or social representation of preceding regimes. Rather, it represented the first ensconcement of a relatively homogeneous and disciplined grouping. The new regime moved with measurable dispatch to implement major programmes which had been on the agenda since the revolution of July 1958: notably the revision and implementation of the Agrarian Reform Law, and the nationalisation of the IPC in June 1972 and of other foreign oil interests by 1975.

Economic Structure under the Ba'th[2]

The commanding economic role of the Iraqi state, directly encompassing the major economic institutions of the society, derives from its formation in the period when the territory was directly tied to the wheel of imperialism, and subsequently from its rentier function in relation to Western oil interests. Direct state control of the oil industry was achieved at a time (1972-5) when the exchange value of crude oil escalated considerably. Oil revenues at the disposal of the regime increased from $487 million in 1968 to $6.7 billion in 1974 and $12.2 billion in 1979 (Table 3.1). The consolidation of political power

Table 3.1: Iraqi Oil Revenues, Selected Years

Year	Revenue ($ million)
1950	19
1953	144
1958	224
1964	353
1968	488
1972	575
1974	5,700
1977	9,600
1979	12,180

Source: Up to 1977, Richard Nyrop (ed.), *Iraq: A Country Study*, Area Handbook Series (American University, Washington, DC, 1979), p. 265. 1979 provisional figure from Economist Intelligence Unit Special, *Iraq: A New Market in a Region of Turmoil* (EIU, London, 1980), report no. 88, p. 31.

under the present regime thus occurred in conjunction with a momentous expansion of the state's economic functions.

Iraq's historically imposed relationship to the world economy has fostered and financed a margin of autonomy of the state and political apparatus in relation to the economic structure of the society. Nevertheless the capacity of the political leadership to develop a more 'modern' economic structure is distinctly constricted by this historical formation, by the vulnerability inherent in its role as supplier of a single, albeit major, commodity to world markets and by reliance on those same markets to provide a growing portion of the goods and services required by Iraq for consumption and capital formation. A review of developments in the major sectors of the Iraqi economy, with particular attention to the implications for class formation, highlights some of the problems facing Iraq's rulers in the 1980s.

Agriculture and the Rural Sector

The regime moved quickly after seizing power to revise and implement the badly lagging agrarian reform programme. Law 117 (1970) further limited the maximum that could be held, eliminated compensation to landowners and abolished payments by beneficiaries (acknowledging the extremity of peasant indebtedness and poverty). According to the official Agricultural Census of 1971, there were 589,387 holdings (from 253,254 in 1957). Despite improved tenure patterns, the top 1 per cent of the landholders still held over 22 per cent of the total (down from more than 55 per cent in 1957) and the lowest 60 per cent owned 14 per cent.[3] In 1973 reform beneficiaries farmed 22.7 per cent of the cultivable land; peasants renting sequestered and state land from the government farmed 34.5 per cent of the total; and private non-beneficiaries held 34.9 per cent.[4]

Since then it can be inferred from scanty statistics that the number of reform beneficiaries has increased while those leasing land from the government have dropped in number. The number of agricultural co-operatives and collective farms has also grown somewhat.

It is difficult to assess changes in rural social structure. The little information available and the experience of other countries suggests that new stratification patterns are emerging, characterised by the rise of middle peasants who directly and through leadership of the co-operatives control allocations of machinery and other inputs. As in the cities and towns, affiliation with the Ba'th smooths this path. The large number of landless peasants forced to work as sharecroppers or wage labourers is vaguely acknowledged in the Political Report of the 8th Regional Congress of the Ba'th Party (held in January 1974).[5] Presumably this phenomenon still exists, and may even have worsened, but it is not confirmed in official statistics.

Within the agricultural sector as a whole the deterioration that began before the revolution has not been appreciably halted. The total arable and total cultivated land have declined, perhaps by as much as 30 per cent between 1958 and 1977.[6] The factors are numerous: soil salinity and lack of drainage investments on the physical side; low prices and inadequate development of marketing and credit functions of the co-operatives on the political level. The most distinguishing feature is demographic: the mass migration from the countryside to the towns and cities threatens a virtual depopulation of the countryside. By one calculation, the number of persons employed in agriculture declined from over 1.5 million in 1973 to 943,890 in 1977, or from 51 per cent to 30 per cent of the total labour force (Table 3.2). As recently as 1975, Iraq and the United Nations had projected an *increase* in agricultural employment to 59 per cent of the total labour force![7]

Table 3.2: Structure of the Iraqi Labour Force, 1977

Agriculture	352,824	591,066	943,890	30.2
Petroleum and mining	2,119	34,716	36,835	1.2
Manufacturing industry	48,618	235,777	284,395	7.9
Electricity, gas and water	949	22,241	23,190	0.7
Construction	5,136	316,560	321,696	10.3
Wholesale and retail trade	16,155	207,949	224,104	7.2
Transport, storage and communications	4,985	172,814	177,799	5.7
Finance, real estate and business services	5,066	26,023	31,089	32.4
Community, social and personal services	86,100	871,879	957,979	
Other	11,979	46,258	58,237	2.0
Unemployed	10,447	64,278	74,725	2.4
Total	544,378	2,589,561	3,133,939	100.0

Source: Central Statistical Organisation, *Annual Abstract of Statistics* (Ministry of Planning, Baghdad, 1978).

There were reports in 1977 that the government tried to restrict peasants from changing their 'profession' on their identity cards.[8] One can assume that the migrants include a disproportionately high number of peasants with skills, precisely those most needed for the agro-industrial projects now planned.

The establishment of schools, clinics and utilities has altered the traditional isolation of rural villages, but the higher level of prosperity in rural areas is due chiefly to the infusion of income from the central government rather than increases in productivity. Field research carried out in more than a hundred villages in Babylon and Nineveh provinces in 1974-5 indicated that continued impoverishment and deteriorating land and living conditions were the main impetus to migration rather than the 'pull' of urban jobs and amenities.[9] Agriculture's share in the domestic product declined to an estimated 5 per cent in 1980. This has put the burden for meeting rising demand for foodstuffs on imports, which have more than doubled since 1977 and stood at $1.4 billion in 1980, more than the total value of Iraqi agricultural production in that year, according to Ministry of Planning forecasts.[10]

Industrialisation and the Manufacturing Sector

The contribution of the manufacturing sector to domestic production rose slowly to a high of 10 per cent in 1973, fell to 4.7 per cent in 1974 after the oil price increase and reached 7.8 per cent in 1976. Tables 3.3 and 3.4 show the growth of large plants (over ten workers) and the public sector share. Small manufacturing workshops also grew

Table 3.3: Large Manufacturing in Iraq

	Firms	Workers
1954	727	44,410
1964	1202	80,066
1976	1479	142,740

Sources: K. Langley, *The Industrialization of Iraq* (Harvard University Press, 1961); Central Statistical Organisation, *Annual Abstract of Statistics* (Ministry of Planning, Baghdad, 1965 and 1977).

in number, especially after the oil price increase. In 1976 they numbered 37,669 and employed 85,460 (including owner/workers).

The greater part of Iraqi manufacturing is light industries based on local raw materials. Food, beverages and tobacco-processing accounted for about one quarter of the large firms, workers and wages, half the input, and 38 per cent of output in 1974. Textiles accounted for about

Table 3.4: Public Sector Share of Large Manufacturing (%)

	Total firms	Total workers	Total wages	Total inputs	Total outputs
1964	22	52	64	55	65
1974	27	74	76	74	74

Source: Central Statistical Organisation, *Annual Abstract of Statistics* (Ministry of Planning, Baghdad, 1965 and 1975).

20 per cent of the firms, 28 per cent of the workers, 17 per cent of input and 19 per cent of output. Twelve large public sector textile firms employed 1,666 workers each, on average. A total of 139 large private textile firms averaged 35 workers each.[11] The value-added per worker was higher in the private sector in food processing and textiles, but public sector dominance in chemicals, oil products and similar capital-intensive industries gave the public sector as a whole a higher input, output and value-added per worker. In the large manufacturing sector between 1974 and 1976 the private sector expanded at a slightly greater rate than the public sector. The main area of private sector growth was in consumer durables.

The relationship between the public and private sectors in large manufacturing is reflected in their employment structures (Table 3.5).

Table 3.5: Employment Structure of Large Manufacturing, 1976 (%)

	Public sector	Private sector
Production workers		
Unskilled	60	40
Skilled	78	22
Technicians and highly skilled	93	7
Non-production		
Services	84	16
Administration/marketing	68	32
High administration	20	80

Source: Calculated from Central Statistical Organisation, *Annual Abstract of Statistics* (Ministry of Planning, Baghdad, 1977).

Average wage scales in 1976 ran from ID 372 per year for unskilled to ID 1,594 for highly skilled experts (ID 1 = *c.* $3). Above-average wages were paid by the public sector for unskilled and non-production workers the private sector paid a substantial premium for its small number of technicians and skilled workers. There was considerable wage differentiation between different industries, public and private.[12]

Large capital-intensive hydrocarbon-based industrial projects have been the centrepiece of the regime's planning since 1973. Their viability is based on projected exports of substantial portions of production. The urea plant at Khor al-Zubair will export a million tons of fertiliser a year, more than half its planned output. A phosphate-based fertiliser plant plans to export 85 per cent of its output. The steel plant at Khor al-Zubair plans to export 1.5 million tons of concentrated ore a year. The $1 billion petrochemical plant there will produce 150,000 tons of polyethylene and polyvinyl chloride and 40,000 tons of caustic soda a year, more than the domestic economy will likely absorb in the foreseeable future. The capital costs of these plants run 50-75 per cent over equivalent costs in industrialised countries. If feedstocks and fuels are not factored in at world market prices, the effect will be a subsidisation of those industries with revenues foregone from the direct export of hydrocarbons.

These projects strengthen Iraq's links to the world market as a provider of intermediate-stage resources and reinforce the pattern of an economy whose export sector is the dynamic core, producing most of the value-added, earning most of the revenues but employing a small fraction of the labour force and reliant on the multinational corporations for capital in the form of technology and skills. Since the oil price increase Iraq has imported machinery, equipment and capital goods worth over $2 billion a year, more than twice the value of the country's entire manufacturing sector. Consultant and service fees alone each year amount to hundreds of millions of dollars — more than twice the value of all Iraq's non-oil exports and more than ten times the total expenditure for local research and development activities.[13]

The Oil Sector

The share of this sector in the national product jumped from 35 per cent in 1970 to 60 per cent in 1974, a level it has since maintained. Its contribution to total government revenues increased from 52 per cent in 1971 to 87 per cent in 1976, and crude oil accounted for some 98 per cent of total exports in 1975. Information concerning production, exports, destinations or purchasers is extremely restricted. From recent editions of the official *Annual Abstract of Statistics* one would not know Iraq ever produced or exported a single barrel of oil. Decisions over markets, prices and production levels are taken by the top leadership. The Oil Affairs Committee of the Revolutionary Command Council became the Follow-Up Committee for Oil Affairs and the Implementation of Agreements in September 1971. Consisting only of Saddam Husain and (until July 1979) Adnan Hamdani, the committee not only directed the oil sector but, under the rationale of circumventing cumbersome bureaucratic procedure, could short-circuit such elemental planning components as competitive bidding by declaring a project to be 'strategic'. Most large industrial and infrastructure schemes are eligible for such designation.

Despite rhetoric concerning the need to diversify the economic structure of Iraq from its dependence on oil exports, the most prominent feature of Iraqi development spending is heavy investment in exploration for additional reserves, and in extending the productivity of existing fields.[14] Nearly one quarter of Iraqi contracts in 1980 were in this sector; nearly half of the total Middle East contracts in this sector were Iraqi.[15]

Construction

This commodity sector now ranks above agriculture and manufacturing in its contribution to the domestic product. Once almost entirely private, there is now a large public sector component which employed 76,479 workers in 1977, far more than the total number of unskilled and semi-skilled workers in both public and private large manufacturing. Average wages for ordinary labourers were relatively high at ID 919.

The prominence of this sector is also reflected in loans by the Estate Bank totalling $223.1 million in 1976. Comparable figures for the Agricultural Bank and the Industrial Bank were $44.6 million and $42.3 million, respectively. Over three-quarters of this construction was buildings rather than infrastructure. More than half the residential buildings and three-quarters of the commercial buildings were in Baghdad.[16] One recent report noted that 'the predilection of leading Iraqis for real estate investment has been acknowledged in the role allotted to the mixed sector in the development of tourism and in meeting Iraq's chronic shortage of hotels'.[17]

Commerce

An Iraqi Chamber of Commerce report in 1973 estimated that the number of retail trade firms had risen from 36,000 in 1965 to 100,000 in 1973, and the number of persons engaged to 200,000. Official figures for 1976 claimed 77,766 establishments and less than 100,000 people engaged full-time. For the few who were not proprietors, salaries averaged ID 349. Retail trade is increasingly dependent on imported goods, 90 per cent of which come through the public sector. Private retail agents receive commissions averaging 10 per cent for serving as distribution networks.[18]

Services

This is now the largest sector in terms of employment: over one million people in 1977. Much of the labour displaced from the agricultural sector in recent years has been absorbed in this sector, and most of it by the state itself. The state is by far the largest single employer. In 1977 the number of government personnel was 580,132, almost as many people as employed by all large public and private manufacturing firms combined (Table 3.6). This does not include the

Table 3.6: Growth of the State Sector

Year	Personnel
1938	9,740
1958	20,031
1968	224,253
1972	385,978
1977	580,132

Source: 1938, 1958 from H. Batatu, *The Old Social Classes and the Revolutionary Movement in Iraq* (Princeton University Press, New Jersey, 1979), p. 482; 1968, 1972 from K. Hameed, 'Manpower and Employment Planning in Iraq and the Syrian Arab Republic', in United Nations, *Studies on Development Problems in Countries of Western Asia, 1975* (United Nations, New York, 1977), p. 34; 1977 from Central Statistical Organisation, *Annual Abstract of Statistics* (Ministry of Planning, Baghdad, 1977), p. 248.

armed forces, an estimated 230,000, or nearly 200,000 pensioners directly dependent on the state for their livelihood. Within the government the largest employer is the Ministry of the Interior, with 136,900 in 1977. Another 40,819 were employed in the Presidential Affairs Department, many of whom, as in the Interior Ministry, were engaged in 'security' assignments.[19] In November 1979 Interior Minister Shakur announced an unspecified expansion of internal security forces 'in order to carry out transactions with citizens with the greatest possible speed'.[20]

Aspects of Class Determination

The basis for the expanding role of the state lies in its access to some

60 per cent of the national product by virtue of its control of the hydrocarbon extraction and export sector. In the sphere of production the largest enterprises are, by definition, public. The structure of public and private sector displays the strategic character of state control of the most capital-intensive and technologically advanced industries, established by contract with large multinational firms. In the sphere of circulation the state is responsible for virtually all external trade. Its control over internal trade is indirect, but, all considered, state owner- ship leaves in the regime's hands the major share of the surplus at the levels of production and exchange.

This control represents, above all, a relationship with millions of Iraqi citizens who have a direct interest in the state's economic decisions and capacities. The manner in which the state – that is, the individuals and institutions who constitute the state – carries out this responsibility and defines this relationship determines its class character.

It seems hardly necessary to point out that there is in Iraq today a rather complete identification of the state with the Arab Ba'th Socialist Party. The 'supreme organ of the state', the Revolutionary Command Council, consists solely of the top leaders of the party, and since 1977 its composition has been identical with the party's Regional Command. More than this, the multifarious organs of the state – civilian and military, economic and political – are headed and staffed by members of the party. Where a position is filled on the basis of skill or technical capacity rather than Ba'th affiliation, a party official is attached to the office to supervise, guide and report on the non- party functionary. The situation as it exists today is thus quite different from any previous period in Iraq's post-revolutionary history, including the early years of Ba'th rule.

Thus it seems reasonable to turn first to the Ba'th Party's own definition of itself with respect to Iraq's social classes. The party defines itself as socialist, but this is sometimes simply a matter of assertion, as when, after 1975, the leadership proclaimed that hence- forth what had been termed the public sector would be called the 'socialist sector'.

Socialism, for the Ba'th, is distinctly not Communist in doctrine or practice, or Marxist in perspective. It can most fairly be categorised as populist. Such is certainly the implication of the party's National Action Charter of November 15, 1971 which proclaims, *inter alia*, that 'While the Revolution (*sic*) is keen in protecting the interests of the toiling masses . . . it is at the same time keen to protect the interests of small and middle merchants'.[21] Perhaps one of the most sophisticated ideological documents of the party in its present configuration is the Political Report of the 8th Regional Congress of January 1974. It takes note of the tendency to confuse 'socialist tenets and state capitalism', and goes on to define the latter as

> a distorted image of socialism. It negates or at least fakes democratic relations in production, freezes the role of the working class and kills its vitality. It makes the bureaucrats the masters and overlords of production . . . It has a distorted view of socialism as a mere economic activity unrelated to other aspects of the life of society.[22]

In a burst of uncharacteristic insight and candidness, the authors of the report acknowledge several pages later that 'most of the measures taken so far resemble state capitalism rather than socialism'.

This report seems to represent the high point of ideological clarity. Speeches and pronouncements by government leaders tend to concentrate more on 'balanced development', 'confronting exploiters', and the like. Adnan Hamdani, the highest authority in the entire realm of economic planning until the summer of 1979, once observed: 'The Ba'th Party is not just a ruling party; it has an ideology based on rapid development of the economy in a limited period of time. For this we need large revenues.'[23] This ideology of 'developmentalism' is one the Ba'th shares with all manner of Third World regimes and agents of industrialised governments as well. It is purposefully 'classless', stressing the development of productive forces (industrialisation) and leaving unsaid any determination of the relations of production. It is, in short, an ideology of capitalist development with a 'national' cover. One is forced to conclude that the Ba'th has not come far from the days in 1963 when then-Secretary-General Ali Saleh Sadi lamented: 'We searched till we wearied for socialist thinkers who could help us, but could find none.'[24]

The State as Boss

The class character of a regime cannot be divined from the social origins of those who staff its highest echelons, nor from its ideology and slogans. The question must rather be asked: In the interests of which class or classes does it function? A determination of this rests on its relationship with the specific classes of Iraqi society, and with international capital.

There is little reason to doubt that the material conditions of the masses of Iraqis have improved in some measure over the last decade. Access to the oil rent has given this regime extraordinary leverage in meeting needs and expectations at the level of distribution of goods and services. This leverage has been adroitly used to ensure popular acquiescence, if not support, for the regime's actions and policies. One instance is the substantial salary increase decreed for all military, security and public sector personnel (more than one fifth of the total labour force) in August 1979. More recently, witness the president's 'guns and butter' policy, which has provided Iraqi consumers with an unprecedented array and quantity of goods (mostly imported) since the war against Iran was launched.

At the level of production the record is less impressive. The production relations of a society determine its structural and institutional needs. Education (for the reproduction of skills and ideology) and security are generally two key responsibilities of a modern state. As we have seen, Iraq's security apparatus has been more than adequately developed. Its investments in education and training have been considerable, but accomplishments have proved more limited.

Structurally, the regime is confronted with the displacement of labour from the rural sector and its absorption for the most part in the notoriously unproductive services sector. Since 1974, the state has expressly become the employer of last resort for all university graduates. This suggests that official unemployment figures bear little relation to the number of individuals who are potentially economically active but are not working. Ironically, the surfeit of non-productive labour in the services sector and the state in particular is matched by a serious labour shortage in productive sectors, from skilled and expert labour in industry to agricultural workers. According to one analysis, industrial projects in the 1976-80 plan called for nearly half a million additional semi-skilled workers, 375,000 craftspersons, and 150,000 degree-holders. The total output of graduates stood at less than 20,000 annually, and most of these were in liberal arts, law, etc. The situation in vocational fields was even more inadequate.[25] It is impossible to say how much this labour 'bottleneck', as opposed to other factors, contributed to the shortcomings of the plan. A recent World Bank study estimates that by 1985 Iraq will depend on non-Iraqis for between 4.3 per cent and 10 per cent of its entire labour force.[26] The outlook may be further complicated if the armed forces draw more heavily on the limited pool of skilled labour.

The difficulty of controlling the labour market is reflected in decrees forbidding private firms from hiring skilled workers who have resigned from the public sector. It is also reflected in the Ba'th's policies towards the working class. Official trade unions are under the direct control of party functionaries. Other labour-organising is forbidden. To resolve acknowledged tensions between management (public and private) and labour, a scheme of worker participation on the boards of directors of firms was instituted: the worker representatives are selected by the party rather than by the workers themselves.

These measures of control are not applied exclusively against workers and wage-earners, of course, but they are an indication that 'socialist' Iraq is not a state that is directed by, or functions particularly on behalf of, Iraqi workers and producers. In its supervision and maintenance of the relations between Iraq's major classes the state must resolve or suppress the contradictions that arise. There are indications that the efforts by the regime to secure working-class support early in its reign, particularly through guarantees of job security, now hamper its efforts to reallocate capital and labour and redefine the terms of their relationship. This was apparent when, in 1976, the regime became seriously concerned with low productivity in both manufacturing and services. It instituted a series of 'productivity seminars' in plants and government agencies. Responsibility was rhetorically shared between management and labour, but there seemed to be little ambiguity in the thrust of the 'solutions': greater surveillance and discipline in the workplace, and tying wage increases (though not salaries) to increases in productivity.[27] One is reminded of Marx's observation on the function of management when the worker, the direct producer, does not own the means of production: 'The greater this antagonism, the greater the role played by supervision.'[28]

There is another aspect to this experience that deserves notice: the clear intent of the state to reproduce within its own agencies, as well as in the public sector enterprises it controls, relations of production, a social division of labour, characteristic of capitalist enterprises: 'the despotism of the factory', to cite Marx again. The Iraqi 'socialist' sector comprises numerous public corporations which reproduce this pattern. In the industrial sector in particular, 'turnkey' contracts with Western multinational corporations specify that management and training be provided in any given plant or enterprise (a petrochemical plant, the state airways, etc.). There is, in other words, a purposeful effort to instil in the most modern and central economic institutions relations of production appropriate to capitalism, not socialism. To the extent that technocratic and managerial personnel from these institutions wield political and social influence in the society, they do so inculcated with an explicitly bourgeois ideology and behavioural experience.

Will the Iraqi Ruling Class Please Stand Up?

A modern state has the function of reproducing and developing the forces of production. This task the Iraqi state is attempting to carry out, in a necessarily imperfect way. A capitalist state must carry out and facilitate this task while at the same time reproducing capitalist relations of production, requiring the development of a bourgeoisie and a proletariat. It is in applying these categories to modern Iraq that the difficulty in specifying the class character of the state becomes apparent.

The difficulty arises in determining the contours of both class poles. Iraq's proletariat now numbers several hundred thousand, but it is clear that most of Iraq's wage-earners are not workers – that is, producers of surplus value. The numerical superiority of Iraqi wage-earners engaged in non-productive work, and identifying with a non-proletarian ideology and outlook, may have the effect of neutralising the working class: though growing in absolute numbers, it remains relatively marginal as a social force.

On the other side of the social divide we must still clarify the identity of Iraq's ruling class. It seems reasonably apparent that, outside the state, there is no large Iraqi bourgeoisie as such whose interests are served by the state. One is left to conclude that the state itself functions as a bourgeoisie, on behalf of the leading elements in the state apparatus. Is this governing class a ruling class? It is tempting to answer in the affirmative, but the increasingly narrow geographical base of the present regime makes us hesitate. Is there a social base that is broader, co-existing and even flourishing as the state leadership itself reverts to localism and personal rule? The answer appears to be yes, although it is not possible at this distance and juncture to identify it with any precision. Clearly it involves identification with the ruling party and privileged access to the social wealth controlled by the state. Some outlines of this base can be inferred from the frequent promulgation of special allowances and privileges for professionals, technicians and top level managers. Allowances – vocational allowance if prohibited from 'moonlighting', geographical allowance depending on proximity to Baghdad, etc. – can total as much as 250 per cent of salary.[29] Privileges include exemption from civil service regulations, including salary limitations.

A social base, however, is not a ruling class. The state, extremely centralised under the direct domination of the president, exercises the powers that in capitalist societies derive from ownership and possession: namely, control of the means of production and determination of the terms and conditions for surplus value extraction. What makes us hesitate from pronouncing the existence, then, of a state bourgeoisie is the lack of coherence within the regime at its highest levels. The state incorporates a bourgeoisie in formation – those who determine its course and functions. The locus of control of political and economic power around a handful of individuals is a point of weakness in the development of Iraq's production relations.

A final observation concerns the general role of the state in advanced or monopoly capitalism and its responsibility not merely for the reproduction of the general conditions but for direct involvement in the actual reproduction of capital. The phenomenon of the state bourgeoisie (or, in Iraq's case, the state functioning on behalf of an incipient, would-be bourgeoisie) may be a structural feature of the current state of development of international capital rather than merely a transition to a 'normal' capitalist society with a leading private sector. Iraq, among other states of the Third World, now participates in the global composition of capital and reproduction of capitalist relations at an unprecedented level, neither co-equal, of course, nor 'dependent' in its relations with the advanced capitalist societies. Its class composition is neither directly nor immediately determined by the mode of its incorporation in the world economy, and is mediated by a state which has come to represent ownership of property. The state itself is strong in its apparatus, but structurally vulnerable and institutionally weak. It is particularly susceptible to the rapidly changing class relations it must embody and reproduce.

Notes

1. Hanna Batatu, *The Old Social Classes and the Revolutionary Movements of Iraq* (Princeton University Press, New Jersey, 1979), p. 806.
2. Revised from a section entitled 'Oil and the State' in 'Iraq and the War in the Gulf', *MERIP Reports*, no. 97 (June 1981).
3. Shakir Issa, 'Rural Income Distribution in Iraq', unpublished mimeo, Development Seminar Working Paper no. 8, School of Oriental and African

Studies, University of London, March 1977, p. 3.

4. Batatu, *The Old Social Classes*, p. 1117.

5. Published as *Revolutionary Iraq* (Ministry of Information, Baghdad, 1974), p. 142.

6. Thirty per cent is Issa's calculation for the decline in arable land based on the 1971 Agricultural Census. According to the government's *Annual Abstract of Statistics* for 1977, p. 59, total cultivated area in 1977 had dropped to the 1971 level.

7. K. Hameed, 'Manpower and Employment Planning in Iraq and the Syrian Arab Republic', in United Nations, *Studies on Development Problems in the Countries of Western Asia, 1975* (United Nations, New York, 1977), p. 30.

8. *Al-Iraq*, 23 June 1977.

9. Atheel al-Jomard, 'Internal Migration in Iraq', in Abbas Kelidar (ed.), *The Integration of Modern Iraq* (Croom Helm, London, 1979).

10. Economist Intelligence Unit, *Iraq: A New Market in a Region of Turmoil* (EIU, London, 1980), Special Report no. 88, pp. 4, 13.

11. Central Statistical Organisation, *Annual Abstract of Statistics, 1977* (Ministry of Planning, Baghdad, 1977). Hereafter *AAS*.

12. Ibid.

13. United Nations Conference on Trade and Development (UNCTAD), *Transfer and Development of Technology in Iraq* (UNCTAD, New York, June 1978), pp. 27, 30.

14. Economist Intelligence Unit, *Iraq*, p. 54.

15. *Middle East Economic Digest*, 25 Jan. 1980.

16. Central Statistical Organisation, *AAS*, 1977.

17. Economist Intelligence Unit, *Iraq*, p. 16.

18. Federation of Iraqi Chambers of Commerce, 'Summary of Annual Report', unpublished mimeo, 1973, pp. 22-6.

19. Central Statistical Organisation, *AAS*, 1977, p. 248.

20. *Al-Thawra*, 18 November 1979.

21. M. Khadduri, *Socialist Iraq* (Middle East Institute, Washington, 1978), p. 222.

22. Government of Iraq, *Revolutionary Iraq*, p. 138.

23. *Middle East Economic Survey*, 20 June 1975.

24. Batatu, *The Old Social Classes*, p. 1014.

25. Economist Intelligence Unit, *Iraq*, pp. 67-8.

26. World Bank, 'Research Project on International Labor Migration and Manpower in the Middle East and North Africa', unpublished mimeo, September 1980, p. 36.

27. *Al-Thawra*, 8 October 1976.

28. Cited in Nicos Poulantzas, *Classes in Contemporary Capitalism* (New Left Books, London, 1978), p. 226.

29. *Al-Thawra*, 17 July 1976.

4 RECENT DEVELOPMENTS IN THE KURDISH ISSUE

Sa'ad Jawad

The Historical Background

The Kurdish issue has constituted a central problem confronting Iraqi governments ever since the state of Iraq was established in 1920. This problem has comprised both internal and external aspects. In the domestic political context the Kurds, on the basis of their ethnic and linguistic difference from the Arab majority, have justifiably pressed for a special status within the Iraqi state. Yet on many occasions that genuine desire has been exploited by external powers with an interest in keeping the contemporary state of Iraq disunited and weak.

The development of the Kurdish issue between 1920 and 1968 reflected this continued interaction between the domestic political context and the international environment. As this writer has shown elsewhere,[1] Turkish and British aspirations helped to create the situation in which the Iraqi Kurds were in almost continuous revolt between 1919 and 1947. Drawing encouragement from international conditions, in 1919 Shaikh Mahmud of Sulaimaniya staged a tribal rebellion in pursuit of autonomy and independence for the Kurdish areas. This rebellion continued through to 1930. From 1927 the Barzani tribe, protesting against the expansion of the central authority and the establishment of police posts in the mountains, took the lead in rebelling against the central government. While the latter rebellion was crushed in 1930, in 1943 the Barzanis again rose in revolt under the leadership of Mulla Mustafa al-Barzani. The Iraqi army's success in crushing the second Barzani revolt in 1946 drove Mulla Mustafa and many of his followers into Iranian Kurdistan, where the Soviet army was in control and was fostering the ephemeral Mahabad Kurdish republic.[2] From this encounter there emerged the Kurdish Democratic Party, for which the Democratic Party for Kurdistan (Iran) served as a prototype.[3]

The period between 1947 (the demise of the Mahabad republic) and 1958 saw a significant division in the Kurdish movement. Kurdish nationalism remained alive among the Kurdish intelligentsia, who had moved

47

from the Kurdish towns and villages to the large cities such as Baghdad, Sulaimaniya and Arbil. The Kurdish Democratic Party (henceforth KDP) was the vehicle through which this nationalism found expression. Under the influence of two young lawyers, Ibrahim Ahmed and Jalal Talabani, the party took a turn to the left.[4] The Kurdish masses, meanwhile, were left under the direct influence of the tribal leaders; they remained tribally motivated and deeply religious. The tribal leaders were soon to find that their tribal, land and other interests lay with the ruling clique in Iraq and thus they chose to support the latter, sometimes against the Kurdish intelligentsia.

After the monarchy was overthrown and a republican regime headed by Abd al-Karim Qasim came to power in 1958, a significant change in government policy towards the Kurds occurred. Qasim released imprisoned Kurds and allowed the return of the exiled Barzanis, headed by Mulla Mustafa. He also assured a Kurdish delegation that visited him of his regime's good intentions towards all national minorities. Moreover, the first republican provisional constitution mentioned the Kurds as partners with the Arabs in the state of Iraq. The position of the Kurds was further enhanced when Qasim came to depend on them to trim the influence and threat of his opponents. In return for their support, Qasim legalised the Kurdistan Democratic Party under the leadership of Mulla Mustafa, allowed Kurdish newspapers to be published and extended armed and financial assistance to the Barzanis.

By the end of 1961, however, the relationship between Qasim and the Kurds had been disrupted. There were two reasons for this. First, as Kurdish influence increased, Qasim began to see in it a threat to his authority. He started, therefore, taking some restrictive measures against the Barzanis and the KDP. He amended the KDP programme, put some of its leaders in prison, closed the Kurdish newspapers and cancelled Kurdish conferences. Second, in June 1961 the Iraqi government began implementing the Agrarian Reform Law (promulgated by Qasim in 1958) in the Kurdish areas. This attempt to limit the size of landholdings was strongly resisted by Kurdish landlords, who claimed that the Kurdish cultivated areas were different in nature from other areas of cultivation in Iraq and required special consideration. Qasim replied by ordering the use of force against the landlords. In the resultant chaos which prevailed over the Kurdish mountains, Kurdish elements hostile to the republican regime in Baghdad rose against it.

It is significant that at that time neither Mulla Mustafa nor the KDP supported the rebellion – indeed, the KDP condemned the rebellion and called on the government to put it down. Qasim, however, saw in this situation the opportunity to strike at all elements of the Kurdish national movement. In September 1961 he ordered the bombardment of Barazan, the home village of Mulla Mustafa, and declared the KDP illegal. Mulla Mustafa and the other leaders of the KDP had no alternative but to join and lead the Kurdish tribal rebellion, declaring it a revolt for national rights.

Between 1961 and 1970 the Kurdish war continued intermittently. Four truces were announced, corresponding to the four changes in regime which Baghdad witnessed,[5] yet all attempts at solving the problem failed. The Kurds sought full autonomy as their primary objective. Iraqi governments, while accepting some measure of self-rule, rejected the idea of an expanded autonomy – regarding this as a step towards separation. Two points of view developed within governing circles as to how the Kurdish problem could be solved: one (maintained largely by army officers) favoured a military solution; the other (maintained largely by civilians) favoured a peaceful approach involving granting the Kurds their basic rights. As the civilians were always in a minority and had no power to enforce their point of view, the military's opinion prevailed.

The Kurdish national movement, too, was divided. A radical faction, centred on Ibrahim Ahmed and Jalal Talabani in the KDP leadership, enjoyed the support of the intelligentsia; while a tribal and rightist faction, headed by Mulla Mustafa, drew support from tribal elements. The latter faction maintained majority support within the Kurdish national movement, and in 1964 Mulla Mustafa was able to ensure his dominance over the movement by removing Ahmed, Talabani and their followers both from the party and from Iraqi Kurdistan.

The March 1970 Manifesto and its Aftermath

A new attempt to come to grips with the Kurdish issue followed the Arab Ba'th Socialist Party's return to power in July 1968 (the Party's first brief taste of power having been between February and November 1963). With a young civilian leadership and a new vision, the Ba'th Party leaders saw in the Kurdish problem a major threat to the existence of the Iraqi state and a dangerous opportunity for foreign elements to interfere in the internal affairs of Iraq. Moreover, embroilment in a war with the Kurds would keep the new government weak and enable the influence of the military to persist, which could in turn make possible a military *coup* against the Ba'th Party (as had occurred in November 1963).

Both intention and necessity, therefore, led the new government to conduct a series of negotiations with Kurdish elements, resulting in the issuing of the Manifesto of 11 March 1970. The March Manifesto gave a considerable boost to the Kurdish national movement: it met fundamental Kurdish demands which previous governments had rejected. The manifesto began by declaring that the Kurds of Iraq were part of the divided Kurdish people, and that the Kurdish national movement was part of the general Iraqi national movement. The government promised the Kurds full recognition of their nationality and autonomy within four years. The Kurdish language was made the primary language in the Kurdish areas, and also an official language which would be taught in addition to Arabic throughout Iraq. A Kurdish vice-president was to be appointed in the central government, together with five Kurdish cabinet ministers (compared with two in most previous Iraqi governments). The Kurds were to be permitted to form their own political and professional organisations, and a certain number of the Kurdish *peshmarga* (armed men) were to be integrated into the Iraqi armed forces as border guards. A general amnesty was declared, with the government undertaking to subsidise the KDP and to assist the remaining *peshmarga* until they were provided with jobs.

The one issue which this far-reaching agreement did not solve satisfactorily was that of Kirkuk. Kirkuk is a province in the north of Iraq with a mixed population of Kurds, Turkomans and Arabs. Most significant is the presence of oil in this area. The Kurds contended that the province should fall within their autonomous region, on grounds of having a Kurdish majority. The government claimed that only some parts of Kirkuk had a Kurdish majority, and therefore only those parts should be included in the autonomous region. It was obvious that the government was unwilling to give up its direct control over a region important to the economy of the whole country. In order to avoid a breakdown in the negotiations over this subject, the two sides agreed that the future of Kirkuk should be left to be determined by a future plebiscite. It was evident that this issue contained the seeds of a future possible split between the two sides.

Despite initial optimism that the March Manifesto would provide the basis for a permanent understanding, by September 1972 the agreement was showing signs of breaking down. The factors leading towards breakdown are clearly stated in the memoranda exchanged between the Ba'th Party and the KDP at this time. An analysis of these memoranda, therefore, is vital to an understanding of what happened. The exchange was initiated by the Ba'th Party in the hope that the deteriorating relations between the two parties – as also the deteriorating situation in Iraqi Kurdistan – could be ameliorated.

The Ba'th Party's memorandum of September 1972, although admitting some mistakes committed by government officials, placed the major share of blame for the worsening situation on the leadership of Mulla Mustafa al-Barzani.[6] Barzani was accused of failing to live up to expectations. After praising the March Manifesto and its accomplishments as the greatest achievement for Kurds and Arabs alike, the memorandum went on to cite the negative acts committed by the KDP and its followers. KDP policy was criticised in three fields. First, in its external relations the KDP was accused of maintaining and strengthening its relations with Iran. The memorandum gave examples of the great quantity of arms and merchandise the KDP was receiving from and through Iran, and the increasing number of KDP members receiving military training in Iran. These moves were regarded as contrary to the security, national integrity and sovereignty of the Iraqi state.

Second, in the field of internal policy the memorandum accused the KDP of working to establish its own and undisputed authority in Iraqi Kurdistan through bypassing, and sometimes defying, the authority of the central government. Mulla Mustafa was accused of not dissolving – and perhaps increasing – his armed *peshmarga* forces, who 'since 1970 have assassinated 379 people, abducted and assaulted 738 people and committed 45 acts of sabotage'.

Third, the KDP was accused of plotting directly and indirectly against the Iraqi regime. This was done through 'sheltering elements [Arab and Kurdish] hostile to the Iraqi revolution, providing them with arms and money, and instructing them in duties that threatened the security and integrity of the state'. The memorandum stated that the KDP was 'encouraging members of the Iraqi armed forces to desert or to commit acts contrary to military discipline'. These policies, the memorandum concluded, were harmful to and destructive of Arab-Kurdish brotherhood, national unity, the Iraqi revolution and the progress of the autonomy plan which was due to be implemented in March 1974.

It was obvious that the government was concerned about the challenge to central government authority posed by Mulla Mustafa and the KDP. The government's concern stemmed not only from Mulla Mustafa's attempts to take advantage of the agreement in order to strengthen the quasi-independent rule he imposed over the areas he controlled, but also from his attempts to impede and oppose certain measures taken by the government which were regarded as essential to the country's international position and future. Among the latter measures were the nationalisation of oil, the implementation of the agrarian reform and the signing of the Iraqi-Soviet treaty of friendship. The stance taken by Mulla Mustafa on these issues, together with his relations with Israel and the CIA (which by that time had become an open secret) put in question the intentions and objectives of Mulla Mustafa and the KDP.

In answer to the Ba'th Party memorandum the KDP sent a yet longer memorandum to the Ba'th leadership. The latter memorandum failed to deny the accusations which had been made, but sought to exonerate the KDP from blame by citing the KDP's own complaints and observations, which it said were the real reasons behind the deteriorating situation. The government was blamed for 'its failure to honour its obligations in the March Manifesto'.[7] Three major undertakings made in the manifesto had not, according to the memorandum, been implemented: first, the KDP had not been given due representation in the legislature and the executive, nor had a Kurdish vice-president for the republic been appointed; second, the demarcation of the proposed autonomous Kurdish region had not been carried out, and finally, the Kurdish areas had not been allocated a special share in the economic plan.

The Ba'th Party's memorandum had, in fact, anticipated these accusations and had provided some justification for the central government's position. The memorandum stated that the Kurds would be able to participate in legislation once a national assembly had been created. The government was pledged to establish such an assembly as soon as was possible, but its establishment was linked to the signing of a 'national charter between the patriotic Iraqi political parties . . . so that the assembly becomes an institution of patriotic coalition and not a floor for negative opposition'.

With regard to appointing a Kurd as a vice-president, the Ba'th leadership declared that it was still honouring its word; it blamed the KDP for failing to choose the right person for the post. What had occurred on this issue is, in fact, both interesting and indicative. Shortly after signing the March Manifesto the KDP submitted the name of its then secretary-general, Habib Mohammed Karim, as its nominee for the post of vice-president. The government rejected this nomination on the ground that Karim was a Fuli Kurd (i.e. of Iranian origin) and as such could not fill so important and sensitive a post. The government asked for another nomination and it suggested itself two other names, one being a member of the KDP's politbureau. The KDP refused and stuck to its initial nomination. Thus the seat remained vacant.

The central government had also, so the Ba'th memorandum contended, shown its willingness to proceed with the demarcation of the proposed Kurdish autonomous area. It was, rather, Mulla Mustafa who had hindered this demarcation by informing a government representative that he would reject the result of any plebiscite in a disputed area – if that plebiscite did not show a Kurdish majority. The two sides were, of course, talking about Kirkuk. With regard to allocating special funds to the Kurdish areas, the government declared that it was already doing so, in addition to allocating generous allowances to the KDP and to Mulla Mustafa's headquarters.

Besides its major complaints, the KDP had other reasons for adopting an intransigent stand. First, there was the role of the Shah of Iran and the CIA who began in September 1972 to furnish Mulla Mustafa with a great deal of material and moral support, thus enabling him to persist in his defiance of the Iraqi government.[8] Second, the Kurdish leaders were alarmed by some abortive attempts on the lives of their leaders, especially on Mulla Mustafa. They interpreted these attempts, which the KDP accused some government circles of organising, as intended to split and dominate the Kurdish national movement. The government's moves towards building up good relations with different Kurdish factions were seen in a similar light. Thus the main problem which had impeded previous attempts at peaceful settlement – that of little confidence and of mistrust – was persisting.

On 9 March 1973 the KDP submitted a detailed plan for autonomy to the government. The government argued that the plan included some demands that were contradictory to the spirit of the March Manifesto. From this point the government seems to have come to the conclusion that it would not be possible to draw up an autonomy plan in collaboration with the KDP; it began, therefore, to draw up its own plan. In September 1973 the government introduced its autonomy plan and invited 'Iraqi progressive, national and independent personalities' to discuss it. This was done in the hope of gaining as much support as possible for the government's point of view. Kurdish elements hostile to Mulla Mustafa were approached, and the secret support of some leading personalities from Mulla Mustafa's KDP was also obtained. The fundamental difference between the Iraqi government plan and the Kurdish plan lay in the extent of the powers allocated to the autonomous authority.

The government's tactics severely angered KDP leaders. The government had chosen to consult other Kurdish factions, together with Arab political groupings, before consulting the main KDP leadership. The KDP therefore stuck to its initial plan. While the government argued that the support it had received through the nationwide discussions was enough to justify its policy, its stance was, in fact, part of a wider policy aimed at showing the KDP that it was not the only representative of the Kurdish people. The government also wanted to involve all national elements in the discussion of possible solutions to the Kurdish problem and thereby make the settlement of the problem a duty of all elements.

Despite the differences, direct negotiations between the government and the KDP started in January 1974.[9] There was, however, no change in the attitude of both sides, and it seemed almost certain that events were moving towards a showdown. On 2 March the talks broke down. Intensive attempts at mediation went on, reaching their climax with the arrival of Mulla Mustafa's son, Idris al-Barzani, in Baghdad on 9 March. But again nothing positive was agreed. The government told Idris that it had bound itself in 1970 to declare Iraqi Kurdistan autonomous by 11 March 1974, and that it was intent on doing so. Thus the KDP was given three final days to consider the government's plan 'with a view to forwarding positive suggestions'. Idris was also informed that, after the government's autonomy plan was announced, the KDP would have a further 15 days within which to comply.[10]

On 11 March 1974 the government announced the Autonomy Law for Iraqi Kurdistan. The KDP rejected this as 'incomplete and lacking the KDP's prior consent'.[11] On the following day Mulla Mustafa ordered his *peshmarga* to occupy border posts and strategic points. Thus four years of peace were ended and war raged again over Iraqi Kurdistan.

Even before this decision, in a show of strength and defiance the KDP had called upon all Iraqi Kurds working in government posts to desert their jobs and join the *peshmarga* in the mountains. This appeal, with which a large number of Kurds complied, proved to be a tactical — and perhaps disastrous — mistake. By issuing it the KDP not only burned all its bridges with the government but also indicated clearly to the government the defiant and separatist intentions of the party. The government could not tolerate such actions. On 6 April the five pro-KDP Kurdish ministers, who were already failing to attend at their offices, were dismissed and five others were appointed. A further decree appointed a Kurd as vice-president of the republic.

The 1974-5 War

Due to the sophistication of the weapons used, the new war was tough and intensive. Both sides were better equipped and organised, but the Iraqi army retained the upper hand. After the initial success of the *peshmarga*, the Iraqi army staged its counter-offensive and in a few months managed to remove the *peshmarga*'s threat to Zakho and Mosul, together with clearing the routes leading from and to the plain.[12] In August 1974 the army launched its main offensive with a view to cornering the *peshmarga* forces and pushing them towards the Iranian border.

The August 1974 offensive, the biggest since the Kurdish conflict had begun in 1961, took the form of a two-pronged thrust that aimed at capturing the Kurdish headquarters and strongholds along the Hamilton Road linking Rawanduz with the Iranian border (Figure 4.1).

Figure 4.1: The Kurdish Areas of Iraq

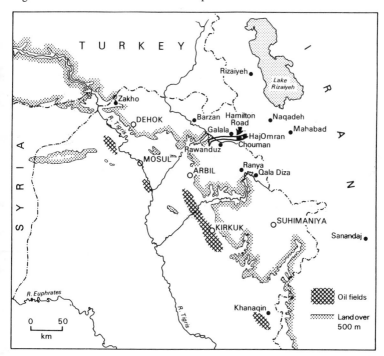

The army duly managed to capture Ranya, Qalat Diza and Rawanduz, thus coming within 20 miles of the KDP headquarters at Chouman.[13] The overall significance of these gains was contested by the KDP, which claimed that it had withdrawn in pursuance of its old and successful tactic of abandoning vulnerable areas in summertime and recapturing them in winter – when the Iraqi army became bogged down in the snowy mountains. By the end of December 1974, however, the strength of the Iraqi army's position was indubitable: the army had not only consolidated its previous gains but had made some fresh gains in difficult terrain, such as capturing the mountain peaks over- looking Chouman, Haj Omran (Mulla Mustafa's headquarters) and the *peshmarga*'s supply lines from Iran. The Iraqi army seemed poised to finish the war in its favour.

Sensing the direction in which events were leading, the Shah of Iran – who was gambling on the success of Mulla Mustafa's forces – began early in 1975 supplying the *peshmarga* with additional sophisticated weapons. When it became clear that the weapons were not sufficient to enable the *peshmarga* to withstand the Iraqi army, units of the Iranian army were sent to fight alongside the *peshmarga*. It was estimated that the Shah sent at least 1,000 men to operate the heavy and long-range field guns, anti-aircraft missiles and anti-tank units.[14] Gradually it became evident that it was only the Iranian support which was enabling the Kurds to hold out.

Iranian involvement in the Kurdish war threatened the area with an open war between Iraq and Iran. Some initial skirmishes between the two armies occurred, bringing home to the Shah the realisation that hostilities would damage his growing ambitions and interests in the Gulf region. Of greater significance, perhaps, was the Shah's need for Iraqi support in the Organisation of Petroleum Exporting Countries (OPEC). These factors, together with the performance of the Iraqi army in Kurdistan, made the Shah reconsider his policy – apparently despite advice from the CIA. The Iraqi government had by this time also realised that only by propitiating the Iranian government could the Kurdish war be ended.

After a series of secret contacts, the Iraqi vice-president (Saddam Husain) and the Shah of Iran met in Algiers in March 1975, during an OPEC summit. The two men agreed to solve the problems between their countries peacefully and promised that their states would refrain from interfering in each other's internal affairs.

The Iraqi-Iranian agreement was not, in fact, as sudden as it first appeared. The agreement was, rather, the result of meetings between the two sides going back to August 1974, when it was announced that an official from the Iraqi Foreign Ministry had met with an Iranian counterpart in Istanbul.[15] These contacts seem to have been productive and in December 1974 the two foreign ministers held a meeting – also in Istanbul.[16] Other contacts between the two foreign ministers occurred in the United Nations.[17] Besides the desire of the two countries to reach a settlement, the progression towards peace was facilitated by the blessing and prodding of other countries, especially Egypt, Jordan, Turkey and Algeria. While the first two wanted to see the Iraqi army and resources free and ready to participate in any action against Israel, Turkey was concerned about the spread of Kurdish activities to its own Kurdish population. Turkey's economic relations with Iraq, moreover, were increasing and the Turkish government did not want to see these much-needed relations damaged or weakened as a result of the Kurdish war. The Algerian government shared Jordanian and Egyptian views regarding Iraq's indispensability to the confrontation states, but was also seeking to cement and safeguard the OPEC organisation, in which Iraq and Iran were leading members.

Due to the secretive nature of the preliminary talks, nothing detailed was revealed at the time about them. Although no agreement was reached 'there was also no disagreement',[18] and it is certain that these preliminary talks successfully laid the ground for the Algiers talks between Vice-President Saddam Husain and the Shah. During the last session of the OPEC meeting, on 6 March 1975, the Iraqi-Iranian *rapprochement* was made public. The central element in the understanding, as far as the Kurdish conflict was concerned, was the agreement 'to establish confidence and security all along the frontiers and to have a strict and efficient control of all subversive infiltration'.[19] As a result of this agreement Iran immediately stopped all aid to the *peshmarga* and withdrew its troops from Iraqi Kurdistan.

Within days of the Iraqi-Iranian understanding, the Kurdish revolt collapsed. The Iraqi government declared a general one-month amnesty to all Kurds and asked the *peshmarga* to lay down their arms. Most Kurds feared reprisals and crossed the border into Iran rather than submit to the Iraqi government. Mulla Mustafa, his family and prominent members of the KDP were among the first to cross. At the end of the amnesty period the Iraqi army moved almost unharassed into the heartland of the KDP, gaining control of all Iraqi Kurdistan. By May 1975, armed activity in Iraqi Kurdistan had come to an end. The number of the Kurds who crossed the borders into Iran was estimated at 50,000 – the majority of these being active and prominent

members of the KDP and its intelligence service, the Paristan. The
Iranian government, concerned at the potential for Iranian Kurdistan
becoming the focus of future Kurdish activity, spread the Iraqi Kurds
over different parts of Iranian Kurdistan – mainly in camps around the
big towns of Mahabad, Sanandaj and Rizaiyeh.[20] Most of the Barzani
family and their close followers were settled in Naqadeh. Mulla
Mustafa himself was settled in Teheran before moving to the United
States. He remained there until he died of cancer in 1979.

The Activities of the Iraqi Kurds in Iran

As soon as they settled in Iran, the Iraqi Kurds split into two major
groups, each putting the blame on the other for the failure of the
Kurdish revolt in Iraq. One group was headed by Jalal Talabani, the
old personal and ideological enemy of Mulla Mustafa. After being
ousted from the KDP by Mulla Mustafa in 1964, Talabani had moved
between Iran, Baghdad and Iraqi Kurdistan, until he finally settled in
Syria following the signature of the March Manifesto in 1970. His aim
throughout had been to gather support against Mulla Mustafa. His
moment finally came when the Shah of Iran signed off Mulla Mustafa
and abandoned his assistance to the Iraqi Kurds. Talabani immediately
moved from Syria to Turkey and Iraq (secretly) to lobby support
against Mulla Mustafa, whom he portrayed as a traitor to the Kurdish
cause. By November 1975, Talabani was able to announce the
establishment of a new Kurdish political organisation, the Kurdistan
Patriotic Union, as a replacement for the KDP. He intended the KPU
to be an umbrella organisation for all Kurdish shades of opinion.
Immediately after its establishment the KPU circulated declarations to
all Kurds in Iran and abroad, and it did succeed in gaining some
popularity among the Kurdish intelligentsia, who had always been dis-
satisfied with the tribal leadership of Mulla Mustafa. The new organisation
adopted a leftist ideology,[21] laying emphasis once more on 'armed
struggle'.

The other group was constituted by the Barzanis and their loyal
supporters. The leadership of this group now fell to Mulla Mustafa's
two youngest sons, Idris and Mas'ud. The group was, in effect, a
continuation of the KDP, whose organisation had been shattered by
military defeat. Seeing Talabani's success in organising cells and
circulating declarations, the two Barzani brothers moved quickly to
reorganise the KDP. The new leadership of the KDP began to publish

announcements even before any organisational structure had been created. To give the party a new and more democratic image, the name 'KDP Provisional Leadership' was adopted, suggesting that the new organisation was going to undergo major changes.[22] Despite this attempt to change the party's image, the Talabani group accused the new leadership of the KDP of being still heavily dependent on the Shah and his secret service, SAVAK. As evidence of this, Talabani pointed to the freedom of movement and of publication which the KDP Provisional Leadership enjoyed in Iran.

In an attempt to improve its wilting reputation among the Kurds, the KDP Provisional Leadership issued a new programme for the party. It made public its willingness to co-operate with all other Kurdish parties and groups. It also tried to stress its 'adherence to socialism' and its belief in 'the force of the workers and the peasantry'. But these announcements did not change the image of the party: most Kurds continued to regard it as linked to, or at least always ready to co-operate with, SAVAK, Israel and the CIA.[23]

The feud between the two Iraqi Kurdish factions also impinged upon their attitude towards the Iranian revolution. As soon as the authority of the late Shah began to show signs of weakness, Talabani's faction leaped to exploit the opportunity. After declaring his full support for the Iranian revolution, Talabani urged the Kurds to assist the Iranian people in their struggle against the Shah, and to work to achieve their national rights and demands.[24] Some reports spoke of successful attacks by armed men loyal to Talabani on isolated army and police posts in Iran.[25] Yet the KDP Provisional Leadership, headed by the two Barzani brothers, was more cautious and thus followed a different course of action. In a declaration circulated in January 1979 it declared its support for the 'struggle of the Iranian people', but at the same time condemned the activities of Talabani and accused his faction of treason.[26]

The attitudes of the two groups towards the Iranian revolution were to develop in an unexpected manner after the success of the revolution. Talabani, who had initially welcomed the revolution, allied himself with the KDP-Iran headed by Ghassemlau; his armed men subsequently took part in actions staged by the KDP-Iran against the new Islamic regime. Differences seem to have arisen between Talabani and Ghassemlau, however, and in May 1980 Talabani was reported to have held talks with Iranian officials to explore possible co-operation. The two Barzani brothers, despite having shown an initially cautious attitude to the revolution, ultimately proved more ready to co-operate

with the Islamic regime. This co-operation was to increase when Iran decided
to use the followers of the KDP Provisional Leadership against the Iraqi
regime (even before the outbreak of war between Iran and Iraq in September
1980). The KDP Provisional Leadership was enabled to gather support
among the Iraqi Kurds living in Iran. Another factor which increased
support for the KDP Provisional Leadership among Iraqi Kurds in Iran at
this time was the role played by Mulla Mustafa's widow (mother of Idris) in
decreasing the differences between her son's faction and other smaller
factions.[27]

The activities of the Iraqi Kurds in Iran, however, made little impact on
the Kurds within Iraq. Contrary to the expectations of many observers, and
despite some isolated incidents and attacks mostly carried out by Kurds living
in Iran, Iraqi Kurdistan has remained relatively peaceful. Three factors
account for this. First, the majority of Kurds appear to have lost faith in the
traditional leadership — partly as a result of their having realised the extent c
that leadership's submission to the Shah's, the CIA's and Israel's interests.
Second, after fifteen years of fighting, Iraqi Kurds have come to conceive of
their demands and prosperity as standing a better chance of fulfilment throw
a national and progressive regime than through continued conflict with such
regime. Third, and perhaps most important, the Iraqi leadership has had son
success in talking directly to the Kurds over the heads of their traditional
leaders, and in carrying out a systematic plan to normalise life in the Kurdish
areas.

Notes

1. S. Jawad, *Iraq and the Kurdish Question 1958-1970* (Ithaca Press, London,
1981), pp. 6-9.

2. For details of the Mahabad experience see W. Eagleton, *The Kurdish
Republic of 1946* (Oxford University Press, London, 1963).

3. See J. Talabani, *Kurdistan wa al-Harakah al-Qawmiah al-Kurdiah* (Kurdistan
and the Kurdish national movement) (Dar al-Tali'a, Beirut, 1971), pp. 145-9.

4. Ibid.

5. In February 1963 Qasim was overthrown by an alliance of Arab nationalist and Ba'thist officers. In November 1963 Abd al-Salam Aref, who had been
appointed president of the republic after Qasim's removal, ousted the Ba'thists
and came to dominate the government. In April 1966 Abd al-Salam Aref was
killed in an air crash. He was succeeded by his brother Abd al-Rahman Aref. The
latter was overthrown by the Arab Ba'th Socialist Party in July 1968.

6. The full text of the Ba'th Party memorandum, from which all information
on this topic given here is taken, can be found in Arab Ba'th Socialist Party,
Likay Yusan al-Salam wa Tata'azzaz al-Wahdah al-Wataniah (So that peace may
be safeguarded and national unity buttressed) (al-Thawrah Publications, Baghdad,
Iraq), pp. 153-86.

7. The full text of the KDP memorandum, from which all information on this topic given here is taken, can be found in Kurdish Democratic Party, *Fi Sabil al-Silm wal Wahdah al-Wataniah, Fi Sabil Tadbiq Ittifaqiat Athar* (Towards peace and national unity, towards the implementation of the March agreement) (al-Taakhi Publications, Baghdad, 1973), pp. 135-93.

8. In 1972 President Nixon, by agreement with the Shah of Iran, ordered the CIA to supply Mulla Mustafa with arms and ammunition worth 16 million dollars. See *Sunday Times*, 15 Feb. 1976; and *New York Times*, 26 Jan. 1976.

9. For further information on these negotiations see S. Husain, *Ahadith fi'l Qadhayah al-Rahinah* (Talks on contemporary issues) (al-Thawrah Publications, Baghdad, 1974), p. 37. Reference may also be made to the KDP's declaration of 12 March 1974, reported in *The Times*, 13 Mar. 1974.

10. Husain, *Ahadith*, p. 43.

11. See the KDP's declaration of 12 March 1974, reported in *The Times*, 13 Mar. 1974.

12. See *The Economist*, 7 Sept. 1974 and 2 Nov. 1974, and *The Times*, 1 Nov. 1974.

13. See *The Economist*, 2 Nov. 1974 and 14 Dec. 1974: and International Institute for Strategic Studies, *Strategic Survey 1974* (IISS Publications, London, 1974), pp. 82-4.

14. *Financial Times*, 24 Mar. 1975.

15. *Financial Times*, 20 Jan. 1975; and *Middle East International*, May 1975.

16. *The Times*, 20 Jan. 1975.

17. C. Kutschera, *Le Mouvement National Kurde* (Flammarion, Paris, 1979), p. 320.

18. *Financial Times*, 20 Jan. 1975.

19. *Guardian*, 7 Mar. 1975.

20. Although there is little information about the role the Iraqi Kurds played in activities in Iranian Kurdistan, it may be significant that the areas where the Iraqi Kurds settled were the first to witness armed activities against the disintegrating Shah's rule and against the Islamic republic.

21. The ideological direction of the KPU was made clear in its first declaration, issued in November 1975.

22. See the declarations issued by the KDP Provisional Leadership dated mid-December 1977 and February 1978.

23. Evidence for this can be found in *Le Monde*, 4-5 Mar. 1979.

24. See *Middle East International*, 2 Feb. 1979.

25. Ibid.

26. Ibid.

27. Mulla Mustafa's widow succeeded in bringing Dr Mahmoud Othman, a ranking member of the old politbureau under Mulla Mustafa, back to the party after he split from it in 1977. Othman, although co-operating with the two Barzani brothers, still keeps a faction working under his name (see *Guardian*, 2 July 1981). She also succeeded in playing down the differences between her son Idris and Mohammed Mahmoud Abd al-Rahman, alias Sami, who had served as minister for four years in the Iraq cabinet after the signature of the March Manifesto in 1970. Abd al-Rahman heads an influential faction inside the KDP. See *Guardian*, 5 Dec. 1979.

5 SADDAM HUSAIN'S POLITICAL THINKING: THE COMPARISON WITH NASSER

Peter Mansfield

Introduction

The title of this chapter may raise two questions: is there any body of ideas which can be identified as Saddam Husain's political thinking? Is there any relevant and useful comparison to be made with the late Gamal Abd al-Nasser? The writer believes that both questions can be answered in the affirmative. It is becoming increasingly apparent that there is such a thing as 'Saddamism' even if it is as difficult to define as 'Nasserism' used to be. As active leaders, the political practice of Saddam and Nasser has to be assessed along with their ideas. The contrasts as well as the similarities between their characters and careers are instructive.

Saddam Husain has now been the principal policymaker of the Iraqi Ba'thist regime for thirteen years. Little is known of his ideas in the West because few of his speeches have been adequately translated and he only very rarely gives interviews to Western journalists. Yet any study of what he has said shows that he must be reckoned as a Third World leader of some importance. In this chapter it is not possible to do more than suggest some reasons why this should be so.

Saddam and Nasser are the two most influential revolutionary leaders to have emerged in the Eastern Arab world since World War II. Part of their importance derives from the natural status of their countries. Control over the Lower Nile and the Suez Canal or over the valley of the Tigris and Euphrates can give a ruler of Egypt or Iraq a stature which leaders of less significant Arab states could not emulate. The presidency of either of these two states, however, does not in itself endow the holder with influence outside the state borders; it has to be combined with a significant and charismatic political personality.

Saddam and Nasser have in common that they were passionately involved in revolutionary nationalist politics from an early age and both came to power in their early thirties. But they had to cope with rather different circumstances in their countries. Egypt—an ancient nation-state—is a relatively easy country to govern. It has a cohesive population, without separatist tendencies, and a strong tradition of powerful central-ised authority. Iraq, with its Arab/Kurdish problem and Sunni/Shi'a division, is the very opposite in this respect. Its national unity is constantly threatened by centrifugal forces. On the other hand Egypt combines its natural internal unity with an equally ancient tradition of alien rule – of subjection to outside powers. Its crucial position at the hinge of three continents has always made it a prime target for imperial ambitions.

Nasser realised early on in his career the role that Egypt's unique situation gave it a chance to play. The idea of Egypt lying within 'three circles' – Arab, Islamic and African – was put forward in his *The Philosophy of the Revolution* (published in 1954) and was further developed after Nasser took part in the Bandung Conference the following year. The common international assumption that Egypt was destined to be a protectorate or appendage of other powers, however, was so overwhelming that Nasser had a constant struggle to establish Egypt's right to play an autonomous role. In contrast, Saddam Husain's first task was to deal with internal enemies.

The difference between the situations facing Nasser and Saddam has been brought out well by Khalid Kishtainy who has translated some of both leaders' speeches:

> Nasser's key words were 'pride' and 'dignity'. Saddam Husain's key words are 'march', 'calculation', 'formula', 'premise', 'resultant', and *'point de départ'*. The words of both respond to the needs of their countries. After centuries of humiliation and servitude, Egypt needs pride, dignity and confidence in herself more than most other things, and Nasser responded to the need with his intimate vernacular and high-sounding words of national exaltation. Iraq's need is quite different. With a long history of anarchy and lawlessness, the Iraqis continued jumping from the frying-pan into the fire and back again until 1968. They seem to have been heeding the words of Alexander the Great when he said that the people of the Orient had become slaves because they hadn't learned to use the word 'No!' Ever since Alexander's death in their midst, the Mesopotamians have taken the words to heart and have said nothing but 'No' to each other and everything. How to make them say 'Yes' became the vexatious problem of all Iraqi statesmen.[1]

It is relevant to our theme that Saddam is a direct successor to Nasser in time. He achieved power in Iraq at the very end of Nasser's life.

Accordingly, he was able to learn from Nasser's experience – his successes and failures. The Iraqi shows considerable admiration for the Egyptian but he is also very critical of some aspects of Nasserism, especially the sentimental and emotional approach to Arab unity and the Palestine question. (The type of feature of Nasserism which Saddam finds deplorable is represented by Ahmed Said and the Voice of the Arabs.)

Like Nasser, Saddam is an ardent reader and self-educator, with an absorbing interest in the moral and material forces of international politics. There is, however, an important difference between them: Saddam derives much of his ideological thinking from Michel Aflak, the founder of the Ba'th Party. Nasser, on the other hand, although he received some stimulus from reading biographies and writings of the forerunners of Arab nationalism and was impressed by a few contemporaries such as Sati' al-Husri, essentially developed his own brand of pan-Arabism, in which Egypt naturally played a central role. Nasser's aim was to convert the Egyptians to his view and many of his speeches took the form of lectures on his conception of Arab nationalism – in the tradition of Egyptian paternalism. Saddam, on the other hand, starts from the assumption that the Arab Ba'th Socialist Party (ABSP) is the only valid expression of pan-Arabism. For him the fact that it is in power in the Iraqi region of the Arab homeland, as he and his colleagues normally refer to their country, is enough to guarantee that the Iraqi people are playing their Arab nationalist role. He also believes that since the rule of the ABSP is essential for the wellbeing of the Iraqis it is sometimes necessary to place the interests of the party before that of the nation. It is worth noting that whereas Nasser had to struggle with what has been called the Pharaonic strain in Egyptian political life – the belief that the people of the Nile Valley have a character and destiny which is distinct from that of other Arabs – Saddam Husain and his fellow ideologists take it for granted that their Babylonian and Assyrian ancestors were Arabs and therefore no conflict arises between their Mesopotamian heritage and modern Arab nationalism.

The differences between the two countries' circumstances are also very relevant to the comparison. Egypt's geographical situation and its weight of population (between a quarter and a third of all Arabs) makes it the natural centre of gravity of the Arab world. Its very modest natural resources and small area of cultivable land, however, reduce its ruler's capacity for independent action. Egypt needs the Arab world as an outlet for its population. (It can also be argued that the Arab world, and especially the pan-Arab ideal, need Egypt – but that is another matter.) Iraq's circumstances are very different. On the one hand it lies on the wing of the Arab world, separated from the political centres of Damascus, Beirut and Cairo by the great Syrian Desert. But it also has great natural resources in relation to its population. It is perfectly possible for an Iraqi regime to isolate itself from the rest of the Arab world in order to concentrate on its domestic problems while at the same time subscribing to all the pan-Arab rhetoric. Saddam Husain has proved this to be so. He has never found himself in the same position as Nasser who, in his latter years, became a prisoner of his own doctrines of pan-Arabism – unable to turn down offers of alliances or unity, however ill-conceived.

The Importance of Strategy

Much of Saddam's thinking is devoted to strategy. Khalid Kishtainy has noted the paradox that Saddam, almost alone among contemporary Arab leaders in being a civilian, has a fondness for military metaphors. 'In his vocabulary we find "battle", "trenches", "fighting", "walls", "battlefield", "bastions", "reserves", "mobilisation", "strategy", "tactics", etc. Problems for him are battles, with enemies and allies outflanking each other's trenches and battlements.'[2] It is also worth noting that whereas Nasser – together with the other Egyptian Free Officers – abandoned his military uniform after the fifth year of the 1952 revolution, Saddam Husain has worn his with increasing frequency since he assumed the rank of honorary general in 1974. One of Saddam's favourite strategies is the tactical retreat or compromise: the clearheaded choice of the lesser of two evils. There are several major examples of this, such as the agreement between the ABSP and the Kurdish Democratic Party in March 1970 (repudiated in 1974), the refusal to allow the Iraqi troops in Jordan to back up the Palestinians in the 1970 civil war and the March 1975 agreement with the Shah of Iran.

This does not mean that Saddam is not prepared to take risks. He believes that the dangers threatening Iraq are such that a purely defensive strategy is inconceivable. But there always has to be careful consideration either that the odds in favour of success are substantial or that the dangers of not taking the risk are far greater than taking them. Such was the thinking behind the nationalisation of the Iraq Petroleum Company in 1972; the nationalisation resulted in an Iraqi triumph nine months later, but only after a period of acute crisis for the Iraqi economy. We can be sure that all previous experiences of major acts of nationalisation of foreign interests were carefully studied, from Mexico to Mossadegh and the Suez Canal Company.

The most recent example of a major strategic decision is the war with Iran. Certainly the risks involved are great and it may turn out to have been a disastrous miscalculation. It was, however, not simply a question of overestimating the weakness of the Iranian armed forces – perhaps with faulty intelligence advice. There is no doubt that Saddam Husain regarded the Khomeini regime as a deadly threat to the position of the ABSP in Iraq and as such it was a challenge that had to be confronted. If this were not so, it is inconceivable that Saddam would have been so rash.

Nasser's reactions to such challenges were generally more emotional. On the question of involvement in war with Israel he was generally cautious, until the near-fatal and still largely unexplained decisions which led to the June 1967 War. In any matter involving the leadership of the pan-Arab national movement, however, he allowed his heart to rule his head from the time of the Suez crisis onwards. A prime example was his involvement in the Yemen in September 1962. It is hard to believe that Saddam Husain would have taken such a decision – although it is also unlikely that such an action would be expected of him, because he has not come close to acquiring the position that Nasser occupied in the Arab World twenty years ago.

Non-alignment: Between East and West

Saddam Husain's attitude towards non-alignment and relations with the superpowers bears a strong resemblance to that of Nasser, allowing for the differences in the circumstances of Iraq and Egypt and the evolution that has taken place in Great Power/Third World relations between the 1950s and 1960s and the 1970s and 1980s. Egypt's key position in the Middle East made it possible for a time for Nasser to play the two superpowers off against each other. Saddam has not enjoyed the same leverage; on the other hand Iraq's oil wealth has made it possible to take a highly pragmatic approach to Iraq's relations with the industrialised countries. Wherever Western or Japanese technology is superior to that of the Communist states – as Iraq generally finds to be the case – it has been chosen when it is available.

In his public statements Saddam Husain has generally been much more friendly towards the Soviet Union than towards the United States – just as Nasser was. But equally like Nasser he has criticised or opposed

Soviet policy on occasions, such as by supporting the Eritreans and Somalis against Ethiopia and more recently by criticising the Soviet invasion of Afghanistan. (Nasser's principal quarrel with the Soviet Union was over Iraq, in 1958-9.) In spite of his bitter differences with the West, Nasser had a much closer rapport with the Western temperament and outlook—especially the Anglo-Saxon—than with the Soviet. The only Soviet leader with whom he had a warm relationship was Nikita Khruschev. His knowledge of and interest in British and American politics was remarkable. Saddam Husain is not as familiar with the Anglo-Saxon idiom but it is unlikely that he feels any personal rapport with East European leaders. (We have it on the authority of Mohamed Heikal that he coined the phrase 'Siberian mentality' to describe the Soviet leadership.)[3]

A favourite theme of Saddam Husain, to which he often returns in his speeches, is the development of new centres of power in the world to replace the monopoly of the two superpowers. He mentions Japan, China in ten or twenty years and a united Europe which he sees forming a productive relationship with the Arab world. These are developments he regards as highly desirable.

On the question of internal relations with the Iraqi Communist Party, there is some similarity to Nasser's attitude towards Egyptian Communists. In both cases the local Communists were entirely subordinated to the power of the state and severely suppressed whenever they were judged to be threatening it. The Iraqi Communist Party was allowed to join the Progressive Pan-Arab Front, together with the KDP, when the Front was established in July 1973. This was, however, at least partly a tactical move resulting from the Soviet-Iraqi accord of the previous year. The Front lasted no more than five years; thereafter the Communist Party was excluded from even a minor share of power as a consequence of its challenge to the ABSP through its political activities in the armed forces. Nasser, on the other hand, never allowed the Egyptian Communist Party even a subordinate role in his regime as a separate entity. Nor did he sign a treaty of friendship with the Soviet Union. In 1965 the Egyptian Communist Party declared itself dissolved and thereafter some leading Egyptian Marxists played a prominent role in the Arab Socialist Union. Nasser, therefore, felt no need to oust the party from the regime and suppress it, but his rejection of any Soviet intervention on behalf of local Communists was entirely the same as Saddam Husain's attitude today.

Political Organisation

As mentioned earlier, Saddam Husain bases all his political thinking on the assumption that the nation's best interests can only be served through the leadership of the ABSP. He maintains that the party is the natural expression of the people's wishes. If the party had not seized the opportunity and carried out the revolution which overthrew the Aref regime in 1968, 'the people would have created the party and the instruments by which a revolution is accomplished'. But the party does exist and did perform its revolutionary task. It continues to derive its inspiration from Aflak, the party ideologist. Saddam describes the Ba'th Party in Syria, which has rejected Aflak, as not being genuinely Ba'thist at all. It is 'apostate', using the word *ridda*, which is the term used of the early Muslims who reverted to paganism after the death of the Prophet.

Saddam often affirms that although the Ba'th is the vanguard of the revolution it must not keep an exclusive hold on power. This, however, is because an exclusive hold on power is unnecessary. As he told a meeting of the Iraqi General Federation of Trade Unions on 25 February 1976:

> It is our opinion that all Iraqis, even those belonging to other political parties, should not feel that there is a contradiction in their belonging to other political parties and at the same time regarding the ABSP as their own party. This is because the ABSP is leading society and the Revolution and because it has proved to them that it is qualified to be their own party through its realisation of the future in stages on the basis of the reality of the present.[4]

Saddam Husain has always been concerned with expanding the narrow base of the party and it is logical that he should pay special attention to youth. 'Let us Win the Young to Safeguard the Future' was the title of his address to the General Federation of Iraqi Youth on 15 February 1976. The party youth organisations begin with the *Tali'a* (vanguards) aged about ten to fifteen, and then the *Futuwwa* (youth) aged about fifteen to twenty. Ba'thist students receive specially favoured treatment. At the same time Saddam constantly shows his concern with the danger that privileged party officials may become detached and arrogant in their attitudes towards the rest of the population and his speeches are full of warnings on this matter. He advises them always to explain decisions and answer criticisms.

Unquestionably he has in mind the experience of the Communist parties in Eastern Europe. 'Democracy' he identifies, not with any parliamentary system (he would agree with Nasser's description of the Western-type parliamentary constitutions adopted by the Arab states after independence as 'sham facades'), but with what he calls 'collective action' — which means action taken by general agreement rather than through the decision of a member of the party cadre. He accepts that some individuals will prove themselves to have outstanding powers of leadership (analogous to that of the ABSP in the state) but they must always be aware of the dangers of elitism.

Nasser never created an effective political organisation to act as an instrument of state power. Much of his energy was spent in trying to create such an organisation, from the Liberation Rally to the National Union and then the Arab Socialist Union, but ultimately he failed. The ASU did not survive long without him. On the other hand, Nasserism had a broader basis in Egypt than the Ba'th has yet achieved in Iraq.

The similarities and contrasts between Saddam and Nasser are of special interest in this respect. From the time of the elimination of Neguib from the regime in 1954 Nasser's personality was dominant in Egypt until his death. Saddam, on the other hand, retained the role of grey eminence for several years after the Ba'th came to power in 1968. Although he began to appear increasingly in the public eye in the late 1970s, it was only after the retirement of President Bakr in 1979 that he emerged as the Sole Leader. Since then — and more specifically since the outbreak of the war with Iran — the cult of his personality has surpassed even that of Nasser in Egypt. It is true that Saddam always gives credit for any action by the state to the ABSP, but this seems to make little impression on the public. It is now possible to talk of 'Saddam's Iraq'.

Socialism and Secularism

The socialist content in Ba'thism is not very specific. It is less a set of socio-economic principles than a rather vague means of national improvement. Saddam says that only certain broad basic conditions need to be fulfilled for a system to be called socialist. As he told a meeting of Iraqi and foreign trade unionists on May Day 1978:

> We believe that when a revolutionary socialist party assumes power, and that power serves as a central instrument for methodically

changing society on the road to building socialism in the service of
the revolutionary classes and strata in society; when the revolutionary authority is a true and realistic reflection of the social forces and
strata expressing their interests; when socialism is an integral part of
the programme of struggle and that of practical implementation by
the state, such a system is called socialist although not all the
executive measures have been applied and not all the social and
economic actions are in full swing.[5]

In the actual application of socialism there is room for pragmatism.
In its broad lines Saddam would accept the economic principles of
Nasser's National Charter of 1962. The Charter said that most of the
economy should be owned by the state – that is, all railways, roads,
ports, airports and other public services, banks and insurance companies,
and the majority of heavy, medium and mining industries. All the
import trade and three-quarters of the export trade must be controlled
by the public sector, which over a period of eight years was also to
take charge of at least one quarter of domestic trade to prevent
monopoly. Private ownership of agricultural land remained within the
limits of the agrarian reform law and private ownership of buildings was
maintained, although 'constant supervision is still essential to prevent
exploitation'. In addition, Nasser's socialism attempted to raise the
living standards of the mass of the population through various means
such as subsidies, price controls and the provision of free social services.
Iraqi Ba'th socialism has been able to carry this much further with the
use of oil revenues, but the principles are much the same. The Stalinist
policy of concentrating on heavy industry to the exclusion of consumer
goods industries, which Nasser specifically rejected as demanding
excessive sacrifices from the people, hardly arises for Iraq because the
oil revenues have made possible an immediate general rise in living
standards.

Saddam Husain often echoes a favourite theme of Nasser – that no
nation can blindly copy the experience of another. Just as Nasser
spoke of Arab Socialism, there is always an Arab dimension in Iraq's
revolution. There are very much the same differences with Marxism –
no class war or dictatorship of the proletariat, and no atheism.

The intellectual attitudes towards Marxism which the two leaders
developed after some years in power are remarkably similar. Nasser's
starting-point was much more hostile. As late as 1955 he wrote a preface
to an anti-Communist tract, *The Reality of Communism*, in which he
rehearsed all the liberal arguments against Marxism, describing it as the

negation of religion, liberty and equality. As relations between Egypt
and the Soviet Union grew much closer in the 1950s he softened his
attitude. He took an interest in Marxist ideas which undoubtedly had
some influence on the Arab Socialism of his National Charter,
although it was primarily in their Yugoslav revisionist form. He
expressed admiration for various Communist nationalist leaders such
as Castro, Ho Chi Minh and Tito, but it is easy to see that it was their
spirit of independence rather than their Communism which he admired.
He also greatly appreciated de Gaulle.

It is no surprise that Saddam Husain's heroes are almost identical.
He speaks more of Lenin than Nasser did, but what he admires most in
Lenin is that he gave Marxism a Russian specificity which Marx would
have been incapable of providing. His views on the reasons why orthodox
Marxism is unsuitable for application to the Arab nation are more
coherently developed than Nasser's were, but the ideas are ones of
which Nasser would certainly have approved. In brief, Saddam Husain
holds that the Arabs have a long history of their own which transcends
Marxist analysis. Certain new African states, for example, may adopt
Marxism because they lack the Arab historical dimension. For the
Arabs to do the same without reservation would be absurd.

As might be expected, Saddam applies a specifically Arab perspective to the Marxist analysis of social class. The Arab nation, he says, has
not known the class structure of certain other nations. While it is true
that there have been social disparities, the division between classes
reflected the relationship between Arabs and non-Arabs more than it
characterised the Arab community itself. In modern times the problems
of the Arab nation were not limited to social questions but were also
derived from the dismemberment of the nation and the struggle against
the Zionist entity. (Saddam has noted that his own personal experience
derives from central Iraq where, in contrast to the north and south of
the country, the humiliating conditions imposed by feudalism hardly
existed.[6])

Saddam Husain shows particular irritation with the orthodox
Marxist assumption that any non-Marxist-Leninist party must necessarily
be petty bourgeois in character. He says that the Iraqi Communists are
correct when they say that 'Iraqi society, for the most part, is revolutionary in its social make-up in the sense that it has a popular revolutionary
structure'. The authority of any petty bourgeoisie would therefore be
rejected by the people. The Ba'th Party is not petty bourgeois and is
not rejected.[7]

The question of attitudes towards Islam and secularism is important in view of the ABSP's sensitivity to the charge of being anti-Islamic, especially during the war with Khomeini's Iran. Saddam follows Aflak's teaching in saying that there is no question of the Ba'th being anti-Islam because Islam is closely bound to the spirit of the Arab Nation. On the other hand, there is to be no truck with religious reactionaries. Any attempt by the ABSP to become a religious party in order to take the religious zealots along with them would be dangerous and divisive. While Saddam accepts that the advent of Islam was a great step forward for the Arab nation, he strongly denies the view that the Arabs made no contribution to civilisation before Islam. Similarly, the Ba'thist revolution has taken the Arab nation a stage further. In a key speech he made to the Party's Information and Cultural Bureau on 11 August 1977 he said:

> When we talk with admiration about religion and heritage we must remember that our philosophy does not consist of religion and heritage themselves. It is rather what is expressed by our ideology and our related policy. Religion and the past with all its factors, traditions and rules of life are essential elements of our society, affecting our traditions and morality. However, our ideology is not the combined outcome of all that is implied by the past and religion. It is an advanced and universal outlook on life, a comprehensive solution to its obstructions and complexes and a means of advancing in a revolutionary way.[8]

Heritage and tradition must be respected and there must be no brutal break with the past while the socialist transformation is taking place. Nothing must stop the 'forward march' — a favourite phrase of Saddam — but it must be at a steady pace. Accordingly, in questions of social change Saddam is a pragmatist, as in other things, and, like Nasser, more of a gradualist than a revolutionary. As regards the emancipation of women, a theme on which he has often spoken, he states the absolute necessity to transform women's role in society. But this can not be done overnight. As he told the Iraqi Law Society on 27 January 1976:

> There should be no halt in the balanced forward movement of our society as a whole and our dynamic role in shedding our backward past. There is, however, no justification for putting forward hasty measures which would place a section of our people — who so far have been with us — in a hostile attitude to the Revolution.[9]

This effectively sums up Saddam's philosophy on social matters.

Notes

1. S. Husain, *On Current Events in Iraq* (Croom Helm, London, 1977), p. ix of K. Kishtainy's introduction.
2. Ibid.
3. M. Heikal, *Sphinx and Commissar* (Collins, London, 1978), p. 279.
4. S. Husain, *Iraq: Revolution in the Service of Humanity* (Z.L. Kaul, New Delhi, no date), p. 16.
5. Reported in *al-Thawrah* (Baghdad), 2 May 1978.
6. See F. Matar, *Saddam Husain ou le Devenir Irakien* (Le Sycomore Editions, Paris, 1981), pp. 147-9.
7. Quoted in A. Iskander, *Saddam Husain: the Fighter, the Thinker, the Man* (Hachette Réalités, Paris, 1980), p. 184.
8. Reported in *al-Thawrah*, 12 Aug. 1977.
9. S. Husain, *On Social and Foreign Affairs in Iraq* (Croom Helm, London, 1979), p. 31.

6 THE EMANCIPATION OF IRAQI WOMEN

Amal al-Sharqi

Historical Background

The term 'emancipation of women' has been applied to so wide a
variety of social, political and ideological attitudes that it has become
one of the most ill-defined terms in modern terminology. It is
appropriate, therefore, to begin with a definition. In this article
'emancipation of women' means the termination of the subordinate
status of women and the achievement of full equality between the
sexes.

Until the beginning of this century the Iraqi woman was the victim
of a complex system of oppression. As other members of society, she
had to share in the general sufferings of a nation which lived in a state
of poverty and backwardness due to its subordination to foreign
occupation and reactionary government. As a woman she had in
addition to suffer the discrimination of a feudal and patriarchal
society that treated women as mere chattels or domestic slaves. Further
to these conditions, which are characteristic of backward, feudal
societies generally, Iraqi society bestowed an additional burden on
women: the veil. Contrary to what some may think, the veil is not a
mere piece of cloth or cover. It is a system of life and a dimensional
restriction which keeps the woman isolated from any positive
influence.

With the emergence of the country from direct colonial rule, and
the introduction of modern forms of political, economic and social
organisation in the 1920s, gradual changes started to take place in the
life of Iraqi women. Schools for girls were opened and, shortly after-
wards, the newly educated woman cautiously ventured into some fields
of work. Some social groups began to change their traditional attitude
towards women, but such change was restricted largely to the upper
and middle classes whose economic and cultural conditions placed them
closest to the process of modernisation. The concept of women's
emancipation held by these latter groups, moreover, only involved a
relatively superficial change of outlook.

The spread of modern ideas was, nevertheless, laying the foundation-

stone for the future progress of Iraqi women. As a result of the
migration of rural people to the towns in search of new avenues of
employment, a significant segment of the population came to be
exposed to urban influences. There was a widespread realisation that
education secured better opportunities for women, so people living on
limited incomes saw an incentive in sending their daughters to school.

Despite such progress as was made, the tendency towards the gradual
emancipation of women did not become consolidated into a coherent
movement. There were two reasons for this. First, the progress was on
an individual basis and was severely limited. Second, there was no
coherent ideological impetus and organisational effort at a mass level.
The consolidation of the women's movement, and the real drive for
the emancipation of women, had to wait until after the Ba'th Party
came to power in July 1968.

Prior to embarking upon an analysis of the Ba'th Party's approach
to this question it would be valuable to describe the actual status of
women in Iraq on the eve of the 1968 revolution. Sixty years of
comparative change and various degrees of exposure to the elements
of modernisation had resulted in Iraqi women ceasing to constitute
one homogeneously oppressed group. By the late 1960s the term
'Iraqi women' actually applied to three distinct social groups, each of
which had its own characteristic features.

The Peasant Woman

In the late sixties the rural population of Iraq formed 44 per cent of
the total population.[1] This meant that nearly half the total number
of women were peasants.

In the backward conditions of the underdeveloped countryside,
women led a difficult and bitter life. They toiled hard, from dawn to
dusk, on manually cultivated farms. They were responsible for all the
dairy work. They had their own household and maternal responsibilities
to fulfil, and they also served as the village 'craftspeople', producing
nearly all the requirements of the peasant's cottage. Despite the active
role they played in the production process, peasant women were
victims of oppressive social conventions which kept them subordinated
to men, forced them into arranged marriages and treated them as mere
productive tools.

The Urban Housewife

The great majority of Iraqi towns were – and still are – fundamentally
rural marketing centres. Such towns are tied to the countryside by the

very nature of their economy; their inhabitants are mostly rural immigrants. It is natural, therefore, for them to be governed by the same social conventions as apply to those living in the countryside.

Thus the urban housewife, who accounted for about 40 per cent of all Iraqi women in the late 1960s, was subject to the same social discriminations as her rural sister. The main difference was that the urban housewife was kept out of the production process, as production in towns was no longer run on a family basis. Wifehood and motherhood were the only careers for which girls were trained. Their idleness burdened the family budget, and their deprivation from any useful outlet for their natural energies threatened to drive them into the dangerous path of the consumer race, to which most women in capitalist and wealthy industrialised societies are attracted.

The Working Woman

The first move towards the salaried employment of women in Iraq came in 1923, when a Teachers' Training Institute was opened. The first generation of working women were mainly employed in teaching, nursing or office work. Despite civil service laws which were completely free of any discrimination against the participation of women, employed women in the late 1960s only made up 14 per cent of the total number of women of working age.[2] This can be attributed to the prevalence of traditional social prejudice regarding the female sex and the limited number of educated women.

It is worthy of note that almost 90 per cent of the employed women were educated, and that the great majority of them belonged to upper and middle class families. The main incentives in employment would appear to have been social and psychological rather than financial. The more needy women were prevented from working by the social inhibitions which prevailed among the lower classes.

The Ideological Background to Ba'thist Programmes

Against the situation outlined above the government which came to power in July 1968 had to work out effective programmes to achieve its objectives: the elimination of differences between various sections of women and the enhancement of the process of women's emancipation

It is important to recognise that the new government's attitudes on the question of women were just one part of its wider ideology. The Ba'th Party saw itself not as a political organisation aiming merely at he achievement of certain political victories, but rather as a mass pan-Arab progressive movement seeking – as its name suggests[3] – the resurrection of the Arab nation and the restoration of the Arabs' historic role among the other nations of the world. The party's approach towards the achievement of this objective was governed by a comprehensive ideology covering all aspects of life in the political, social and cultural fields. The revolution of July 1968 was seen as bringing to fruition the party's struggle against the old, reactionary regime, and initiating the drive towards establishing a modern and progressive society.

In undertaking the responsibility for reconstructing Arab society the party could not underestimate the negative effects which the subordination of women exerted upon society. Nor could it neglect the value of the role which Arab women could play in future progress. The party's constitution, laid down in 1947, stated that 'the Arab woman enjoys the full rights of the Arab citizen', and that 'the party should struggle to raise the general standard of women in order to make them worthy of those rights.'[4]

The party rejected a limited 'feminine' treatment of the question of women because this would deprive emancipation of the great momentum achieved through a comprehensive treatment. Instead, it stressed the necessity of regarding the liberation of women as an integral part of the liberation of the whole people.

The report of the Ba'th Party's Sixth National Conference (held in 1963) identified the inferior status of women as 'an integral part of the ideology of a feudal and tribal society', against which the party's struggle was aimed. The report went on to point out that 'education alone is not enough to realise women's liberation in a revolutionary way'. It also warned against 'dependence upon the slow progress of liberation', as this was likely to 'render the pace of Arab progress unbalanced and without harmony'. Finally, the report stated: 'The emancipation of women is one of the major responsibilities of the national socialist revolution.'[5]

That, then, was the ideological approach of the Arab Ba'th Socialist Party to the question of women's emancipation when it came to power in 1968. Actual experience has enriched that ideological stand. Subsequent statements emanating from party sources have placed yet more emphasis on the relationship between the emancipation of women and the achievement of the rest of the party's revolutionary aims. The report of the party's Eighth Regional (Iraqi) Conference held in 1974 stated that the backwardness of Arab women in economic, social and cultural fields is now one of the most serious obstructions in the path of the modern Arab renaissance . . . With the preservation of the present backward status of the Arab woman and the absence of real equality between men and women, there can never be any real achievement of unity, liberty and socialism . . .

As leader of social change in all fields, the Arab Ba'th Socialist Party assumes direct and full responsibility for the emancipation of women.[6]

A similar perspective is brought out by President Saddam Husain in his book *'An al-Thawrah wal Mar'a* (On revolution and women):

The achievement of the full emancipation of women is as necessary for enriching the drive for progressiveness with double energy as it is essential for encountering the fatal challenges that face us in the present stage . . .

. . . Any segregation of women or restriction of their full participation in public life deprives the homeland of half its product ive and struggling capacity.[7]

The Ba'thist revolution needed women as a basic potentiality, while women needed the revolution as a means of liberation. When the two needs met, the process of emancipation was put into full gear — as a mass movement.

The emancipation of women in Iraq, then, is regarded as one of the main national aims, for the achievement of which all potentialities, both men's and women's, are mobilised and all revolutionary momentum is recruited. It has gone beyond the limits of exclusive 'feminine' interests and surpassed the aggressive, sectoral attitude that fights segregation with segregation, to become a positive and constructive mass movement directly linked with the progress and welfare of society as a whole.

The Programmes for Emancipation

In the Ba'th Party's analysis, five factors were regarded as basic causes of the suppressed condition of women:

(1) The generally backward economic and social conditions prevailing in the country;

(2) The limited educational opportunities for women;
(3) The limited number of women involved in the productive process;
(4) Discriminatory treatment of women in some legislation; and
(5) Social prejudice against women.

Two different paths were followed in seeking to change the status of women in Iraq. The first was indirect: raising the living standards of society as a whole, such that those problems which stemmed from low standards of living could be confronted. The second involved a direct approach, laying down an overall plan to promote women's education, to bring about their full participation in the production process, to improve their legal position and to eliminate social prejudice against them. The measures taken in these different fields will now be examined.

General Standard of Living

Following Iraq's nationalisation of the oil industry in 1972, and the oil price rises of 1973-4, Iraq entered a period of unprecedented social change and economic growth. With a centralised and socialist policy the government vastly increased its budget so as to implement a gigantic development plan. The main aims of the plan were to industrialise the economy, to mechanise agriculture, to extend social, educational and health services and to raise the general standard of living. The government's overall control of the distribution of wealth, wages and prices ensured a well-balanced growth in individual incomes. Table 6.1 shows the rise in national income *per capita* which occurred between 1970 and 1979.

Table 6.1: National Income *per capita*, 1970 and 1979

Year	*Per capita* share of national income (Iraqi dinars)
1970	95.3
1979	763.8

Source: Central Statistical Organisation, *Annual Abstract of Statistics 1979* (Ministry of Planning, Baghdad, 1980).

One effect of the economic development which has taken place is that the urban sector of the population has increased. Whereas the rural population made up 44 per cent of total population in 1967, in 1977 this figure had dropped to 36 per cent.[8] Meanwhile, the development plan has begun to bring living conditions in rural areas closer to those in the towns. The overall improvement in standards of living, under new production relations, has naturally brought benefits to both men and women.

Education

Despite primary education for girls having begun early in the century, with the first secondary school for girls opening in 1929, the number of educated women remained comparatively limited in the mid-1960s. The opportunity for girls to pursue their education was effectively open only to those who came from wealthy and middle-class families in the cities.

The year 1974 constituted a turning-point in the Iraqi educational system: education was made free at all levels. This involved not only exemption from study fees but also free books and all other educational requirements. School expenses, therefore, were no longer an obstacle in the way of enrolment of lower-class girls. A further turning-point came in the school year 1979-80: education at primary school level was made obligatory for all Iraqi children. As a result of the latter ruling the number of girls enrolled at the primary school level increased sharply that year—reaching a total of 211,265, as against 209,612 boys.[9]

Tables 6.2-6.5 show how the percentage of girls at all educational levels increased between 1970 and 1980.

Table 6.2: Percentage of Girls at Primary Level, 1970/1 and 1979/80

School year	No. of girls	Percentage
1970/1	318,524	29
1979/80	1,165,856	45

Table 6.3: Percentage of Girls at Secondary Level, 1970/1 and 1979/80

School year	No. of girls	Percentage
1970/1	88,595	29
1979/80	278,485	31

Table 6.4: Percentage of Women at University Level, 1970/1 and 1979/80

School year	No. of women	Percentage
1970/1	9,212	23
1979/80	28,647	31

Table 6.5: Percentage Increase of Girls/Women at all Educational Levels, 1970/1 and 1979/80

Educational level	School year 1970/1	School year 1979/80	Percentage of increase
Primary level	318,524	1,165,856	366
Secondary level	88,595	278,485	314
University level	9,212	28,647	310

Sources: Central Statistical Organisation, *Annual Abstract of Statistics 1979* (Ministry of Planning, Baghdad, 1980).

Even in vocational and specialised education, traditionally regarded as an exclusively male preserve, women were successfully directed into a variety of different branches. This is evident from Table 6.6.

Table 6.6: Percentage of Girls/Women in Vocational and Specialised Fields of Education, 1979/80

Branch	Percentage
Vocational training	28
Commercial training	77
Medicine	44
Agronomy and veterinary	20
Abstract sciences	39
Management and economics	38
Electrical engineering	25
Control and system engineering	42
Civil engineering	18
Metallurgical engineering	37
Mechanical engineering	15
Chemical engineering	64
Architecture	23

Source: General Federation of Iraqi Women, *Iraq's Programme of Action to Improve the Status of Women* (GFIW, Baghdad, 1981).

The most important of the factors accounting for the rapid increase in girls' and women's education are free education, the rise of individual income, the spread of social enlightenment and the availability of wider employment opportunities for women. The latter opportunities made women's education worthwhile and rewarding in the public eye.

While the government's programmes thus paved the way towards full equality in education for the new generation, the older generation of women also had their share in the educational drive. A country-wide anti-illiteracy campaign was started on 1 December 1978 – aimed at eradicating illiteracy among all Iraqi citizens between 15 and 45 years of age. The number of illiterate women covered by the campaign was 1,535,940, which represented 66 per cent of the total number of women in this age group. The 36-month campaign was carried out in all districts of the country's cities, villages, mountains and deserts.[10]

In the first year of the campaign illiteracy was eliminated in twelve governorates out of the eighteen in Iraq. Graduates of anti-illiteracy centres were enrolled in special state schools which could give them an education equivalent to that offered in primary schools. Enrolment in anti-illiteracy centres and subsequently state schools (for adults) was made obligatory for both men and women between the ages of 15 and 45.

Women at Work

Giving women financial independence is a crucial element in emancipation – hence the significance attached to the participation of women in the production process. For women, work also serves an educational purpose, carrying them beyond the limits of their traditional interests and drawing them into involvement in the progressive movements of society. The employment of women has, moreover, become a necessity for Iraq in view of the urgent need for manpower in a country with no more than 13 million people and a gigantic development plan.

Legislation was introduced to ensure that Iraqi women enjoy equal opportunity of employment, equal pay and equal chances of promotion in all fields of work without exception. In 1974, a governmental regulation made it obligatory for all state establishments to adopt clear policies aimed at raising the number of women employed in all positions and at all levels. Thanks to this encouragement, the percentage of women in the total non-agricultural workforce rose from 7 per cent in 1968 to 19 per cent in 1980. Figures regarding the participation of women in the agricultural sector are not available – and would be difficult to come by, as much of the agricultural work is undertaken on a family basis. The annual percentage rise in the number of working women is currently estimated at 11.6 per cent.[11]

One significant trend in the employment of women during the 1970s relates to the educational background of those employed. In 1968 women constituted 26 per cent of the high school graduates employed in the public sector, but only 4 per cent of the uneducated workers in that sector. This pattern had not changed greatly by 1972: although women now made up 30 per cent of high school graduates employed in the public sector, they still only accounted for 4 per cent of the uneducated workers. With the implementation of the national development plan, a more significant shift began to occur. Uneducated women were now increasingly drawn into the labour market such that in 1975, only one year after the plan's inception, they made up no less than 10 per cent of the uneducated workers.[12]

These figures reveal the invisible, but close, relationship between the progress of women's emancipation and that of social and economic development. They also indicate that emancipation need not be limited to a privileged group. It is the employment of lower class women that can bring about real revolutionary change in society, alleviating directly a multitude of social ailments.

Women and Legislation

The obstacles to the improvement of women's position in Iraq have been more of a social than a legal nature. In university education, for example, there never was any restriction whatsoever against the enrolment of women, and it was purely social restrictions that limited the number of women. There were, however, some legal shortcomings and the government has sought to eliminate these through new laws or through amendments to old laws, giving women full equality of rights and obligations.

Reform began in 1970 with the passing of a new agrarian reform law. This provided that women could own their own land on an equal footing with men. It was followed by a law on agricultural co-operatives, granting every woman who worked on a co-operative farm the right of equal wages with men. According to the provisions of this law, peasant women became full members of agricultural co-operatives.[13]

A number of amendments to the labour and civil service laws assured women of an equal footing with men in employment, guaranteeing equal pay, equal allowances, equal leave and equal chances of promotion. Other laws provided for the employment of women in the armed forces and the air force, for married women to gain the same tax-exemption enjoyed by married men, and for women to receive children's allowances in case of divorce or widowhood, and both children's and marital allowances if the husband did not benefit from these allowances. Retirement age for women was reduced to 55, while that for men remained at 60.

New labour and civil service laws ensured good conditions for the working mother. One month's paid leave was granted to an expectant mother before childbirth, and six weeks paid leave after delivery. She was also entitled to six months half-paid maternity leave, to be taken at any time she chose between the birth of the child and its fifth birthday. The law forbade expectant mothers to be employed on dangerous or difficult work and limited their daily working hours to seven. It also provided for two half-hour breaks a day for a nursing mother when her baby was kept at a crêche attached to the factory; or else the two breaks could be combined to allow a one-hour break when the child was at a nearby nursery.

The amended Personal Status Law (1978) introduced a radical change to the legal position of women within the family circle. The provisions of this law enabled the right of divorce to be granted to both men and women in cases such as persistent dispute, adultery, incurable disease or long absence of the spouse. The law prohibited parents or anyone else from forcing girls into unwanted marriages or from preventing marriage between two adults. It imposed a penalty of imprisonment on men who failed to register their marriages at court, thus putting an end to the illegal practice of polygamy.

In the case of divorce, the Personal Status Law also gave the custody of children under ten years of age to the mother unless the court was convinced that the mother's guardianship was harmful to the child. Judges were given the right to prolong the period of a mother's custody, when this was deemed desirable, until the child was fifteen years old. Thereafter the child would decide for himself or herself with which parent to stay permanently.

Eliminating Social Prejudice

The centralised nature of the Iraqi state makes it possible for any line or policy adopted by the government to be carried out on all levels at the same time. In the attempts to eliminate social prejudice against women a comprehensive programme has been undertaken by all state establishments and people's organisations. At work, any distinct contribution by women is rewarded and publicised. In the information media, the image of women as active partners and equal citizens is replacing that of sex objects or subordinate mates. In social and public activities, women have been encouraged to play active roles and to occupy responsible positions.

A prominent role in this programme is played by the General Federation of Iraqi Women. This extensive and popular organisation both initiates and implements programmes aimed at raising the social, economic, cultural and health standards of women. It co-operates with government establishments and other people's organisations for the achievement of its aims. It contributes to promoting women's work and performance through open discussions held at worksites — attended by all working staff, and possibly by relevant ministers or heads of departments. The participation of the federation in arts, sports and other public activities has contributed significantly to the emerging image of the new Iraqi woman.

The emphasis given in this chapter to official measures does not imply that Iraqi women themselves maintain a passive attitude to emancipation. They have, rather, grasped eagerly the opportunities which have become available. The number of women university graduates employed is currently almost equivalent to the total number of women graduates, which suggests that they are making full and proper use of their education. The contribution of women covers a wide variety of fields. They now account for 46 per cent of teachers, 29 per cent of doctors, 46 per cent of dentists, 70 per cent of pharmacists, 15 per cent of accountants, 14 per cent of factory workers and 16 per cent of civil servants. There is even a small number in senior management (4 per cent of the total). Although the latter proportion is limited, it is indicative of the significant prospects of promotion available.[14]

Among less conventional professions to which Iraqi women are attracted are archaeology, geology and engineering. A number of women engineers hold key positions in the oil industry and on irrigation projects. In the Ministry of Oil, for example, the percentage of women employed in designing oil projects stood at 37 per cent in 1980, while 30 per cent of construction supervisors at the same ministry were women.[15] Journalism, too, is becoming popular, with most women journalists choosing to work as reporters and editors on national newspapers and magazines rather than on specialised women's publications.

Women have also become active in political life. The 1980 National

Assembly elections brought nineteen women members to the new assembly. Similarly, they have been elected to positions of authority in a variety of government establishments and institutions. An indication of the fundamental change of attitudes occurring in Iraq is the election by Iraqi peasants of a woman onto the executive board for agricultural co-operatives.

In general cultural and social life, some women have become trend-setters in poetry and painting. Iraqi women join the people's army on an equal footing with men, and they are equal members of youth centres and sports clubs. In short, women are taking up new positions and increasing their presence in all fields, where they are being warmly welcomed.

Conclusion

The material presented in this chapter gives evidence of the long distance which Iraqi women have covered towards the achievement of complete emancipation. An equally long distance may lie ahead, but a framework has been created which secures the future. The solid work is done, the seed is sown and women are justified in their confidence that further progress shall be made. The Iraqi experience shows that no limited treatment or 'sectoral' effort can lead to the emancipation of women in society; it is only when sound analysis, comprehensive solutions, political will and mass efforts are combined that this major objective becomes attainable.

Notes

1. Central Statistical Organisation, *Annual Abstract of Statistics 1969* (Ministry of Planning, Baghdad, 1970).

2. Ibid.

3. The Arabic word *ba'th* means 'resurrection'.

4. The constitution of the Arab Ba'th Socialist Party was accepted at the party's founding congress, held on 7 April 1947.

5. Arab Ba'th Socialist Party, *Report of the Sixth National Conference of the Arab Ba'th Socialist Party (1963)* (al-Thawrah Publications, Baghdad, 1963).

6. Arab Ba'th Socialist Party, *Report of the Eighth Regional Congress of the Arab Ba'th Socialist Party (1974)* (al-Thawrah Publications, Baghdad, 1974).

7. S. Husain, *'An al-Thawrah wal Mar'a* (On revolution and women) (General Federation of Iraqi Women, Baghdad, 1978).

8. Central Statistical Organisation, *Annual Abstract of Statistics, 1967* (Ministry of Planning, Baghdad, 1968): and Central Statistical Organisation,

Annual Abstract of Statistics 1977 (Ministry of Planning, Baghdad, 1978).

9. Central Statistical Organisation, *Annual Abstract of Statistics 1980* (Ministry of Planning, Baghdad, 1981).

10. For the information contained in this paragraph see General Federation of Iraqi Women, *Iraq's Programme of Action to Improve the Status of Women* (GFIW, Baghdad, 1981).

11. Ibid.

12. Ibid.

13. All information on legislation given here is taken from the texts of the relevant laws, as published by the Ministry of Justice, Baghdad.

14. General Federation of Iraqi Women, *Iraq's Programme.*

15. Ibid.

7 REVOLUTION WITHIN THE REVOLUTION? WOMEN AND THE STATE IN IRAQ

Amal Rassam

The Ideological Setting

In common with other Third World countries Iraq shares the challenge of modernising its economic, political and social systems. In the political sphere, the regime's stated task is to develop an effective state apparatus and nationwide institutions with integrative functions. In the social sphere, the goal is to restructure the society in such a way as to minimise inequality, and ensure a more equitable distribution of goods and services among the citizenry. In the language of the Ba'th, the ruling party, this programme entails a 'total and permanent revolution', one of whose features is the 'liberation of women' and their full integration into the transformational process.[1]

This chapter will examine some of the issues involved in the attempt by the Ba'th to effect changes in women's roles and status. As will become clear, some of these issues are specific to Iraq, others have far wider implications as they extend to Arab-Muslim societies in general. By no means is this exercise meant to be a balance sheet of the Ba'th's achievement in this area; the regime has been in power for a period of no more than half a generation and it is unrealistic, if not outright foolish, to expect any general assessment. At best, one can begin to identify trends, problems and paradoxes as they emerge.

The organising questions to which the enquiry will be addressed include the following: What image do women assume in the ideology of the Ba'th? How does this relate to the reality of their position in the society? How are broad ideological commitments translated into concrete policies by the state? How is legislation used as an instrument for change by the political elite? What structural and cultural constraints determine the shape of change in Iraq? What is the relation between 'cultural authenticity' and 'revolutionary change'?

The Arab Ba'th Socialist Party, which came to power in Iraq in 1968, has articulated a vision of a future society 'free from the old, obsolete, and exploitative relationships that held the peasant, the tribesman and the woman prisoner in their own society'.[2] But whereas the Ba'th state-led initiatives to alter the lot of the peasant and tribesman have been bold and systematic (these include sweeping land reform, rural education and extension of services, breaking down the power of the landlords and the shaikhs, etc.), this has not been the case for the women. Suffice it to point out that in the area most under the direction of the state, namely that of legislation, the Ba'th-sponsored reforms in the Code of Personal Status lag behind those of Tunis and even Egypt, two Arab countries that make no claims to 'total revolution' or to a radical overhaul of the social order. Before going into some of the reasons for the caution and ambivalence which the regime displays in its efforts to transform women's status, the image of women as it appears in the ideology of the Ba'th will be presented.

> The liberation of the Arab woman and her release from her
> antiquated economic, social and legal bonds is one of the main aims
> of the Arab Ba'th Socialist Party . . . The Party must therefore work
> tirelessly toward legal equality and the provision of equal
> opportunities at work. It is the duty of the Party and its
> organization to fight against the backward concepts which relegate
> the role of women to a marginal and secondary place. Such concepts
> conflict with our Arab and Islamic heritage and are in fact alien and
> harmful. They also conflict with the values and concepts of the
> Party, the Revolution and the needs of modern times . . . The
> liberation of women can be done through the complete political
> and economic liberation of society. The Arab Ba'th Socialist Party
> has a leading role to play in the liberation of women since it leads
> the process of social and cultural change.[3]

The statement is fairly straightforward; the party takes it upon itself to liberate the woman from *all* bonds, economic, social and legal. The political report, however, does not spell out the nature of these bonds nor how the party intends to go about effecting this process of liberation. The clearest and most systematic statement by the Ba'th on women, at least to this writer's knowledge, is the one made by Dr Elias Farah, one of the party's theoreticians, in a speech entitled 'The Woman in the Ideology and Struggle of the Arab Ba'th Socialist Party'. The speech was delivered in December 1975 to a conference/workshop held by the Federation of Iraqi Women (al-Ittihad al-Nisa'i al-Iraqi).[4]

Farah points out that the general constitution of the Ba'th Party, drafted in 1947, grants the Arab woman full citizenship rights and promises that the party would strive to ensure that they fully enjoy these rights. The constitution also states that the family is the primary cell of the nation whose duty is to protect and nurture it. Marriage is considered a national duty which the state must encourage, facilitate and supervise, and procreation is the duty of the family, the state being charged with fostering the children's health and education. Farah proceeds then to link 'the problem of the Arab woman' with the general problem of national development and liberation, arguing that any attempt to improve the status of women which does not call for a basic transformation of the class structure and its supporting ideology is bound to fail.

> The Arab woman is doubly dispossessed, being a woman in a dispossessed society . . . The Party is committed to undertake the struggle to liberate the Arab woman in a fundamental and real sense. The Arab Ba'th believes in the equality of men and women and is committed to support all efforts undertaken by women to ensure their liberation as it [i.e., the Ba'th] refuses to divide Arab society into free men and enslaved women.[5]

The Arab woman, Farah adds, suffers special liabilities in such areas as education, choice of profession, opportunity of work, salaries and wages, marriage and divorce and in political participation, all of which give a special urgency to the question of women and to their role in safeguarding the revolution. As he puts it,

> the success of the Ba'th Revolution depends, to a large extent, on the mobilisation of women and on their positive contribution to the new social order. To that end, they must be liberated from all economic, social and legal constraints.[6]

After a critical review of the role of women in the revolutionary ideologies of the Marxists, Maoists and the Vietnamese, Farah goes on to maintain that, even though the revolutionary struggle of the Arab woman has taken many forms, it can still be seen as part of one historical movement towards emancipation and self-realisation. He identifies certain watershed dates in that history: the year 1922 in Egypt, when women defied their society and went out unveiled; 1929, when the first Conference of Arab Women was organised in Palestine; 1932, the year women organised and led demonstrations protesting against British support of Zionist activity in Palestine; 1949, when women won the vote in Syria; and 1954, when Algerian women actively joined the FLN in the Aures mountains.

While all these achievements may be impressive for their time and place, they failed to generate enough momentum and force, writes Farah, to radically alter the condition of women. This, he adds, is largely the result of viewing 'the problem of women' as separate and separable from that of the total society. To ensure the full participation of women and their equality in all spheres,

> the Party has specified its duties towards ensuring the liberation, *tahrir*, of Arab women. These duties are:
> 1. To struggle against the negative image of women and to work towards doing away with all backward and traditional attitudes.
> 2. To develop practical programmes which will allow the women to participate effectively in public life and in the struggle for their own liberation.
> 3. To remove all constraints that prevent the realisation of women's full potential and their humanity.
> 4. To reject all superficial bourgeois solutions to women's problems, especially those that contradict the positive aspects of Arab tradition and those that are anti-socialist.
> 5. To struggle against all outdated and backward customs and traditions and to make the liberation of women an indivisible part of the struggle for a new Arab socialist society.[7]

Despite the sloganeering quality of much of Farah's address, it is nonetheless the clearest statement we have on the attitude of the Ba'th towards women and their public resolve to free women and involve them as full partners in the revolutionary struggle. This stance has been amplified in many pamphlets and publications put out by the Federation of Iraqi Women, the organ of the party charged with women's issues.[8]

The Federation sponsors and operates a number of programmes aimed at women. These include 'consciousness-raising' conferences and meetings, television and radio programmes that offer advice and information to women and rural centres where women come to learn to read, sew and embroider. But these programmes, useful and important as they may be, can hardly be expected to 'liberate' women. One then has to look elsewhere to gauge the structural changes and to see the role that the Ba'th plays in transforming women's lives.

Economic Participation

The most significant area of structural change is perhaps the economic one; here significant changes in the role of women are taking place as a result of their increasing participation in the wage labour market. The Ba'th's direct contribution to this process (which is, of course, a near-universal one) consists in their emphasis on education and training for *both* men and women, their encouragement of women's participation in the labour market and lastly in their sponsorship of a Unified Labour Code (1970) that equalises the status of men and women on the job. As the single largest employer in the country, the government is in a position to enforce the Code and to ensure the equality of women employees in matters of pay, pensions and benefits.

As the Iraqis themselves are aware, however, the equality is limited to a narrow sphere and involves a small percentage of women. Available statistics indicate, for example, that the number of women working in government administration has doubled between the years 1968 and 1977; that total, nevertheless, is still no more than 14.8 per cent. In 1968, women made up 26 per cent of the educated (professional) working population in Iraq but only 4.3 per cent of the unskilled working population. The latter figure had increased to 10 per cent by 1975. The breakdown of the non-agricultural working population for 1976 indicated the following: women made up 38.5 per cent of those in the field of education, 31 per cent in medicine, 25 per cent of all laboratory technicians, 15 per cent in accounting and related fields, 11 per cent in factories, 4 per cent in engineering and 3 per cent in high government posts.[9]

In a survey carried out by the Ministry of Planning in 1971, it was reported that women made up 40.6 per cent of agricultural labour but that the percentage of women working for wages in that sector was only 2.5 per cent; of the latter only around 5 per cent were permanently employed (i.e. not seasonal labourers). When one recalls that approximately 70 per cent of *all* women of working age are in the agricultural sector (those in industry constitute no more than 10.4 per cent of the urban working population) the implications are clear: women still provide a source of 'cheap' labour. This is disguised in terms of the traditional division of labour within the family, which refers to women's work both within and outside the home (i.e. in the fields) as 'domestic work'.[10] It is interesting to note here that the agrarian reforms promulgated by the regime did little to ameliorate the situation for women. For example, according to Dr al-Attiya, landownership is still vested in the family as a unit with the males as 'heads of household'; women in Iraq, in fact, make up no more than 4 per cent of those who own agricultural property. In addition, women are under-represented in the agricultural co-operatives: in 1976, out of a membership total of about 272,131, women accounted for 98,422 members. When it comes to dividing the shares of the co-operative's profit, the wife's contribution in labour is not taken into account; this is contrary to the by-laws of the co-operatives which allows shares to *all* who participate in the agricultural work.[11]

Without labouring the point, it is clear that, despite some strides in this area, women's participation in the wage labour market is still very limited and it is difficult at this juncture to evaluate its impact on the personal and social autonomy of the woman.

Legislation on Personal Status

One area where, as mentioned earlier, one would have expected the regime to translate its ideological commitments into policy is that of personal status. But, so far, the Ba'th have not enacted any radical family legislation; as will become evident, the amendments they introduced into the 1959 Code of Personal Status are primarily reformist in nature and mild at that. These amendments, however, are worth examining in some detail both for their intrinsic interest and for the light they shed on the regime's view of society.

Legislation is not only an important instrument of social change but family legislation, in particular, is acknowledged to be a key to social modernisation. Progressive governments therefore generally devote considerable resources to the preparation and implementation of new family laws. The extreme case in the Middle East is, of course, that of Ataturk who, in 1926, repealed the Ottoman Law of Family Rights (based on the Islamic *shari'a*) and substituted a new civil code based on the Swiss one. His example has not, so far, been emulated in any other Muslim country. In Tunisia Bourguiba's Code of Personal Status (1956) has gone furthest in the direction of Ataturk but without overtly acknowledging a break with Islamic tradition.

The Iraqi Code of Personal Status was promulgated in 1959 under the pre-Ba'th regime of Qasim. This was the first time that the various laws and statutes concerned with personal and family status were systematised and organised into one coherent legal document. The unified code applies to all Iraqi citizens of the Muslim faith. It should

be noted that *qadis* (judges) have the right to refer to Hanafi or
Ja'afari rules in cases where they deem the law to be unclear, inadequate or inappropriate.

In 1978, the Ba'th promulgated an amended Code of Personal
Status, or *Qanun al-Ahwal al-Shakhsiyya*.[12] In the preamble, the Code
states that the new amendments are based on 'the principles of the
Islamic *shari'a*, but only those that are suited to the spirit of today, and
on legal precedents set in Iraqi courts, especially the High Court
(*mahkamat al-tamyiz*), and on the principles of justice'. Rather than
go through the amendments one by one, a few shall be selected here and
their significance discussed.

The first has to do with the question of eligibility for marriage, or
ahliyat al-zawaj. Whereas previously it was required that both men and
women be sixteen years of age and have the consent of the father or
guardian, the 1978 amendment lowered the minimum age of marriage
to fifteen, but stipulated that the permission of the *qadi* is required in
the case of minors. The lowering of the age of marriage was intended,
in part, to address the reality of early marriages for women – especially
in rural Iraq. What was important, however, was the new clause which
stated that

> in the case where the guardian refuses to allow marriage and where
> the *qadi* sees no valid reason for this refusal, he, the *qadi*, asks the
> guardian to reconsider within a set time period; should the guardian
> still refuse, the *qadi* has authority to permit the marriage.

The authority granted to the judge (who is appointed by the Iraqi
state) to overrule the wishes of the father of a minor can only be
interpreted as a challenge to the patriarch and as an attempt to erode
the power of the patriarchal family by granting the young (both men
and women) more autonomy in their lives. This also seems to be the
aim behind the new article which seeks to discourage and eliminate
forced marriage (*jabr*), an issue that was completely ignored in the
1959 Code. *Jabr* refers to the traditional customary right to force a
woman to marry a man without taking her wishes into consideration.
Among tribal (and some non-tribal) groups it was manifest in the right
of a man to his father's brother's daughter (*bint al-'amm*) or conversely
his right to forbid her from marrying anyone else if he himself did not
want her in marriage; this negative right is known as *nahwa*. *Jabr* and
nahwa are recognised customary rights of the patriarch and of other
male kin (e.g. paternal uncle, paternal cousin, etc.), and are the

corollaries of strict patrilineality and of the effort to maintain solidarity among agnates through the control of women.

The 1978 legislation considered forced marriage to be void if not already consummated, and, where consummated, special provisions were made for divorce should one or other of the two parties so desire. Penalties were specified for those found guilty of forcing marriage upon a man or woman, and what is of special interest is that the legislation differentiated in this regard between two categories of relatives. First, the parents may in such cases be penalised by imprisonment for a period of no more than three years, the payment of an unspecified fine or both. Second, for relatives other than parents, including brothers, uncles, cousins and some other kinsmen (*aghyar*) the penalty is imprisonment for a period of no less than three years and no more than ten.

The clear separation of the nuclear family from the larger extended one (which includes the uncles, cousins, etc.) and the rejection of the traditional authority of the kinsmen *vis-à-vis* the women of the group are clearly consistent with the aforementioned intent of the legislation to undermine the power of the extended kin group and its hold over the life of the individual member.

In Iraq, as elsewhere in the Middle East, the individual's relationship to the state was traditionally mediated through a strong and cohesive kin group, family and tribe. The tribe provided the basic source of identity and was the primary focus of loyalty as well as the political unit of action. Tribes had their own laws and territory, and through the practice of endogamy tended to be socially encysted. Loyalty was to the shaikh, who in most cases (at least in this century) held the power of life and death over his tribesmen. Political modernisation implies, among other things, the freeing of the individual from the familial and tribal matrix and his reintegration into the nation-state. In one sense, this means that state institutions come to assume more and more the authority, prerogatives and duties traditionally associated with the patriarch and the tribal shaikh. This is not the place to discuss the transformation of the concept of 'tribe' (*ashirah*) in Iraq; suffice it only to point out that tribes are no longer viable political units of action. Important as they may remain for purposes of social identification, and even though they may still act as voluntary associations for mutual aid and support (in cases of rural immigrants to cities, for example), tribal affiliation is no longer a sufficient basis for political mobilisation as it used to be in Iraq as recently as the 1940s.[13] This transformation in the nature and function of tribal groupings is partially the result of natural evolutionary processes; governmental policies, however, certainly accelerated the transformation.

It is ironic that in the two areas where women are most directly disadvantaged legally, namely those of polygamy and divorce, the 1978 legislation had only minor reforms to offer. Concerning polygamy (or, more correctly, polygyny), the 1978 Code decreed that although valid under the *shari'a*, an additional marriage must first be cleared by the *qadi* and registered in court. For the failure to register a second marriage (which implies clearing it with the judge), 'the penalty is imprisonment for a period of no less than three years and no more than five'.

In decreeing a tough prison sentence and excluding fines, the legislation obviously sought to discourage the abuse of women by making it difficult for the men to contract impulsive second marriages. The law also added that a wife could now initiate divorce proceedings if her husband took a second wife without permission of the *qadi*. The assumption throughout is that the *qadi*s are modern in outlook and reformist in spirit and would see to it that a woman's legal rights are safeguarded.

Concerning divorce, perhaps the single most significant reform introduced was with respect to adultery. The new code substituted the term *khiyana zawjiyya* (marital infidelity) for the older term *zina* (fornication). The law now stated that *either* party may ask for a divorce in the case of adultery being committed by the other partner. This gets around the symbolic and practical implications of the earlier condition of *zina* where a husband's infidelity was not considered adultery and valid cause for divorce unless it was committed within the confines of the conjugal home. A woman's adultery, on the other hand, was considered *zina* no matter where it took place. The term *zina* has strong connotations in Islamic culture, tied as it is to concepts of purity of women and to their role as guardians of male honour. By removing the term *zina* and substituting the more neutral and 'secular' one of *khiyana zawjiyya* the legislation drew attention away from the question of honour to the responsibility of both husband and wife to live up to the marital commitment. It is interesting, however, to note here that Article 216 of the Iraqi Criminal Code states that whosoever finds his wife committing *zina* and kills her on the spot *may* be sentenced to prison for a period of no more than three years! The reverse does not apparently hold for the wife who, if she were to kill her husband under the same circumstances, would be charged with murder.

'Cultural Authenticity' and 'Revolutionary Change'

The above examples serve the purpose of indicating how the ideology of the Ba'th with regard to women and to the role of the family is being put into practice through legislation. While the legislation seeks to free the individual from the hold of the local group (family and tribe) in order to integrate him as a citizen into the new nation-state, it seems to balk at freeing the woman from the constraints of the *shari'a*-based rules and laws that serve to limit her full autonomy and which confer on her a status secondary to that of the man.

The extreme caution and moderation exhibited by the regime in this area may be partly explained by the reluctance of the government to provoke the more conservative elements among the religious establishment who could conceivably mobilise a following on the issue of women. It is suggested here, however, that the reasons go much deeper than that and involve a basic dilemma, one which is shared throughout the Islamic world. The Iraqi leadership, no less than the Pakistani or the Saudi ones, seems to entertain a basic ambivalence with regard to the role of women and their 'proper place' in society. While such leaderships call for the participation of women in the development process, they all seem to balk at the full emancipation of women from the social and legal bonds that perpetuate their status as permanent wards of their male kin, be they fathers, husbands or brothers.

The dilemma, it will be suggested, consists in what are perceived as the contradictory demands of modernisation and development and those of 'cultural authenticity', a term used here to refer to the core values and structure of meaning that distinguish the culture and impart to it its special ethos. In Arab-Islamic societies, this ethos is to a large extent bound up with Islam and the Islamic heritage which, in addition to imparting a sense of identity and pride in culture, also clearly and directly regulate the most intimate area of interpersonal and familial relations at whose core lies the 'question of women'. However they are interpreted, and regardless of whether they are followed to the letter or totally ignored, 'Islamic values' and notions of proper and improper behaviour still inform the lifestyle of the overwhelming majority of the Middle East. These values and notions are clearly and emphatically expressed in the perennial debates and arguments which link the emancipation of women (however interpreted) to the moral corruption of the society and to the degradation of the faith. Whether this perception is valid or not is beside the point; what is important is that the issue has been perceived in those terms and that it continues to be so.

An important reason for the ambivalence exhibited over the question of women, then, may have to do with the linkage of women to the 'culture core' and with the implicit assumption that a radical change in the position of women implies a deterioration if not outright corruption of the culture. This basic assumption seems to be shared across political and ideological boundaries, lying as it does at the deeper levels of the shared 'cultural bedrock'.

In countries like Saudi Arabia and today's Iran, the dilemma is muted (at least for the time being), as women are presumably in their 'proper Islamic place'. This is not the case in Iraq, Algeria or Syria, where the dilemma assumes a more dissonant expression as it directly clashes with the stated ideology of the regime. The same basic problem, however, is confronting both types of regime: namely how to maintain a sense of identity and cultural continuity in the face of massive change. Given the current cultural onslaught of the West, the issue assumes sharp urgency. In such a context, then, women become the symbolic representatives of the purity and authenticity of the culture. This is, of course, consistent with their traditional role as the representatives of male and family honour. As the repositories of cultural purity and the guarantors of its continuity, women must submit to the rules and regulations that are seen to preserve and perpetuate this perceived authenticity. Like the culture core which they are made to represent, they, too, must be 'protected' from radical change.[14] Hence the dilemma.

Writers such as F. Fanon and A. Memmi have explored the phenomenon whereby colonised societies defend themselves against the coloniser by emphasising and elaborating certain aspects of their native tradition, which then come to serve as symbolic boundaries against the foreigner. Writing of the Algerian experience, under the French, P. Bourdieu has termed this form of cultural retrenchment 'colonial traditionalism'. He writes:

> Colonial traditionalism had come to replace the traditionalism of the traditional society. As a result, ways of behaviour that in appearance had remained unchanged were really endowed with a very different meaning and function, because of the fact that they are now set in relation to a totally new frame of reference. The veil and the chechia (the men's distinctive cap) for example, had been in the traditional context mere vestimentary details endowed with an almost forgotten significance . . . In the colonial situation, however, they take on the functions of signs that are being consciously utilised to express

resistance to the foreign order and to foreign values as well.[15]

It is contended here that much of the same syndrome can be evoked to explain the observed reluctance of even the most secularist and progressive Arab regimes, like that of Iraq, to bring about radical transformation in the personal status of women. As long as women are perceived, consciously or unconsciously, as the symbols and repositories of cultural purity and authenticity, their full liberation will continue to pose a dilemma. If the Ba'th state succeeds in resolving this dilemma and truly manages to liberate women, it will have succeeded in bringing about a revolution within its 'total revolution'.

Notes

1. See Arab Ba'th Socialist Party, *Revolutionary Iraq: 1968-73* (the political report adopted by the eighth regional congress of the Arab Ba'th Socialist Party) (al-Thawrah Publications, Baghdad, 1974), pp. 184-5.
2. Ibid.
3. Ibid.
4. The speech was published in pamphlet form by the Federation of Iraqi Women. See E. Farah, *Al-Mar'a fi Fikr wa Nidhal Hizb al-Ba'th al-'Arabi al-Ishtiraki* (Women in the ideology and struggle of the Arab Ba'th Socialist Party) (Federation of Iraqi Women, Baghdad, 1976). The excerpts quoted from Farah's speech are translated by the writer.
5. Ibid., p. 13.
6. Ibid., p. 13.
7. Ibid., p. 11.
8. The Federation produces a journal, entitled *Majallat al-Mar'a* (Woman's journal). See also S. Husain, *'An al-Thawrah wal Mar'a* (On the revolution and women) (Federation of Iraqi Women, Baghdad, 1975).
9. These figures are taken from A.Y. al-Zaydi, 'Bahth 'an Dor al-Mar'a fi'l Khalij al-'Arabi' (A study of women in the Arab Gulf), in M. al-Najjar (ed.), *Man and Society in the Arab Gulf* (Centre for Arab Gulf Studies Publications, Basra, 1979), vol. 2, pp. 149-232.
10. F. al-Attiya, 'Culture and Social Change and their Impact on the Participation of Women in National Development in the Arab Gulf Region', in M. al-Najjar (ed.), *Man and Society in the Arab Gulf* (Centre for Arab Gulf Publications, Basra, 1979), vol. 1, pp. 100-39.
11. Ibid.
12. The amended code was published in *al-Thawrah* newspaper on 20 Feb. 1978. A special memoir on the code was made available through the Ministry of Justice.
13. On this issue reference may be made to A. al-Wardi, *Tabi'at al-Mujtama' al-Iraqi* (The nature of Iraqi society) (al-Ani Press, Baghdad, 1972).
14. The psycho-sexual and cultural dimensions of this argument are more fully explored in a work which the writer has in progress, entitled 'Women, Power and Cultural Authenticity in Arab Society'.
15. P. Bourdieu, *The Algerians* (Beacon Press, Boston, 1961), p. 125.

8 THE ERADICATION OF ILLITERACY IN IRAQ

Alya Sousa

Introduction

When the modern state of Iraq was formed in 1921 the country
suffered from a variety of deep schisms. Prominent among these was
the huge gap which separated the urban and rural populations. The
rural population was itself divided on the basis of the tribal system
of organisation, being united only in the common suffering of
primitive socio-economic conditions. The urban centres were mostly
internally divided on the basis of ethnic and religious divisions — with
each ethnic or religious community organising its own communal life.
In the north of the country, moreover, there were the Kurds and
other smaller non-Arab or non-Muslim groupings, each possessing a
sense of identity of its own. Thus, the most challenging problem
which faced the nascent state was that of social and national
integration of all the different groups which, through centuries of
Ottoman rule, had become accustomed to living in isolation from one
another. All governments since 1921 — although in different ways —
have conceived of education as the principal means whereby
integration could be achieved.

The base from which the educational system developed after 1921
was extremely narrow. The old Ottoman provinces of Baghdad, Mosul
and Basra, which form the Iraq of today, had been only slightly
affected by the cultural revival witnessed by some other Arab
provinces of the Ottoman Empire in the nineteenth century. Modern
schools were extremely few in number and access to them was
limited to a very small wealthy elite. Traditional education was
provided for by traditional religious institutions, basically in the form
of the *Katatib* (sing. *Kuttab* : elementary school) at which small children
received basic religious education by a *mulla.*[1] In spite of their
primitiveness and unsuitability, the *Katatib* continued to serve as the
principal centre of primary education until the end of Ottoman rule
and the passing of the country into British hands after World War I.

Despite the existence under the Ottomans of a few government
schools, together with the *Katatib* and some foreign and private

missionary schools, the percentage of literacy did not exceed 0.5 per cent.[2] The period between the British occupation and the 1958 revolution witnessed some important developments on the educational and social levels. The *Katatib* gradually gave way to public primary schools, such that by 1958 only two recognised *Katatib* remained. The relative expansion in primary education, however, was unable to match the increase in the population. Thus, the percentage of illiteracy registered in 1957 was 81.71 per cent, ranging from 91.51 per cent in rural areas to 63.3 per cent in urban centres, and from 91.6 per cent among women to 72.4 per cent among men.[3]

Under the post-1958 republican regime education received more serious attention. Education was made compulsory and the number of pupils admitted to primary level increased from 430,000 in 1957-8 to 849,000 in 1963, then to 926,000 in 1965. Despite the legislation of compulsory education, however, it was not until the 1970s that the measure was fully implemented and all children were, in fact, attending school.

The expansion of the educational system, however, necessarily focused exclusively on school-age children. To bring some enlightenment to the illiterate sections of the adult population required a different approach. From the 1920s onwards, therefore, schemes were proposed – both at official and private levels – to reduce or eradicate illiteracy. The first attempt made by the *Ahali* grouping to organise politically was the Society for Combating Illiteracy, which emerged in the 1930s.[4] The schemes which were implemented before 1958, however, achieved little or no success. By 1963 a framework of illiteracy centres had been established (330 for men and 56 for women, falling to 323 for men and 45 for women in 1965[5]), but the impact was limited.

The causes of the failure or limited success of illiteracy eradication schemes before 1968 are to be found principally in the lack of an overall vision. For a clear strategy to solve the problem, illiteracy needed to be viewed within its political dimension – involving the phenomenon of cultural illiteracy as well as that of alphabetical illiteracy. The approach to the problem, moreover, lacked the necessary determination and dedication. Other factors contributing to failure were the absence of accurate statistical information on the numbers, age groups, employment, sex and distribution of illiterates; the insufficiency and inadequacy of the texts prescribed for adult learners; the lack of adequate funds to provide suitable learning conditions; and the low motivation among adult learners in the absence of mature guidance.

During the 1950s and 1960s Iraq's population was growing very quickly.[6] Even if the number of literates was increasing, therefore, this did not necessarily – and did not in fact – raise the proportion of the population which was literate. To combat illiteracy decisively, therefore, a compulsory and comprehensive scheme was necessary.

The Programmes of the Ba'th Party and Government

The Arab Ba'th Socialist Party had consistently stated that illiteracy was not just an educational, social and economic problem, but a central political issue with far-reaching implications.[7] The issue was mentioned in the Party's first manifesto in 1947, and in the Report of the Sixth National Conference (1963) the Party leadership committed itself to the eradication of illiteracy:

> Illiteracy is an obstacle to the fulfilment of the objectives of the Arab Nation . . .
> The building-up of socialism and the practice of democracy necessitate the complete and immediate eradication of illiteracy and the mobilisation of all potentialities to fulfil this mission with immediacy and success.[8]

The objective of eradicating illiteracy was incorporated in Article 27 of the Provisional Constitution adopted following the Ba'th's take-over of power in 1968, and the Report of the Eighth Regional Congress of the Party stated that

> The coming stage must witness a reappraisal of the means previously employed in this field in order to achieve a transition from the phase of reducing illiteracy to the phase of its complete eradication . .
> The noble aim of eradicating illiteracy is one of the main fields of our strife and activity. On its success will depend the determination of many vital political, economic and social issues in this country . . .[9]

The unprecedented boom in the Iraqi economy which followed the nationalisation of the oil industry in 1972 and the oil price rises of 1973 created the framework within which the age-old problem of illiteracy could be solved.

The legislative basis which laid the guidelines for educational policies in the 1970s was set by three laws. An Illiteracy Eradication Law was promulgated in 1971. This was followed by a Free Education Law in 1974, whereby the state undertook the responsibility of covering all financial costs at all educational stages – from kindergartens to universities. In 1976, a further Compulsory Education Law was passed, making primary schooling compulsory for all children between 6 and 15, and committing the state to providing all the necessary facilities.

The period between the promulgation of the Illiteracy Eradication Law (1971) and the initiation of the national comprehensive campaign for the eradication of illiteracy in December 1978 was spent in creating the infrastructural base for eradicating illiteracy. Measures were taken to train literacy teachers and administrative personnel through a National Training Centre for Fundamental Education which was created for this purpose. A number of decrees were passed with the object of encouraging illiterate citizens to enrol at literacy centres; literacy was made a condition for employment in government departments.

A conference to discuss appropriate preparatory measures for the conduct of the comprehensive national campaign was held in May 1976, attended by non-Iraqi – as well as Iraqi – experts. In the same year a Supreme Council for the Eradication of Illiteracy was created, with members drawn from relevant ministries and organisations (the Ministries of Planning, Education, Health, Defence and Social Welfare; the trade unions; farmers' co-operatives; and volunteer societies) and others serving in their capacities as educational experts or social workers.

The Supreme Council sought to mobilise educationalists, statisticians, psychologists, social workers and religious and community leaders for the campaign. In order to provide the necessary data regarding the number of illiterates, their age groups, sex, income and ethnic and geographical distributions, a general census was carried out in November 1977. The census revealed that there were 2,212,630 people between the ages of 15 and 45 who did not have the basic skills of reading and writing. Of these, there were 676,693 men and 1,535,937 women[10] – the percentage of women coming to 69.42 per cent of the total. The percentage of illiterates in rural areas averaged 48.67 per cent of the rural population, while the governorate of Baghdad alone held one-fifth of the total number of illiterates.[11]

In May 1978, the National Comprehensive Campaign for Compulsory Literacy Law was issued, making the eradication of illiteracy a national issue towards which all the country's facilities on both official and popular levels were to be oriented. The law specified the objectives to be achieved as follows: to teach reading, writing and arithmetic; to develop professional skills; to help illiterates raise their cultural, economic and social standards of living; to promote national consciousness among illiterates; and to encourage those who gained literacy. The campaign aimed at eradicating the illiteracy of all those between the ages of 15 and 45 whose illiteracy had been revealed in the 1977 census — within a fixed limit of 36 months. The time limit was later reduced to 21 months. Male students were enrolled in two stages, females in four. The law made regular attendance at illiteracy eradication classes obligatory, and laid down punitive measures to deal with those who failed to comply with its provisions.

An extensive publicity programme preceded and accompanied the campaign, which was duly launched on 1 December 1978. Trade unions and popular organisations played a decisive role in carrying out the decisions and recommendations of the Supreme Council.[12] The mass media was fully employed to familiarise the public with the objectives and seriousness of the campaign and the benefits to be reaped therefrom. Special programmes were broadcast on radio and television, and exhibitions depicting the various aspects of the battle against ignorance were offered to the public. Daily evening literacy lessons were televised on all channels of the national networks.[13]

All schools and public buildings were used as literacy classrooms. The circumstances and special needs of each village and community were taken into consideration. Literacy classes on large ships and oil tankers were required by law. Marsh-dwellers had their own 'floating schools', and travelling schools were instituted for the nomads. The handicapped, the disabled and the blind were enabled to attend special literacy centres equipped with the requisite teaching aids. Prisoners were told that any progress they showed in learning would be taken into consideration in remission of sentences.

Literacy teachers were recruited from among primary-school teachers, government employees, university students and volunteers. Most of these were offered special training programmes. The texts employed in the literacy centres were geared to the needs of the individuals attending the classes, with a basic differentiation being made between peasants, workers, housewives and soldiers. The difference lay in the presentation rather than the content. Terms and information were used which related to the occupational functions of each group; in this context the opportunity was taken to promote each group's consciousness of the significance of its role in society, together with the consciousness of individuals as to obligations as citizens.

There were other significant elements of the campaign. The emphasis which the Ba'th Party places on 'the full emancipation of women from social, economic, cultural and legal restrictions',[14] meant that special facilities were provided to ensure that practical difficulties did not inhibit women from attending. Nurseries were opened in many literacy centres, to which women could bring their children. The campaign also took into account the local needs of the Kurdish autonomous region: the instruction in this region was carried out in Kurdish, with all the relevant texts produced also in Kurdish. The scale of the literacy campaign, and the range of the different facilities which had to be offered, naturally required substantial resources. The 1976 conference had recommended the allocation of ID 66.95 million (ID 1 = c. $3) for the campaign, but this figure was subsequently raised to ID 236 million.

The instruction in basic skills of reading and writing was only the first stage in the literacy campaign. Following the completion of the first stage in all parts of the country in 1980 a second stage was initiated. The latter takes the form of 'popular schools', intended to enable learners to develop their skills of reading and writing and at the same time study a variety of subjects ranging from arithmetic to geography and to basic science. English is taught in the last two years. Upon graduation from the popular school learners will then be able to enrol in any evening secondary school and so further their education.[15] It is expected that the popular school stage will be completed by the end of 1983.

Evaluation of the Campaign

On the basis of the material just presented some observations can be made regarding the value and effectiveness of literacy campaigns — especially from the perspective of the contribution they can make to social integration and economic development. It must be admitted that only tentative conclusions can be reached; the full effect of the literacy campaign on economic production will only become apparent in the long term — when the illiterates of the age group over 45 (for whom participation was not compulsory) have disappeared from the scene. Research in other parts of the world has sought to quantify the effects of education on levels of production: in the United States it has been suggested that 21-29 per cent of increases in productivity are attributable to rising standards of education; in Japan 27 per cent of productivity increases have been attributed to education; in the Soviet Union the productivity of a worker who has completed elementary school education has been estimated as being equivalent to one and one-half times that of an illiterate worker of the same age and function. Soviet workers with secondary education are said to be twice as productive – and those with higher education four times as productive – as their illiterate counterparts.[16]

The principal effect of the literacy campaign has been to deliver a shock to the country's social infrastructure in a manner which will facilitate significant social changes. Two major types of impact are discernible – both stem from the obligatory nature of the enrolment in literacy classes. First, a large number of women who rarely left their homes in the past now have the opportunity of mixing in society, acquainting themselves with the world around them and even participating in the social activities organised at the literacy centres. The campaign has, therefore, constituted a serious blow to the remaining forms of segregation; previously illiterate women have become conscious of the means whereby they can break out of the oppressive forms of social control to which they were formerly subjected.

Second, the poorer elements in society generally have been brought into contact with modern ideas. The textbooks prepared for the literacy classes have deliberately diffused modern concepts of law and order, punctuality, cleanliness, patriotism, women's liberation and child care. Such exposure should contribute to the replacement of traditional sets of values by new sets of values more appropriate to the needs of the developing economy. The spreading of new ideas, however, also has a more critical significance. As explained earlier, the Ba'th Party's objective in eradicating alphabetical illiteracy is considered as no more than a means of combating cultural illiteracy. The Ba'th strategy aims at raising the social, economic and cultural levels of the lower classes in this manner – such that the gap separating them from other elements in society is bridged and social cohesion is reinforced. Cultural and social alienation should disappear. If the strategy is indeed successful, this would be the most significant achievement of the literacy campaign.

As would be expected, the implementation of the campaign did not proceed without difficulties and problems – despite the considerable support and attention it received from all governmental departments and popular organisations. One problem was that of the 'psychological barrier' among adult learners, due to the new demands and norms of behaviour imposed by regular class attendance. This problem was especially acute among tribal people and villagers, in whose view learning was associated with children; men considered their enrolment at school as constituting a slight on their manhood. Among the major technical complications was the insufficient number of teachers – even though all primary-school teachers were compulsorily recruited. This insufficiency made it necessary to recruit additional teachers from among college students, public department employees and volunteers, not all of whom received special adult education training. School-buildings were also sometimes insufficient, despite the rapid expansion which had taken place. In some cases buildings had to be used by day as well as by night, and this conflicted with the daily work schedule of those who were enrolled – thus leading to absenteeism.

The problem of absenteeism does not generally seem to have been very acute. Of the total number of illiterates who were supposed to attend the literacy classes (2,063,075) only 343,309 (about 16 per cent) did not attend. It is significant, moreover, that 8.63 per cent of those who attended the literacy classes were above the age of 45 – i.e. they were attending on a voluntary basis and not because attendance was compulsory.[17] The rate of absenteeism has, without doubt, been affected by the outbreak of war with Iran, but the war has not seriously impeded the effectiveness of the campaign.

Unlike previous literacy projects the campaign has made provision for continuing discussion of the problems which are encountered, such that the methods and materials used can be modified and improved. A specialised monthly magazine (*al-Ma'rifa*) was established for this purpose and, in conjunction with the Arab League Educational, Scientific and Cultural Organisation, the Supreme Council created a 'Body of Evaluation' such that all aspects of the implementation of the campaign could be evaluated.

Finally, a key element in Iraq's literacy campaign has been the conception (mentioned above) that instruction in reading and writing only constitute a first step towards further learning. The principle of continued education and self-education has been established. Arrangements are currently being made for the continuation of adult education after the popular school stage. There are plans to establish an Iraqi Union for Adult Education and a Centre for Adult Education. The former would be concerned with co-ordinating activities and potentialities related to adult education, and the latter with ensuring that adequate materials (publications, films, etc.) are available for adult education.

Whatever deficiencies may have occurred, Iraq's literacy campaign has come to constitute an essential element in developing Iraq's society and economy. The international approval won by the campaign[17] suggests that other Arab countries could be well advised to follow the procedures and practices adopted in Iraq.

Notes

1. Similar schools existed in the Christian and Jewish communities. See A. al-Hilali, *History of Education in Iraq in the Ottoman Period* (al-Ani Press, Baghdad, 1959).

2. M. al-Rawi and Q. Qaranba, *Readings in Illiteracy Eradication and Adult Teaching* (al-Thawrah Press, Baghdad, 1981), p. 208.

3. A. Jasim, 'Patterns of Social Life in Iraq', *Social Sciences Bulletin* (Baghdad, vol. 2, no. 2, July 1977, p. 16.

4. For the Ahali group's activities against illiteracy see F. Wakil, *The Ahali Group in Iraq* (el-Ani Press, Baghdad, 1979), pp. 124-40.

5. Al-Rawi and Qaramba, *Readings*, p. 223.

6. The population of Iraq rose from 4,816,000 in 1947 to 6,337,400 in 1957, to 8,097,230 in 1965, to 10,823,000 in 1974 and to 12,000,497 in 1977.

7. See E. Farah, *The Political Dimensions of the Comprehensive National Campaign for the Eradication of Illiteracy* (al-Thawrah Press, Baghdad, 1976).

8. Arab Ba'th Socialist Party, *Report of the Sixth National Conference* (al-Thawrah Press, Baghdad, 1964), p. 23.

9. Arab Ba'th Socialist Party, *The 1968 Revolution in Iraq* (Ithaca Press, London, 1964), p. 174.

10. Supreme Council of the Comprehensive National Campaign for Compulsory Literacy, *The Illiteracy Eradication Campaign: Review and Statistics* (SCCNCCL, Baghdad, 1980).

11. Out of a population in 1977 of 12,000,497, the census revealed that there were 4,500,000 in the 15-45 age-group.

12. See, for example, K. Shawkat, 'The Role of Professional and Popular Organisations in the Comprehensive National Campaign for Compulsory Literacy', *Al-Mu'allim al-Jadid*, vol. 40, no. 2 (1979).

13. S. Amin, 'Television in the Service of Literacy', *Al-Mu'allim al-Jadid*, vol. 40, no. 2 (1979).

14. Ba'th Party, *The 1968 Revolution*, p. 173.

15. H. Hamid, 'The Popular Schools: a Step towards the Cultural Level', *Education of the Masses* (Baghdad), vol. 6, no. 15 (Sept. 1979), p. 207.

16. S. Azb, 'The Iraqi Experience in Illiteracy Eradication: a Survey', *Ta'lim al-Jamahir* (Baghdad), no. 16 (Jan. 1980), p. 64.

17. Evidence of the international approval is provided by the United Nations Educational, Scientific and Cultural Organisation (UNESCO) having made an award on the basis of the campaign's achievements. The Nadezhda K. Krupskaya prize (a UNESCO prize intended to 'reward remarkable and effective contributions in the field of illiteracy eradication') was awarded to the Supreme Council of the National Comprehensive Campaign for Literacy in Iraq, in August 1979, for having 'harnassed in a remarkable way the country's full energies in promoting a far-reaching literacy campaign'.

9 UNITED STATES-IRAQ RELATIONS: A SPRING THAW?

Barry Rubin

Introduction

Speaking about relations between Iraq and the United States is reminiscent of George Bernard Shaw's satirical article 'On the Origins and History of the Snakes of Ireland'. There are no snakes in Ireland and, since 1967, there have been no diplomatic relations between Baghdad and Washington. Preoccupation with this formal break, however, should not obscure other real and potential ties between the two countries.

The most obvious of these links is trade, though the most important, many observers thought in recent years, might become some loose and subtle strategic alignment. Statistics clearly demonstrate, and American business is well aware, that Iraq has increasingly turned towards the West, and to a large extent towards the United States, for the technologies and products required for development. On the political and strategic side there may be some parallel interests which would inspire some parallel, if not explicitly co-operative, efforts. The most important of these is preventing any spread of Soviet influence into the all-important Arab/Persian Gulf region.

These factors have led some to overstate the possibilities for current or future interaction or even alliance. The most extreme case is the ridiculous Iranian conspiracy theory about a US-Iraq plot against Teheran. Given the great barriers separating Washington and Baghdad — their continuing mutual mistrust and differences over the Arab-Israeli conflict in particular — even far more cautious and less ambitious assessments may be wrong. Yet certain mutual interests and mutual objectives could lead to a new era in the relationship. Such potentialities are well worth exploring.

Relations before 1968

In a real sense, the two countries have never been particularly close in the past. If Britain was Iraq's principal great power ally until 1958, the Soviet Union took that role in later years. The United States remained a distant and secondary actor in Iraq's conduct of foreign relations.

Although American companies had a 23.75 per cent share in the Iraq Petroleum Company (IPC), the venture was dominated by British interests. The disproportion was even greater on the political level. When the United States decided to raise the level of its Baghdad representation to minister in 1944 the Foreign Office objected lest this threaten the British ambassador's precedence. Iraq was little better than a British colony, wrote US diplomat Loy Henderson in March 1944, and he criticised the British-backed Iraqi government for its repression and narrow base. The British made it clear that Iraq should remain in its sphere and discouraged any US political or economic foothold there.[1]

While some Iraqi politicians sought closer relations with the United States during the next few years to balance British influence, these initiatives were never fully pursued. While the United States became the main Western ally of Saudi Arabia and Turkey in the late 1940s and assumed the senior Western role in Egypt, Iran, Lebanon and even Jordan in the early and middle 1950s, Iraq remained a British stronghold.

Before the July 1958 *coup*, which ended the Hashimite monarchy and the long string of pro-British regimes, two issues had a great effect on US-Iraq relations: Palestine and the question of regional security arrangements. On the former, Iraq, like other Arab countries, opposed Israel's creation and was bitterly angry at American policy. This disagreement did not destroy existing co-operation between the two countries but it did lay the basis for great strains in the future.[2]

Growing Arab nationalism and anti-Western feeling, alongside increased regional instability, also threatened the traditional Anglo-Iraqi alliance. An attempt to revise those arrangements through the January 1948 Portsmouth Treaty was prevented by violent street clashes between government and opposition. Alignment with Western powers was becoming identified with surrender of Arab interests to an external imperialism.

By the mid-1950s, when Secretary of State John Foster Dulles was assembling a chain of pacts and treaties to contain the USSR, Washington preferred bilateral links with Iraq. London, however, pressed for Iraq's inclusion in a multinational arrangement. Aware of Arab, and particularly Egyptian, opposition to any initiative seeming to divide the Arab world, Dulles cabled the US Embassy in Baghdad in

April 1954: 'If Iraqi leaders are justified in their fears of public reaction and repercussions in other Arab States, agreement may well cause difficulties out of proportion to benefits'. Instead of joining the newly created Turkey-Pakistan accord, Iraq signed a military aid agreement with the United States on 21 April 1954.[3]

The US programme in Iraq was initially small, involving only eleven US advisers and $9 million in assistance for the first year.[4] Events, however, moved quickly. Iraq signed a pact with Turkey in February 1955 and another one with Britain two months later. By November 1955 the Baghdad Pact organisation had taken shape in the face of strong opposition by Gamal Abd al-Nasser and his allies. The Suez crisis of 1956 heightened the nationalist legitimacy of the latter elements and further undermined Britain's role in the region.

Although the United States never fully joined the Baghdad Pact, the organisation was identified with American as well as with British interests. The increasingly unpopular regime in Baghdad was also viewed as linked to Western aims. Thus the July 1958 *coup* produced a regime whose attitudes mixed hatred for the old establishment and structures with strong distrust of Western governments, based on their stands towards both Iraqi and regional issues.

The Qasim regime withdrew from the Baghdad Pact in March 1959 and terminated the bilateral military assistance agreement two months later. It briefly severed relations when the United States recognised Kuwait in 1961. During the 1960s Iraq's increasing hostility and radicalism played a central role in the growing US-Iran alliance. The sale of F-4 fighter planes to the Shah, for example, was justified within the American government as matching Soviet sales to the Iraqis. Previously, despite frequent pleas and demands from the Shah, the United States had been reluctant to grant Iran large amounts of military aid. Iranian forces, Washington argued, could not possibly be large enough to counter the most likely security threat – a direct Soviet invasion from the north. Instead, they should be organised so as to serve as a 'trip-wire' in any such eventuality and to maintain internal stability.[5]

With the rise of radical Arab forces, the Shah's attention shifted towards the south and the Gulf. The West's growing dependence on Arab oil and Britain's intention of withdrawing from the region added to American concerns. The Shah could not counter the USSR but he could conceivably prevent internal upheavals in the newly independent small Arab shaikhdoms and face down Nasserist or Iraqi influence. These were the main considerations which set the Nixon administration on the course of dependence on the Shah and towards a massive military build-up for that country.

While the United States and Iraq were moving into positions which made them enemies, some links remained. A cultural co-operation agreement was signed in January 1961, a Food for Peace arrangement commenced in August 1963, a US Export-Import Bank Loan was made in 1965 and an Agricultural Commodities Agreement was negotiated in December 1966. After the end of Abd al-Karim Qasim's five-year reign in 1963 the ruling Aref brothers made attempts to renew economic and commercial ties with the West. Particularly significant in this regard were Prime Minister Bazzaz's 1966 and 1967 visits to Britain and the United States, respectively. Two other events, however, reversed these trends: the 1967 Arab-Israeli war and the 1968 Ba'thist revolution in Iraq.[6] Immediately after the June 1967 war Iraq severed diplomatic relations with the United States, suspended oil shipments, refused US aircraft overflight rights and announced a boycott of American goods.

The 1968 Take-over and the Early Years of the Ba'thist Rule

When the Ba'th came to power in 1968 the new regime did not want to reverse an apparently militant nationalist step taken by its predecessors. The Ba'th itself was outspokenly pan-Arab, domestically socialist, favoured alliance with the USSR, supported revolutions against conservative regimes abroad and took an activist line on the question of Israel. Reconciliation with the United States, identified with capitalism, imperialism, the pre-1958 monarchy and the Ba'th's foreign rivals and Israel as well, hardly constituted a priority for Baghdad.

The United States held equally unfavourable perceptions of Iraq, as a radical state, an ally of the Soviet Union and a destabilising, revolutionary force in the region. Washington supported Iran, which held similar views. The Shah's decision to police the Gulf was symbolised by his seizure of three strategic islands near the Gulf's gateway, the Straits of Hormuz — a step which led Iraq to break relations with Iran and an apparently complicit Britain. The Iranian monarch then ordered $2 billion in military aircraft from the United States, the biggest single deal concluded by the Pentagon up to that time.

During his May 1972 visit to Teheran, US President Richard Nixon promised to sell Iran any non-nuclear weapon it wanted in unlimited quantities, to provide technicians for training Iran's military and to help Iran support the Kurdish nationalist insurgency against Iraq. These two first decisions led to a rapid increase in the Shah's arsenal and played a role in creating the conditions which were to lead to the Iranian revolution.

Given Iran's fear and mistrust of Iraq and Baghdad's attempts to undermine Iran by supporting that country's Arab minority, Teheran responded by aiding and arming the Iraqi Kurds. Both the State Department and the CIA had serious reservations over such a move but they were overruled by the White House. Iranian support for the Iraqi Kurds continued until the Shah was able to negotiate a treaty with Iraq in March 1975, settling their border dispute and pledging both sides to stop supporting each other's dissidents; Teheran then abandoned the Kurds. Washington went along with this decision. Iraqi knowledge of the United States' collaboration with Iran on the Kurdish issue inevitably increased antagonism towards the United States, and Baghdad's 1972 Friendship Treaty with the USSR, moving the two countries closer than they had ever been before, had a similar effect on US attitudes towards Iraq. The earlier hostility became integrated into Cold War alignments.

Iraq's alignment with the Soviet Union, however, was not unconditional. Saddam Husain, the most influential personality in the regime, realised very well that his Arab nationalist aims often meshed poorly with those of the Soviet Union. Ba'thist ideology viewed many aspects of world politics similarly to Moscow's analyses – they shared opposition to the regional *status quo*, and the USSR's willingness to supply large quantities of arms was a powerful incentive for alliance. Yet, Husain told an American interviewer in July 1973, Iraq wanted independence from foreign interference and neutrality in great power conflicts. 'Iraqis can not drink oil,' he explained, 'and our markets are in the West and Japan'. While Iraq saw US policies as hostile, 'I will never close the door on any positive development in those policies through which relations might be changed'.[7]

Indeed, while Iraq nationalised the IPC in 1972 and the concessionary rights of Exxon and Mobil the following year – the day after the October 1973 Arab-Israeli war began – Iraq did increasingly turn towards trade with the United States. The income generated from the steep and rapid rises in petroleum prices made Iraq an active and attractive commercial partner. While the speedier pace and wider scope of such well-financed efforts were one reason for the expansion of economic links, Iraqi dissatisfaction with the quality of Eastern bloc goods was another. 'When we need commodities or services which our economy can not provide at this time,' said Tariq Aziz, then Minister of Information, in November 1976, 'we will seek to purchase them from the United States if an American firm is the top bidder. But this will not necessarily lead to deeper political relations'.[8] This last point was true and Western expectations to the contrary often seemed based on some naive version of economic determinism.

The United States imported $123 million worth of oil from Iraq in 1976 and $671 million in 1979. By the first half of 1980, US imports of oil amounted to 37,000 barrels a day from Iraq. Although the value of these interactions was high, Iraq was only ninth among American suppliers. The United States was, therefore, not highly dependent on Iraq as a supplier, nor was the American oil market of crucial importance to Iraq. In 1979 the United States took only 3.2 per cent of Iraq's oil exports. On a broader strategic plane, however, such important US allies as France, Italy and Japan were major customers.[9]

US exports to Iraq, meanwhile, grew from $382 million in 1976 to around $700 million in 1980. The US share of Iraq's import market, which totalled an estimated $5.5 billion in 1979, remained relatively steady over those years, growing somewhat since then. American companies, however, provided many of the most advanced technology goods. Moreover, even though Iraq took a hard line on the Arab boycott of Israel regulations, these were sometimes waived for US manufacturers when their product was particularly needed. American exports included planes, communications equipment and an entire petrochemical plant. By 1976, twenty-two US companies already had branches or offices in Iraq.[10]

The lack of formal relations did not damage this interchange. The US interests section in Baghdad, located in the Belgian embassy, and the Iraqi interests section in Washington, placed in the Indian embassy, expanded as necessary to meet the demands. They also allowed a modicum of communication between the two governments.

New Elements in the Relationship: the late 1970s and early 1980s

The Carter administration, which came to office in January 1977, repeatedly declared its willingness to reopen formal relations with Iraq.[11] It is worth noting, however, that the US interests section in Baghdad was already larger than most of the embassies in the city, while a low profile avoided its becoming a target for anti-Americanism. In addition to the commercial and communications functions, the US consular staff was able to issue visas for an estimated 2,500 Iraqis studying in America in 1980, triple the number only three years earlier.

Despite periodic rumours of a changed Iraqi policy over recognition, Baghdad's position remained remarkably consistent. Saddam Husain's February 1979 statement that relations would be re-established when it was found to be in the Arab world's interests, for example, was almost identical with his formula six years earlier.[12]

From 1977 onwards US motives for attempting to improve relations with Iraq were of two kinds—relevant to two distinct periods. At first, the Carter administration was concerned to play down the East-West aspect of Third World conflicts and did not adopt its predecessor's view of Iraq solely as a Soviet ally. After the USSR's invasion of Afghanistan, however, and the accession of the more conservative Reagan administration, Iraq was seen by some as a potential ally in maintaining regional stability and in opposing Soviet expansionism.

These conceptions were based on a fresh assessment of Iraq's possible role in the area. There was, first, a realisation of the increasing importance and strength of Iraq itself. Iraq was OPEC's second largest petroleum exporter, with an annual income approaching $30 billion a year. Impressive economic projects and the apparent stability of the Ba'thist government also drew much attention. The growing military might of Iraq, though often overestimated as the Iran-Iraq war was to show, nevertheless made that country strong relative to its neighbours in the Gulf. The possibility of Iraq playing a significant role, moreover, was strengthened by the effective removal from the scene of the two countries in the Middle East Muslim world whose armed power and political influence most exceeded Baghdad's: Egypt and Iran. By signing the Camp David accords Egypt was isolated among the Arab states; ironically this move made another Arab-Israeli war less likely and hence allowed increased inter-Arab conflict. Egypt's isolation, at any rate, offered dramatic possibilities for Iraq's long-held Arab leadership ambitions.

The fall of the Shah removed a leader who had openly sought primacy in the Gulf region. His support from the United States and his huge stores of modern military equipment, including the largest naval forces in the Gulf, had overshadowed Iraq and must have constituted a factor in that country's decision to settle its border dispute in 1975. While the Iranian revolution created a power vacuum in sub-regional affairs, it also produced a Khomeinist regime which sought to fill it in a manner opposed to both Iraqi and US interests.

The Islamic Republic of Iran made no secret of its ideological mission to spread similar revolutions throughout the area. Although this effort consisted mostly of radio broadcasts and preachers despatched to the Arab side of the Gulf, Iraq received special attention. A terrorist group, the al-Da'wa Party, sought to raise revolt among Iraq's majority Shi'a Muslim community and an assassination attempt against Tariq Aziz was acknowledged by figures close to Iran's government. Iraq in turn began to support Iranian Arabs in that country's oil-rich Khuzistan province (called 'Arabistan' by the Iraqis). This gradually escalating conflict led to a series of border clashes and finally to Iraq's September 1980 invasion of Iran.

Another factor affecting US-Iraq relations was the growing rift between Baghdad and Moscow. From the mid-1950s onwards the USSR had invested much time and money to gain footholds in the radical Arab states. These governments, however, generally preferred Arab nationalism to Communism, and their own objectives to those of the Soviet Union. Although interests often coincided, differing stands and goals caused strains; increases in Soviet influence created Arab fears that this merely represented a new form of imperialism. The result was setbacks or stalemates in the Soviet Union's relations with a number of countries.

In the late 1970s the Soviets began shifting attention from the core Arab world to the Middle East periphery. Rather than support existing independent left-nationalist regimes Moscow sought to create and maintain dependent Marxist regimes over which it could exercise greater leverage. Such was the model followed with greater or lesser success in Afghanistan, Ethiopia and the People's Democratic Republic of Yemen.

The presence of Soviet or Soviet-surrogate troops and of many military and civilian advisers in these dependent Marxist regimes was designed to give Moscow some control over which faction and individuals would rule. Pressure for the creation of a united, pro-Moscow Marxist party and the penetration of key institutions, like secret police and intelligence, were aimed to tie any such country irretrievably to the USSR.

Observing these developments, the Iraqi government became concerned over their domestic and regional significance. Baghdad certainly wanted Soviet support in combating Western influence, but it had no intention of helping the USSR gain hegemony over the region. On the one hand, Iraq's Arab nationalist principles set it against any foreign power's intervention in local affairs; on the other, Iraq wanted to project its own influence throughout the region.

It was for such reasons that Iraq rejected the USSR's invasion and occupation of Afghanistan and voted to condemn this action in the United Nations. Iraq's conflicts with Syria and with the People's Democratic Republic of Yemen were both heightened by the closer links which the latter states maintained with the Soviet Union and, in turn, further estranged Iraq from the USSR. Moscow's refusal to re-supply Iraq during its war with Iran, though the door was kept open by some covert shipments through Eastern European countries, produced another grievance. Moscow's distaste for Saddam Husain and continued ties with and assistance for the Iraqi Communist Party were also issues of contention. When that party continued, despite Iraqi government warnings, to organise in the army, a bloody purge was begun against the Communists.

While Iraqi policies and perceptions were changing, the same could be said of American perspectives. The Gulf was becoming more important for US interests at the same time as it was becoming more unstable. The Iranian revolution and the Soviet invasion of Afghanistan had far-reaching effects on Washington's thinking, and for the first time in US history the Gulf became a primary area of concern.

American dependence on Gulf oil and the hostage crisis with Iran brought home to every US citizen the significance of the Gulf area. The Soviet threat to the region seemed to make this a matter of particular importance and urgency. While the main emphasis in the US response was placed on ties with Saudi Arabia and the smaller Arab emirates of the Gulf, Iraq's power created a great deal of interest and speculation over its future role. The fact that Iraq was patching up its relations with the Arab states of the Gulf and was moving away from the USSR altered the image of Baghdad held by American policymakers.

This was the context in which President Carter's adviser on national security affairs, Zbigniew Brzezinski, made his much-cited comments in an April 1980 television interview:

> We desire good relations with all Arab countries. We see no fundamental incompatibility of interests between the United States and Iraq. We feel that Iraq desires to be independent, that Iraq wishes a secure Persian Gulf, and we do not feel that American-Iraq relations need to be frozen in antagonism.

Brzezinski added that this did not mean the United States was encouraging any Iraqi actions against Iran: 'We are not interested in the eruption of hostilities in the Persian Gulf.' If Iran faced the dangers of isolation or even partition, it was because of the attitude of the Teheran regime, he continued, in breaking so sharply with the United States. At any rate, 'the road towards improvement' of US-Iraq relations would be 'a long one'.[13]

Assistant Secretary of State Harold Saunders, in his September 1980 congressional testimony, mentioned 'the legacy of Iraq's support for radical groups engaged in terrorism', while noting Baghdad's enhanced regional and international role. 'We are encouraged,' he concluded, 'by signs that Iraq has developed a greater harmony with Arab neighbours on the Gulf'.[14] A short time later, Secretary of State Edmund Muskie's meeting with Iraqi Foreign Minister Sa'adun Hammadi at the United Nations symbolised the new level of communications between the two countries.

At the outbreak of the Iran-Iraq war the United States declared its neutrality. Given Iran's hostility and the continued holding of fifty-two American hostages, as well as the pattern of US interests, no other course of action would have been plausible. The Iraqis were nervous, however, lest the United States help Iran, if only as a means of securing the hostages' release. For its part, Iran claimed that Iraq was operating as an American agent in making the attack — a wild fantasy even by the Teheran regime's standards.

Actually, the United States hoped for a quick end to a conflict which threatened to add to regional instability and to provide new opportunities for the USSR. The United States was particularly opposed, Muskie said, 'to the dismemberment of Iran'. The Iraqi newspaper *al-Thawra* responded with concern that this might presage American assistance to prevent an Iranian collapse: 'We can easily relate the American regime's public hints on its readiness to supply the Persian regime with arms and ammunition to save it from an inevitable defeat.'[15]

As the months went by, however, the United States did not intervene on Iran's behalf. Even after the hostages were released on 20 January 1981 the American government sent no arms to Iran, even from among the $550 million worth of equipment already ordered and paid for by the Shah's regime.

Appreciation for this behaviour — or an attempt to encourage its continuity — brought some cautious optimism from Baghdad regarding the resumption of relations. In an interview the day before Iran released the hostages Saddam Husain used the traditional Iraqi formula on US-Iraq relations, but with a somewhat more encouraging emphasis. Diplomatic ties with the United States could not be normalised because of the Palestine question, he explained. 'However, when America's relationship with the Arabs becomes positive and its views on our rights become just, we might restore our diplomatic relations with it.' He went on to define the kind of change which could occur in American policy: 'The United States does not amend its policy radically but partially, and in the form of merely minor, temporary and transient touches.' Minor changes should not be thought major radical transformations, but positive transformations should be encouraged.[16] The same language could equally well be used to characterise the American perspective on Iraqi foreign policy.

Iraqi officials also had some hopeful words to say about the new Reagan administration. Deputy Prime Minister Tariq Aziz expressed the desire that it 'will make efforts to understand Arab situations and issues in a fair, just and equitable manner', and compared it favourably to its predecessors.[17] The new US Secretary of State, Alexander Haig, responded in kind. He called for a strategic 'consensus' to counter Soviet expansionism and spoke in this context of improved relations with Iraq, remarking on 'some shift' in Iraqi policies caused in part by 'a greater sense of concern about the behaviour of Soviet imperialism in the Middle Eastern area'.[18] A few days later, the State Department lifted a freeze on the sale of five Boeing passenger planes, which could be converted to troop transports, to Iraq.

Clearly the issue of formal relations was a secondary one on which little dramatic progress seemed likely. 'Many nations have relations with Iraq,' said one US official, 'but they have not been able to have the exchange of ideas and dialogue we have had over the last few years through the interests sections'. Trade and commercial relations also seemed likely to continue their increase without any diplomatic shifts. Although the Iraqi government preferred to avoid buying from American companies if goods of equal price and quality were available elsewhere, in many cases this requirement could not be met. Closer ties between Baghdad and America's Western European allies on commercial transactions also seemed probable.

After Israel's raid on Iraq's nuclear reactor in June 1981 the United States and Iraq negotiated through United Nations' channels to produce a compromise resolution on the issue. Yet the attack, which employed American-built aircraft, pointed up the continued distance between the two countries. High Iraqi officials implied that the United States had advance knowledge of the strike.

Concluding Perspective

Extensive mistrust between the United States and Iraq in recent years
has manifested itself over two principal issues: Gulf security and the
Arab-Israeli conflict.

In the early 1970s the United States adopted a Nixon Doctrine
approach in dealing with the Gulf. This meant that Washington would
depend on local countries – Saudi Arabia and particularly Iran – to
maintain regional stability; it would not directly intervene. The Shah's
fall, however, disillusioned many Americans on the value of the
indirect approach and the Reagan administration became particularly
prone to such thinking. The new government favoured the direct
projection of American power and emphasised its willingness to
intervene in regional affairs. Reagan Middle East policy originally
stressed three principles: the primacy of the Gulf area, the primacy of
the Soviet threat and the primacy of military responses to these
problems.

To these three priorities the local Arab states seemed to counterpose,
respectively, the importance of the Palestine question, the dangers of
local state conflicts or internal upheavals and the utility of diplomatic
and economic responses. They preferred a collective security
arrangement involving only local states, an idea which was contained
in Iraq's 8 March 1980 Arab Charter and which appeared in the
negotiations leading up to the establishment of the Gulf Co-operation
Council.

Many American policymakers had great difficulty in understanding
these sentiments. Although there was some talk of encouraging Middle
Eastern governments to play the major role in security – and even
consideration of Iraq making a major contribution towards this end –
such conceptions were overshadowed by discussions over potential
bases, the Rapid Deployment Force, etc. The idea that many Gulf
Arabs equated US intervention with Soviet intervention and that
aspects of US policy might actually be counterproductive to achieving
US objectives was not easily accepted. At the same time, however, the
continued inability of regional states to produce an indigenous security
arrangement was also a factor which had to be taken into account.

Despite these differences Iraq did not go out of its way to attack
US policies after the beginning of the war with Iran. Both its need to
neutralise any American support for Iran and to develop good relations
with the Arab states of the Gulf dictated such caution. Baghdad
opposed great power intervention but remained quiet about American

supplies of arms and AWACs (radar) planes to Saudi Arabia and about American facilities in Oman and elsewhere. The impact of Gulf security issues on US-Iraq relations would be determined by the specific future of regional instability and by whether any American interventions actually took place.

The effect of the Palestine question and of the Arab-Israeli conflict on US-Iraq relations is a complex problem, much of which lies outside the scope of this study. It can be said, however, that the United States is unlikely to change its policy to the extent Iraq desires and it is equally unlikely that Baghdad would revise its stand so that conflict on the issue would disappear. Differences on this question, therefore, can be expected to continue – whether relations improve or deteriorate.

While for Iraq, as for other Arab states, the Palestine question is both an emotional and politically central issue, it is not clear whether changes in the Arab-Israeli situation will deeply affect Iraqi policy towards the Gulf. Iraq, moreover, is not a front-line state and even the strongest rhetoric from Baghdad tends not to have great material effect on the issue. The unlikelihood of a speedy comprehensive settlement is not liable to bring any new, direct clash between the United States and Iraq. Although bilateral co-operation will always be limited by this factor, there are other and more immediate barriers; its removal would not, for example, reconcile Iraq to escalated American intervention in the Gulf.

Similarly, as a leader of the non-aligned movement, Iraq would hardly be likely to ally itself openly or closely with the United States. The Baghdad government takes its ideology seriously and is aware that its enemies would use against it any implication that it was becoming identified with the United States. Iraq's own political culture – the Portsmouth Treaty and Baghdad Pact experience are obvious examples – illustrates the price that may be paid for alliance with the West.

On the American side Washington's policy towards Iraq depends heavily on the attitude taken by Saudi Arabia and the other Gulf Arab states. Is Iraq's current moderation towards them to be seen as merely tactical and temporary, in part as a means to obtain support in the conflict with Iran? Or does Iraq see the new orientation as a means of breaking out of its past isolation? In short, is Iraq seeking to project power and influence in the Gulf as an ally of the moderates rather than as a revolutionary force? Future crises and opportunities will put this to the test.

There may be some material forces pushing Iraq towards making its regional friends the same as those of the United States. If Iran and

Syria remain Iraq's enemies, Saudi Arabia, Jordan, Kuwait, the United Arab Emirates and other such moderate states must be its allies. The war with Iran demonstrates to Baghdad its need for secure supply routes which, given geographical circumstances, must lie through these countries.

The Gulf Arabs certainly want to woo Iraq away from the USSR, but they also worry about Iraqi threats or subversion against them, noting their past experience in this regard. Ironically, Iraq's mixed military showing against Iran might reassure them, both in terms of Baghdad's limited military ability and of the importance of their support.

Iraq, for its part, has co-ordinated its moves with Saudi Arabia and has refrained from criticising the Saudi-sponsored Gulf Co-operation Council. Baghdad's gestures towards the United States might also be intended to reassure those neighbours. Just as Washington must decide the mix between direct projection of power and dependence on its Gulf allies, the United States must also decide whether and to what extent Iraq should be integrated into such a strategy.

While the risk of antagonism with Iran run by an overbearing US approach to the Gulf is great, over-optimism on the degree of identity between US and Iraqi interests also runs some risks. An example of this problem is the proposal to sell US-built gas-turbine engines for installation in four Italian-made frigates destined for Iraq's navy. This would extend Baghdad's patrolling capacity to the Straits of Hormuz, the mouth of the Gulf. While the Carter administration pressed for the sale, Congress opposed it on the basis of Iraqi support for terrorist movements. The Iran-Iraq war temporarily suspended the issue; the broader question has not yet been resolved. The fundamental consideration is whether the United States considers Iraq an implicit ally or a threat to American interests in the Gulf—in its own right or in conjunction with a renewed Soviet-Iraqi alliance.

The ease with which Iraqi policy could swing towards restoring past close relations with the USSR or towards a break with other Arab states friendly to the United States must be a major concern for Washington policymakers. Supplies of Soviet arms, sent through Eastern European countries, have continued throughout the Iran-Iraq war, as have Baghdad's claims of ideological affinity with Moscow. At the same time, Iraq's continued belief in a revolutionary mission *vis-à-vis* other Arab states and the difficulty in divining Iraq's post-war policy in the region also raises doubts. Finally, despite the apparent stability of the Iraqi government, the possibility of an overnight change at the top can never be discounted.

The US-Iraq relationship is not going to become the central aspect of American policy in the Gulf. Washington sees Iraq as an important actor there but not as the region's new leader. Moreover, any bilateral dealings will always be secondary to and subject to the more important US-Saudi link. The many unanswered questions about Iraqi objectives and perceptions towards the United States and towards the Gulf will limit any major *rapprochement.*

For its part, Iraq does not seek an alliance with the United States but, at most, some minimum basis for co-existence. It seeks to neutralise Washington in terms of the Iran-Iraq war and to prevent any American hostility from jeopardising Iraq's new relations with the Arab states of the Gulf. Baghdad is also seeking to convince the United States not to intervene in the region and to refrain from expanding its military presence there. Iraqi suspicion that American forces in the Gulf might be used against Iraq or against Iraqi interests is a very real factor.

The best way for Iraq to gain leverage over US policy would be to demonstrate that it has no intention of undermining other Arab states in the Gulf and will help build constructive Arab security alternatives to direct US involvement through a workable regional system. It is possible that Iraq sees the United States, up to a point, as a beneficial counterweight to Soviet power in the region. Even in the latter case, however, Iraq would without doubt prefer a balance between the two great powers rather than an American build-up of influence.

While drastic change in the US-Iraq relationship is unlikely, it may be entering a new era of parallel efforts and constructive dialogue. This lies somewhere between estrangement and alliance; if not an arm's-length relationship, it may at least be an elbow-length one.

Notes

1. B. Rubin, *The Great Powers in the Middle East 1941-1947: The Road to the Cold War* (Frank Cass, London, 1980), pp. 137-8.

2. For a discussion of Iraq's role in the Palestine question, see B. Rubin, *The Arab States and the Palestine Conflict* (Syracuse University Press, New York, 1981).

3. Dulles to US Embassy Baghdad, April 9, 1954, RG319, Box 2672, File 500-US Military Aid to Iraq, Cairo Post File, Washington National Records Center.

4. US House of Representatives, Committee on Foreign Affairs, *Selected Executive Session Hearings*, vol. XII, Mutual Security Program Part 4, pp. 262-72.

5. On the history and development of the US-Iran relationship, see B. Rubin,

Paved with Good Intentions: The American Experience and Iran (Oxford University Press, London, 1980).

6. M. Khadduri, *Socialist Iraq* (Middle East Institute, Washington, 1978), p. 172, suggests that this *rapprochement* with the West was one cause of the 1968 revolution.

7. *Washington Post*, 15 July 1973.

8. Ibid., 14 Nov. 1976.

9. Sources: International Monetary Fund, *Direction of Trade*; CIA, *International Energy Statistical Review*, 24 Feb. 1981.

10. International Monetary Fund, *Direction of Trade*. US Department of Commerce figures are different but show the same trends.

11. See, for example, *The Department of State Bulletin*, 4 July 1977, p. 3, for the text of Carter's 13 June 1977 speech, and the 10 Oct. 1977 issue, p. 463.

12. *Washington Post*, 15 Feb. 1979.

13. Transcript of interview, 'MacNeil/Lehrer Report', 14 Apr. 1980.

14. US Department of State, Bureau of Public Affairs, testimony before the House of Representatives Committee on Foreign Affairs, 3 Sept. 1980, current policy paper no. 215.

15. *Washington Post*, 21 Oct. 1980; *al-Thawra*, 23 Oct. 1980. See also Saddam Husain's interview in *al-Qabas*, 17 Jan. 1981.

16. Interview in *al-Anba*, 19 Jan. 1981.

17. Interview in *al-Sharq al-Awsat*, 2 Feb. 1981.

18. *New York Times*, 20 Mar. 1981. In April, Deputy Assistant Secretary of State Morris Draper met with Foreign Minister Hammadi in Baghdad. His mission to re-establish relations, however, seemed to enjoy little more success than a similar one undertaken by Under-Secretary of State Philip Habib for President Carter in May 1977. In an *al-Thawra* interview, 5 April 1981, Hammadi reaffirmed Iraq's traditional line on the issue.

10 IRAQI POLICIES TOWARDS THE ARAB STATES OF THE GULF, 1958-1981

Tim Niblock

Perspective

Western policymakers concerned with security in the Arab Gulf area have – since the 1958 revolution in Iraq – generally purveyed an image of a 'radical, socialist and Soviet-oriented' Iraq posing a threat to the 'conservative, moderate and pro-Western' Gulf states of the Arabian peninsula (Saudi Arabia, Kuwait, Bahrain, Qatar, the United Arab Emirates and Oman). Journalists writing from the same viewpoint produce maps of the 'arc of crisis' in the Gulf and Indian Ocean, indicating the threats to security by placing hammers and sickles in Afghanistan, Iraq, the People's Democratic Republic of Yemen and Ethiopia. The image purveyed is then used to justify Western involvement in the maintenance of Gulf security – whether by providing military support for the more conservative regimes or by a direct Western military presence in the vicinity of the Gulf.

The contention of this chapter is that the Western governmental image is misguided. Iraq's relations with the Gulf states on the Arabian peninsula have indeed frequently been strained. The strains, however, have not sprung from Iraq's pursuit of policies which – intentionally or unintentionally – undermine the conservative regimes of the Gulf. On the contrary, over most of the period since 1958 Iraqi governments have displayed (some would say regrettably) a willingness to work closely with these regimes. The problems, rather, have arisen from specific differences of interest, perception and objective, largely related to the role which non-Arab powers (whether the Western powers or Iran) should be permitted to play in the Gulf.

One indication that the causes of tension between Iraq and its Arab Gulf neighbours do not lie in the radical threat to the conservative monarchies is found in the historical origins of the issues around which conflict has occurred. Many of these already caused strains when Iraq was governed by a conservative pro-Western monarchy (i.e. before 1958). What did change – gradually – after 1958 (and more noticeably after 1968) was Iraq's interest in playing, and ability to play, a Gulf role.

125

Whereas formerly Iraqi foreign policy, at the regional level, had concerned itself mainly with the Fertile Crescent area, Egypt, Turkey and Iran, the growing international importance of the Gulf drew Iraqi governments into increasing involvement with developments there. The scope for differing interests and perceptions leading to direct conflicts between Iraq and its Gulf neighbours accordingly increased.

Britain's withdrawal from the Gulf (announced in January 1968 and completed in November 1971) created a context within which powers could manoeuvre for position and influence, with a view to 'filling the vacuum'. The government of Iraq was intent on ensuring that Britain's dominance would not be replaced either by a more indirect (but none-theless effective) Western dominance, or by an Iranian dominance. The pursuit of this objective led to a tense relationship not just (unsurprisingly) with Iran but also at times with the Arabian peninsula Gulf states. This followed, first, from the willingness of some Arab Gulf states to co-operate with Iran (under a framework strongly supported by the United States) in the maintenance of Gulf security — on terms which, in Iraqi eyes, ensured both an Iranian and a broadly Western dominance. Second, it followed from the strategic requirements of Iraq's Gulf role: to play such a role Iraq needed a strategically secure outlet into the Gulf, and this led to territorial conflict with both Iran and Kuwait. Iraq's two major points of access to the Gulf were from Basra through the Shatt al-Arab waterway (whose sovereignty was disputed with Iran) and at the port of Umm Qasr (whose sea-lanes were dominated by the Kuwaiti islands of Warba and Bubiyan).[1] It seemed that an effective Gulf role for Iraq, backed up by naval power, was dependent either on Iran recognising Iraqi sovereignty over the entire Shatt or else on Kuwait ceding control over Warba and Bubiyan. The confrontation with Kuwait which ensued (mainly between 1972 and 1974) was to have damaging effects on Iraq's relationship with other Gulf states.

Since 1975 Iraq's relations with the Gulf states of the Arabian peninsula have steadily improved. Although Iraq is not a member of the newly established Gulf Co-operation Council, she has been a participant in many of the co-operative arrangements among the Arab Gulf states which have come to exist in recent years. This improved relationship is not, except in the idiosyncratic case of Oman, an effect of Iraq being any more eager than before for good relations with these states; the eagerness had, as will be contended, been present well before 1975. It is, rather, an effect of the major inhibition to the development of closer relations — differences over the need to resist 'Iranian domination of the Gulf' – being removed. The March 1975 Iran-Iraq agreement led to Iraq itself establishing a workable relationship with Iran. Since the fall of the Shah Iraq and the Gulf states of the peninsula have shared a common apprehension of the new Iranian regime.

If the thesis put forward in this chapter is correct, the manoeuvrings of the Western powers to 'protect the security of the Gulf' may be counterproductive. It has been the attempts to draw Arab Gulf states into security arrangements with non-Arab powers (the Western powers themselves, together with a strongly Western-supported Iran) which have created sporadic differences between Iraq and its neighbours on the Arabian peninsula. Instability, in short, has issued from the very arrangements which were intended to prevent it, and not from the threat posed by a 'radical Iraq' to the 'conservative monarchies' of the Arab Gulf.[2]

While the focus of this chapter is on Iraq's relations with the Arabian peninsula Gulf states, the description and analysis of these relations must inevitably take account of developments in Iraq's relationship with Iran – for the latter relationship has constituted a crucial influence on the character of the former.

Pre-1958

Iraq's policies towards the Arab Gulf before the 1958 revolution in no sense form a continuum with those pursued after 1958. There are, nevertheless, some elements of pre-1958 policy which help towards an understanding of the policies developed after 1958.

The main characteristic of Iraqi policy towards the Gulf before 1958 was, as suggested above, the secondary role it played in Iraq's regional policy. The concentration was on the Fertile Crescent, Egypt, Turkey and Iran. Iraq had been a party to the Sa'adabad Pact of 1937, which brought it into a defensive alliance with Turkey, Iran and Afghanistan; had entered into a further mutual defence agreement with Turkey in 1946; had come together with Turkey in February 1955 to form a regional security structure, later known as the Baghdad Pact and joined by Iran, Pakistan and Britain; and early in 1958 was planning to form a federation with its fellow-Hashimite kingdom, Jordan. Rivalry with Nasser's Egypt provided one of the mainsprings of foreign policy in the years leading up to 1958.

The secondary (or perhaps tertiary) role played by the Gulf in Iraq's regional policy reflected a number of different political and economic realities. First, the country's main oil installations at this time – before the Rumaila oil fields of southern Iraq had been developed – were located in northern Iraq. The oil was transported to overseas markets not through the Gulf but by pipeline across Syria and Turkey. Second, agricultural and industrial development was concentrated in central and northern Iraq; the parts of Iraq close to the Gulf generally suffered from economic neglect, and the communications network – which might have encouraged contact with the adjacent areas of the Gulf – was severely underdeveloped. Third, Britain's protectorate over the smaller Gulf states left Iraq with little opportunity to play a Gulf role. For most of the period between Iraq's independence in 1932 and 1958 British influence in Baghdad was sufficient to ensure that Iraq did not champion the liberation of the Gulf emirates from colonial control.

There was, nevertheless, some contact between Iraq and other Gulf states. For geographical and historical reasons the strongest contact was with the shaikhdom of Kuwait. Long-established economic ties existed between Kuwait and southern Iraq: Kuwait was dependent on Iraq for the supply of grain, fruit, vegetables and even fresh water (transported by boat from the Shatt al-Arab), and Kuwaiti ships carried much of the trade of southern Iraq. The Shaikh of Kuwait, as also some of the more prominent Kuwaiti merchant families, owned date plantations in the vicinity of Basra. Three aspects of Iraqi policy towards Kuwait at this time had some bearing on policies which were pursued after 1958.

First, for one brief period in the 1930s the government of Iraq appeared to be prepared to give support and encouragement to nationalist tendencies in the Gulf shaikhdoms – with attention focused primarily on Kuwait. King Ghazi ibn Faisal (1933-8) appears to have taken a personal interest in this matter. In 1936, at King Ghazi's instigation, an 'Association of Arabs of the Gulf' was established in Basra, committed to cultivating links with nationalist groupings in the Gulf shaikhdoms.[3] The activities of the Association were complemented by broadcasts directed towards the Gulf emanating from a transmitter in King Ghazi's palace in Baghdad.

This Iraqi involvement in promoting anti-colonial tendencies in the Gulf reached its climax in 1938 when the Advisory Council in Kuwait passed resolutions 'contrasting unfavourably the poverty of Kuwait with the wealth of Iraq, and advocating union between the two'.[4] Broadcasts from King Ghazi's transmitter at this time described the Shaikh of Kuwait as 'an out-of-date feudal despot whose backward rule

contrasted with the enlightened regime existing in Iraq. Kuwait . . .
would be much better off merged with her northern neighbour'.[5] The
Shaikh of Kuwait disbanded the Advisory Council and disowned its
resolutions. At the time of the popular demonstrations which followed
the Shaikh's action King Ghazi raised the possibility of Iraq intervening
in Kuwait and incorporating it.[6] No moves towards that end were
taken, however, and the Iraq government's 'forward nationalist' role in
the area came to an abrupt end in April 1938 when King Ghazi died in
a car accident.

Second, Iraqi governments before 1958 had involved themselves in
seeking a delineation of the border with Kuwait, in a manner favourable to Iraq. The whole question of the legitimacy of Kuwait's
separation from Iraq affected the Iraq government's handling of this
issue. In 1932 the Iraqi Prime Minister Nuri al-Sa'id, following
correspondence with the Shaikh of Kuwait, affirmed that the frontier
between Iraq and Kuwait lay along a line which the Shaikh of Kuwait
had proposed.[7] The latter line was based on the frontiers defined in the
Anglo-Turkish agreement of 1913; the islands of Warba and Bubiyan
were included within Kuwaiti territory. The physical delimitation of
the border, however, was not carried out – apparently because the
Iraqi government was uneasy about offering any further measure of
de jure recognition to Kuwait's separate existence.[8]

In 1951, when the Shaikh of Kuwait requested that arrangements
for the physical delimitation of the border be initiated, the government
of Iraq expressed its willingness to co-operate provided the island of
Warba was ceded to Iraq.[9] The Iraqi government's new interest in
Warba stemmed from the development of the port of Umm Qasr
during World War II; the port's sea-lanes, as mentioned above, passed
through the narrow channel between Warba and the mainland. While
the port, which had been constructed so as to facilitate the transport
through Iraq of goods destined for the Soviet Union, was dismantled
after the war (and was not reconstructed until 1960-1), the possible
future importance of sovereignty over Warba had become clear. The
Shaikh of Kuwait refused to accept any modification in the frontiers
of his shaikhdom as defined in earlier agreements.[10] In 1954 the Iraqi
government put forward an additional claim to some 4 kilometres of
Kuwaiti-controlled coastline west of Warba and Bubiyan (in the region
of Khor al-Sabiya).[11] When the Shaikh of Kuwait rejected this claim
also, the British government proposed that Kuwait should lease the
island of Warba to Iraq. That, too, proved unacceptable and was
formally rejected by the Shaikh in 1956.[12]

Third, discussions took place between Kuwait and Iraq as to the
feasibility of building a water pipeline from the Shatt al-Arab to
Kuwait, obviating the need to bring water by boat (i.e. before the
construction of desalination plants and the discovery and exploitation
of substantial quantities of groundwater had rendered Kuwait self-
sufficient in this valuable commodity). The proposal for such a pipeline
was first made in 1936 but was rejected by the British authorities in
Kuwait – apparently on the grounds that the shaikhdom would become
over-dependent on Iraq.[13] The project was resurrected in 1955 and
negotiations took place. The two sides, however, were not able to reach
agreement: the government of Iraq was not prepared to accept the
Shaikh of Kuwait's request that a 30-metre stretch on either side of
the pipeline be ceded to Kuwait, nor would it agree to the construction
of the installations deemed necessary by the Kuwaiti side.[14] A proposal
by Britain that Iraq should 'exchange' the Shatt al-Arab water for a
lease on the island of Warba failed to resolve the deadlock.[15]

A final aspect of Iraqi policy towards Kuwait before 1958 was Nuri
al-Said's attempt to draw Kuwait into the federation which Iraq and
Jordan were seeking to establish. In return for Kuwait's adhesion, the
government of Iraq offered to demarcate the Iraq-Kuwait border (in
accordance with the 1913 Anglo-Turkish Treaty), to supply Kuwait
with piped water from the Shatt al-Arab and to guarantee continuation
of the existing degree of autonomy enjoyed by the Shaikh of Kuwait.[16]
The Iraqi advances were rejected, apparently on British advice. With
the overthrow of Iraq's Hashimite dynasty in July 1958, in any case,
the federation issue lost its relevance.

In comparison with Iraq's involvement with Kuwait, the contacts
between the Iraqi government and other Gulf states on the Arabian
peninsula were minimal. In the case of the small shaikhdoms of the
lower Gulf, indeed, there seems to have been virtually no expression of
Iraqi governmental interest and no contact. Relations between Iraq and
Saudi Arabia, sharing a long common border and both being sovereign
states, were necessarily rather more substantial. The early stages of the
relationship between these two states was marked by a coolness
stemming from the Saudi-Hashimite rivalry which had occurred in the
Hijaz. King Faisal of Iraq and King Abd al-Aziz ibn Saud appear,
however, to have established a reasonable relationship at their first
meeting in 1930 (on the British warship, HMS *Lupin*) and in April
1936 the two states concluded a Treaty of Arab Brotherhood and
Alliance.[17] The Treaty obliged each side, in the case of aggression by a
third party, to come to the aid of the other. The relationship, however,

never became particularly significant to either side; trade remained insubstantial and Saudi Arabia declined an invitation to join the Baghdad Pact.

The early years of independent Iraq's relationship with Iran were marked by severe differences regarding the delimitation of their common border – especially on the Shatt al-Arab. The conclusion of a boundary treaty on 4 July 1937 brought to an end the overt confront-ation. The treaty, following the main lines of the 1847 Treaty of Erzerum, defined the border as running along the low-water mark on the Iranian side, except for an 8-kilometre stretch in the vicinity of Abadan where the median line – *thalweg* – would constitute the border.[18] The border issue, however, was not completely closed: the Iranian government sporadically voiced its discontent with the treaty's provisions, claiming that the treaty had been 'imposed on Iran to satisfy British strategic interests'. The two governments' shared concern with regional security and with countering the 'Communist threat' (i.e. through the Sa'adabad Pact and the Baghdad Pact) ensured that differences over the border were not allowed to escalate.

1958-63

Despite the significant changes brought about by the July 1958 revolution in Iraq, and despite it being from this time that Western powers began to conceive of Iraq as a disruptive force in the Gulf, Iraqi government policies towards the Gulf area did not undergo a fundamental change under the Qasim regime. The focus of regional policy remained elsewhere: on relations with Egypt (first marked by friendship but soon characterised by rivalry), on the Palestine issue and on relations with the Arab countries at the other end of the Fertile Crescent. Notwithstanding the occasional denunciation of British imperialism in the Gulf, little practical interest was taken in the affairs of the lower Gulf and relations with Saudi Arabia remained insubstantial. Kuwait alone, among the various states and shaikhdoms on the Arab side of the Gulf, attracted serious governmental interest – at least between 1961 and 1963.

The genesis, during the Qasim regime, of Western concern over Iraq disrupting the stability of the Gulf was based on two developments: Qasim's apparent threat to incorporate Kuwait within Iraq in 1961 and the confrontation with Iran over the Shatt al-Arab in 1959-60. Western concern was, no doubt, fortified by the expansion of Iraq's relations with the Soviet Union and by the role played by the Communist Party in domestic Iraqi politics. Neither in the case of Kuwait nor in that of Iran, however, was the Iraqi government raising a new issue. As shown above, the pre-1958 regime had maintained an equivocal attitude to Kuwait's separate existence, and Iran had retained serious reservations regarding the provisions of the 1937 border treaty.

What had changed—bringing formerly submerged issues to overt conflict—were circumstances. Kuwaiti independence in June 1961 forced the Iraqi government to take a definitive stance: either to recognise the new state or to reject its legitimacy. Whether the pre-1958 regime would have taken a different stance than that adopted by Qasim must remain speculative. In the case of the Shatt al-Arab conflict, the factors which had previously led Iran and Iraq to subordinate their differences there to a higher concern no longer held. The two countries were no longer partners in a common effort to counter the 'Communist threat' through a Western-supported security system. It is perhaps significant that the conflict on the Shatt did not take place until after Iraq had formally withdrawn from the Baghdad Pact—an act which was carried through on 24 March 1959.

The crisis over Kuwait developed rapidly. On 19 June 1961 the 1899 treaty guaranteeing British protection for Kuwait was abrogated and Britain recognised the independence of Kuwait. Six days later, on 25 June, Qasim held a press conference in which he announced that, as Kuwait was an integral part of Iraq,

> . . . a presidential decree will shortly be issued appointing the present, honorable Shaikh of Kuwait as the Kaim Makam [prefect] of the Kuwait district of the Basra Liwa [province]. We shall warn the Shaikh not to disregard the rights of the Kuwaiti people who are among the people of Iraq. If he acts rashly, he will receive severe punishment and be considered a saboteur. . . The Republic of Iraq has decided to protect the Iraqi people in Kuwait and to demand the land, arbitrarily held by imperialism, which belongs to Iraq.[19]

Despite Qasim's insistence that he would not resort to force, the presumption (in the outside world) that war was impending was strengthened by a rising—though possibly irrelevant—chorus of rhetoric from the Iraqi communications media. Baghdad Radio announced that the army's chief-of-staff had cabled Qasim, affirming that the entire Iraqi army was at the Prime Minister's 'beck and call'. The slogan 'On Saturday we shall be in Kuwait' was broadcast, as also were telegrams from different elements of the Iraqi population urging Qasim 'to extend his declaration of sovereignty over Kuwait to all the other . . . territories along the shore of the Arabian Gulf'.[20]

The outcome of these pronouncements is well known. A state of emergency was declared in Kuwait, and Kuwait's limited armed forces were placed on alert. Messages of support for Kuwait were forthcoming from other Arab countries. On 1 July, at Kuwait's request, British and Saudi troops arrived in Kuwait, to be replaced in September by an Arab peace-keeping force established under the Arab League (with units from Jordan, Saudi Arabia, Sudan, Tunisia and – briefly – the United Arab Republic). Early in 1963 (even before Qasim's regime had been over-thrown) the decision to withdraw the peacekeeping force was taken – on the grounds that the threat to Kuwait's sovereignty no longer existed.

Iraq's image in the Western world as a 'radical expansionist threat' to the other states and shaikhdoms of the Arab Gulf may seem a natural effect of the developments which occurred over Kuwait. As mentioned earlier, however, Kuwait had always constituted a special case to Iraqi governments. Between July 1958 and April 1961 Qasim's attitude to Kuwait appeared no different from that of former governments – combining a grudging acceptance of Kuwait's separation with a reluctance to give overt recognition either to this separation or to the common border. Qasim's first public statement on Kuwait (in April 1961) followed the circulation of rumours that Kuwait, on becoming independent, would join the British Commonwealth.[21] The possibility of such an outcome was strongly denounced. It was apparently from this time that Qasim began gathering evidence to substantiate a historical claim to Kuwait.[22] Whether Qasim was, in fact, intent on a military invasion of Kuwait, or was hoping to use the claim over Kuwait as a bargaining counter in subsequent negotiations, remains conjecture. A bargaining counter would certainly have been of value, both so as to ensure a favourable border settlement (the re-construction of Umm Qasr port in 1960-1 had raised again the issue of control over Warba island) and so as to persuade the government of Kuwait to abrogate its defence treaty with Britain. The latter required and justified a continuing British military presence in, or close to, the Gulf. It is significant, moreover, that Iraqi's 'radical threat' to Kuwait in 1961 took the form of a traditional inter-state conflict, not subversion of an existing government.

The confrontation with Iran developed with a similar abruptness. Following indications of Iranian unease with the provisions of the 1937 treaty, the Iraqi government itself in December 1959 questioned the validity of certain aspects of the treaty—specifically with regard to the 8-kilometre stretch in the vicinity of Abadan where the border followed the river's median line.[23] Iraq requested the return to Iraqi control of all the roadsteads outside the Iranian ports of Abadan, Khorramshahr and Khosrowbad. In January 1960, while border clashes between the two states were occurring, Iran accused Iraq of violating the treaty in two respects: by failing to respond to repeated Iranian proposals for the establishment of a joint Shatt al-Arab committee (as envisaged by the treaty), and by using the fees collected by the Basra Port Authority for purposes other than river development. Due to these infringements, and to the Iraq government's 'incitement of its people against Iran', Iran declared that henceforth the border would follow the median line of the Shatt. Relations between the two states remained tense for the remainder of Qasim's rule.

The Qasim regime's lack of practical interest in the affairs of the Lower Gulf stemmed not only from its conception of the regional priorities as lying elsewhere. There was, at least between 1961 and 1963, little potential for Iraq to expand its contacts with the British-protected shaikhdoms. The crisis over Kuwait exerted an inhibiting influence over such contacts. This also held true for relations with Saudi Arabia: Saudi support for Kuwait, characterised by King Saud's assurance to the Shaikh of Kuwait that 'Kuwait and Saudi Arabia are one country, what affects Kuwait affects Saudi Arabia',[24] inevitably limited the prospects for developing Iraqi-Saudi relations.

1963-8

During the regime of the two Arefs Iraqi policies towards the Gulf began to reflect, and to respond to, the growing international importance of the Gulf area. While the continued British presence in the Lower Gulf restricted the potential for local states to exert influence outside their own borders, the desire of Iraq to play a role began to be evident. The change of regimes in Baghdad made possible the development of a new relationship with Kuwait, built on the abandonment of Qasim's historical claims, and this in turn facilitated the establishment of Iraqi contacts with the shaikhdoms of the Lower Gulf. Despite a series of border incidents with Iran in 1965-6, stemming from the activities of Kurdish insurgents (in rebellion against the Iraq government) close to the border, Iraqi-Iranian relations generally tended more towards co-operation than conflict. Iraq under the Arefs, in fact, stood in need of a co-operative Iran; Iranian support for the Kurdish insurgents could easily have rendered the Iraqi government's hold on the Kurdish areas untenable.

The development in Iraqi-Kuwaiti relations was perhaps the most significant element of Iraq's new posture in the Gulf, providing some evidence of the type of co-operative links which Iraq would later seek to forge with other Arab Gulf states. Kuwait had been one of the first states to welcome the inception of a new Iraqi regime on 8 February 1963. Following the exchange of friendly telegrams, the government of Iraq on 8 February lifted all the restrictions which the Qasim regime had imposed on travel to and from Kuwait.[25] On 5 April the Kuwait Government responded to the Iraqi indications of goodwill by announcing that henceforward it would encourage private Kuwaiti investment in Iraq.[26] Following the first government-to-government visits between the two states in early May, the framework which the new Iraqi regime was proposing for the solution of differences became known: in return for Iraq's recognition of a sovereign Kuwait, Kuwait would revoke its defence treaty with Britain, declare its intention of working towards closer relations with Iraq in the long term and, as a short-term indication of its special significance to Iraq, offer a financial contribution to the Iraqi economy.[27] Three months of sporadic negotiation ensued and an agreement appears to have been reached at the end of September 1963.[28] This was cemented and endorsed in the course of the Kuwaiti Prime Minister's visit to Baghdad at the beginning of October.[29] Iraq formally extended recognition to Kuwait, while the Kuwait government announced that it 'would terminate the agreement with Britain at the appropriate time'.[30] On 21 October the two countries signed an agreement for a £30 million interest-free Kuwaiti loan for Iraq.[31]

The establishment of normal relations between Iraq and Kuwait led on to co-operation in a number of different fields. First, the attempt was made to create a broad framework for economic co-operation and co-ordination between the two states. In early October 1964 delegations from the two sides opened negotiations to this end, and on 25 October an agreement was signed lifting all customs duties and internal taxes formerly levied on agricultural and industrial goods, animal products and mineral resources traded between Iraq and Kuwait.[32] While the low level of trade between the two countries limited the significance of the agreement, the introduction of free trade could be expected to increase the complementarity of the economies in the longer term. Further trade talks were held in January 1967 and the two governments determined to encourage barter deals with a view to promoting an expansion of trade.[33]

Second, the old project (mentioned above) to pipe fresh water from the Shatt al-Arab to Kuwait was resurrected and a preliminary agreement on this was signed on 11 February 1964.[34] Technical studies followed, but the implementation of the project had to await the Kuwait government's final approval. This was never given.

Third, the level of Kuwaiti public and private investment in Iraq steadily increased. In January 1964 talks were held to examine the potential for the two countries to undertake joint industrial projects,[35] and on 13 January the Iraq government announced measures to encourage Kuwaiti capital investment in Iraq.[36] Loans from the Kuwait Fund for Arab Economic Development for a paper mill in Basra and for the Samarra Barrage duly became available in October 1966 and October 1967, respectively.[37] Following the visit of the Iraqi Prime Minister to Kuwait in January 1968, a joint committee was established to study co-operation in the iron and steel, sulphur and petrochemical industries.[38] The deliberations of the latter committee seem to have facilitated the formation of an Iraqi-Kuwaiti company to exploit the sulphur deposits at Mishrak (Iraq).[39]

Fourth, serious attempts were undertaken to reach a final border settlement. When the Emir of Kuwait visited Iraq in June 1966 the two sides agreed to establish a demarcation committee which would examine all issues pertaining to the border and produce some recommendations.[40] Due to a disagreement as to the framework within which the demarcation committee would work, and the failure of government-to-government talks in January 1967 to solve the problem,[41] the demarcation committee did not actually begin work until October 1967. Despite the goodwill and seriousness of purpose displayed on both sides, the nature of the problem which had delayed the committee's establishment, and which subsequently aborted its deliberations, indicated the complications ensuing from Iraq's desire to play a more active Gulf role. Such a role increased the priority given by the Iraqi government to secure access into the Gulf, and hence led to the re-assertion of Iraqi claims on the islands of Warba and Bubiyan.[42]

Further aspects of the co-operative relationship developed between Iraq and Kuwait over this period were the visits exchanged by government leaders (the Emir of Kuwait visiting Baghdad in June 1966 and June 1968, President Aref visiting Kuwait in December 1966 and the Iraqi Prime Minister also visiting Kuwait in January 1968), the conclusion of an agreement in February 1966 for the establishment of a joint radio communications system,[43] Kuwait's support for Iraq in its conflict with the Iraq Petroleum Company[44] and the co-ordinated approval given by the two governments to the prospects of a federation in the Lower Gulf.[45]

The moves made by the Iraqi government between 1963 and 1968 to establish closer contacts with the shaikhdoms of the Lower Gulf were intimately connected with an Arab League initiative in this area. The first 'political' visits by Iraqi officials to the Lower Gulf, in fact, occurred within the context of an Arab League delegation. An Arab League 'Arab Brotherhood Mission' – the first of its kind – toured the Lower Gulf in October 1964, holding talks with shaikhs on the political development of the region and on the assistance in economic, social and educational fields which the Arab League could provide.[46] The mission was led by Abd al-Khalig Hassouna, Secretary-General of the Arab League, and was composed of two Iraqi, two Saudi and two Kuwaiti members.

The Arab League initiative, however, did not provide the motivation for Iraq's establishment of closer contacts with the Gulf shaikhdoms. That motivation was already present. The initiative, rather, made available a context within which the pursuit of closer contacts could be conducted. At the time of the Arab Brotherhood Mission's tour of the Gulf President Aref extended invitations to the rulers of all Gulf shaikhdoms to visit Baghdad. The rulers of Ajman and Ras al-Khaimah duly undertook such visits in October 1967,[47] and the ruler of Bahrain in December.[48] It seems that discussions covered the means whereby independent statehood could be achieved and contacts with Iraq strengthened. The Kuwait government formally supported Iraqi attempts to persuade the Gulf shaikhs to abandon British protection, and facilitated some of the contacts.[49]

The reaction of Gulf rulers to the Iraqi and Arab League initiatives was generally cautious, influenced no doubt by the negative attitude adopted by the British authorities in the area. The attraction of aid from the Arab League was offset by Britain's decision to establish a new Trucial States Development Fund. The Arab Brotherhood Mission's tour, however, was to have some less direct repercussions on Iraq's role in the region. In June 1965 Shaikh Saqr al-Qasimi of Sharjah was deposed – apparently due in part to the positive attitude he had taken towards the Arab League's involvement in the Gulf. The Shaikh proceeded to Baghdad, where he was provided with facilities to issue a statement sharply critical of British policy.[50] It was from Baghdad also,

in April 1966, that Shaikh Saqr announced his support for collaboration among the different movements waging liberation struggles in
Muscat, Oman and the Gulf shaikhdoms.[51] In August 1967 it was
reported that Shaikh Saqr had held friendly talks with Iraqi
government leaders on 'general Arab issues'.[52]

Despite Iraqi contacts with an individual who had taken on an
opposition role (with respect to the established situation in the Lower
Gulf), however, Iraqi government policy was not directed towards
undermining existing regimes. The objective was to remove the
British presence, not to change the structure or form of authority
within each state (possibly excepting Sharjah). Reasonably cordial
relations were maintained with the ruler of Bahrain even while
(from June 1966 to 1968) the Iraq government was denouncing the
provision of new military facilities for the British in his territory.
Following the June 1967 war the ruler made gifts to Iraq and the
United Arab Republic to 'relieve difficulties resulting from the
conflict',[53] and in March 1968 when the ruler visited Baghdad Iraq
pledged 'cultural, scientific and technical support for the emirates'.[54]
Iraq was one of the first states to welcome the proposed formation of a
federation among the traditional shaikhdoms of the Lower Gulf—
evidently because such a development, although ensconcing traditional
forces in power, would facilitate Britain's withdrawal.[55]

Non-political links between Iraq and the Gulf states were also
expanded at this time. In February 1966 an Iraqi trade mission toured
the Gulf surveying the market for Iraqi goods—especially cement.[56] A
very modest expansion of trade ensued. In 1968, shortly before the
demise of the Aref regime, the Iraqi government began to establish
commercial and cultural offices in the Lower Gulf.[57]

Iraq's relationship with Iran between 1963 and 1968 was mostly of
a co-operative nature. This was, as suggested above, a necessity to the
governments of Abd al-Salam and Abd al-Rahman Aref: the coherence
of the Iraqi state stood in danger should Iran extend support to the
Kurdish insurgents. The two countries resumed diplomatic relations in
August 1963 (broken since Iran recognised Kuwait's independence) and
in the same month concluded an agreement on co-operation in oil
production.[58] The latter agreement involved arrangements for sharing
the Naft-i-Shah-Khanerquin oil field, which straddles the border, and for
jointly exploiting oil resources located in disputed territorial waters. In
March 1964 an Iraqi mission held talks in Teheran with a view to settling
the two countries' differences on the Shatt al-Arab.[59] Although the latter
talks led to no agreement the tenor of discussion appears to have been friendl

In December 1965 Iraqi troops, while pursuing Kurdish insurgents, became involved in a clash with Iranian police at an Iranian border post; shortly thereafter Iraqi planes bombed an Iranian border village.[60] The Iranian government quickly summoned its troops up to the border, warned Iraq to stop the raids and demanded that negotiations be initiated for a final settlement of the Shatt al-Arab problem.[61] The situation, however, was not allowed to run out of hand: on 30 December President Aref reaffirmed Iraq's desire for friendly relations with Iran,[62] and in early January the two sides held talks.[63] It was agreed to establish a joint committee to recommend procedures to prevent border incidents occurring. Thereafter, despite a further minor border incident in May,[64] relations between the two countries steadily improved.

Two economic agreements in 1967 expanded the scope of the developing relationship between Iran and Iraq. In March 1967, following the visit of President Aref to Iran, the governments signed a further agreement covering co-operation in oil exploitation,[65] and on 3 May an economic agreement aimed at promoting trade between the two countries was signed.[66] The latter agreement envisaged an expansion of trade on forty named items and the establishment of a joint committee to promote further economic exchange. A further indication of the direction which Iraqi-Iranian relations were taking was an Iraqi government statement on 28 June 1968 expressing willingness to work with Iran to maintain the security of the Gulf.[67] The latter scheme would have involved joint use of the Shatt al-Arab.

Unlike the other spheres of Iraq's Gulf policy under the Aref regime, little change occurred in relations with Saudi Arabia. This relationship remained tense and insubstantial. Although Saudi Arabia's opposition to Arab League involvement in the Gulf shaikhdoms, and its contributions to the British-inspired Trucial States Development Fund, created resentment in Baghdad, the major factor affecting Iraqi-Saudi relations was not in the Gulf but in Yemen. Given the severity of the conflict in Yemen between the Egyptian-backed republican government and the Saudi-based royalist insurgents, it is hardly surprising that the Aref regime's pursuit of a 'unified political command' with Egypt limited the prospects for an improved Saudi-Iraqi relationship.

1968-75

This period covers the years between the rise to power of the 'second

Ba'thist regime' (the first having survived briefly between February 1963 and November 1963) and the conclusion of the Iraq-Iran agreement of March 1975. The central characteristic of Iraq's policies towards the Gulf over these years was constituted by an increased determination to play a role in the Gulf region—a role defined in terms of ensuring that no non-Arab power (whether local or global) assumed the role from which Britain was withdrawing. The critical relationship, inevitably, came to be that with Iran. An important element in the Iraqi government's chosen role involved the cultivation of close links with the Arab states of the Gulf. Ultimately, however, the development of conflict in Iraq-Iran relations came to affect Iraq's relationship with the Arab states, as also did the strategic requirements of Iraq's active Gulf role (i.e. with regard to secure access to and from the port of Umm Qasr).

The problems which arose with Iran can only be understood in the context of the policies towards Gulf security which Iran—with the United States government's encouragement and support—was pursuing. In the Western powers' deliberations about security arrangements in the Gulf after Britain's withdrawal, no serious consideration seems to have been given to drawing Iraq into such arrangements—even under the 'moderate' Aref regime. The twin-pillar policy, as developed by the United States government, envisaged the Western powers entrusting Gulf security to Iran and Saudi Arabia, and providing military support to that end. There could be no doubt that militarily Iran was expected to play (and was capable of playing) the greater role.

Iran stepped with enthusiasm into the allotted role: a sudden and substantial increase in the Iranian defence budget in February 1970 was described as necessary 'so as to enable Iran to take up its responsibilities in the Gulf';[68] the development of Bandar Abbas port, and the shift to Bandar Abbas from Khorramshahr of Iranian naval headquarters in 1972, emphasised Iran's growing naval power;[69] on 23 March 1973 the Iranian government announced that, in conjunction with Oman, its navy would inspect ships passing through the Straits of Hormuz;[70] and in newspaper interviews given in 1973 the Shah talked of Iran's role as 'guardian and protector of 60 per cent of the world's oil reserves',[71] and of Iran's duty to dominate the Gulf.[72] In short, when these developments are taken together with Iran's seizure of Abu Musa and the Tunb islands in November 1971, and the despatch of Iranian troops to Oman in 1973 to assist Sultan Qaboos in his struggle with the Popular Front, a 'Pax Iranica' appeared to be descending on the Gulf.

Given the objectives which the Iranian government was pursuing, and given the policy espoused by the new Iraqi government, it is scarcely surprising that a conflictual relationship developed between the two states. A further element of conflict, moreover, followed naturally from the importance which the new Iraqi government attached to a Gulf role: the issue of sovereignty over the Shatt al-Arab became more significant than before (because secure access to the Gulf had become crucial). Nevertheless, the deterioration of relations between the two states cannot be conceived as the deliberate intention of the new Iraqi regime. There was, on the contrary, some attempt to construct a workable relationship with Iran. In December 1968 the Iraqi defence minister visited Iran to discuss the promotion of co-operative relations; the talks were described as 'fruitful'.[73] In February 1969 the joint committees on economic co-operation and the border were re-activated.[74]

By April 1969 the wide divergence between the two states' claims on the Shatt al-Arab had become apparent. The discussion in the joint committee having led nowhere, the Iranian government formally denounced the 1937 agreement on 19 April—declaring that henceforward Iranian ships plying the Shatt al-Arab would no longer pay Iraqi tolls and would not fly the Iraqi flag.[75] The Iraqi government reacted by accusing Iran of having taken a 'unilateral action contravening the principles of international law', repeating Iraq's claim to the whole Shatt al-Arab. The realities of Iranian power were apparent when, after Iraq had warned that ships not complying with Iraqi regulations would be prevented from entering the Shatt, an Iranian cargo ship with naval and air escort was despatched through the estuary to the Gulf. For the six years which followed, use of the Shatt was on the terms laid down by Iran.

The course of the Iraqi-Iranian conflict which occurred between 1969 and 1975 will not be covered here in detail. The important point is that relations reached, and remained at, a low ebb. Over this period each side regularly accused the other of sending infiltrators and insurgents across the border; border clashes occurred frequently between 1972 and 1974; trade sanctions were imposed on both sides; bitter exchanges broke out over Iran's seizure of the Tunb islands and her 'compromise agreement' with the ruler of Sharjah over Abu Musa; and ultimately Iran came to extend support to Iraq's Kurdish insurgents. While attempts to reach an accommodation between the two countries had been initiated at the time of the October 1973 Arab-Israeli War, it was ultimately the threat to the coherence of the Iraqi state posed by the development of the Kurdish conflict during 1974 which brought about the March 1975 Algiers agreement. The latter, formalised in the Baghdad Treaty of 13 June 1975, involved the two sides agreeing:

(1) To make a definitive demarcation of their land borders in accordance with the Constantinople Protocol of 1913 and the minutes of the Committee for the Demarcation of Borders of 1914.

(2) To define their maritime borders in accordance with the *thalweg* line, i.e. the median line in the Shatt al-Arab.

(3) To restore security and mutual confidence along their common frontiers and to establish control which would put an end to 'all infiltrations of a subversive character from either side'.

(4) To restore the traditional ties of good neighbourly relations so as to ensure that the region would remain secure from foreign intervention.[76]

Iraq's confrontation with Iran was to have a decided relevance for its relationship with the other Arab states of the Gulf. The critical interactions here are most evident in the case of Iraqi-Saudi relations. The new Iraqi regime started with an eagerness to improve relations with Saudi Arabia, in the hope that co-operation between the two countries could ensure a specifically Arab role in the maintenance of Gulf security. Talks to this end, specifically with regard to creating a joint deterrent naval force for the Arab Gulf, were held in September 1968.[77] It soon became apparent, however, that, following Western policy, the Saudi government was intent on managing Gulf security in alliance with Iran, not Iraq. Moves towards cementing the Saudi-Iranian umbrella for the Gulf took place during the Shah's visit to Saudi Arabia in November 1968.[78]

Despite further attempts by the Iraq government, in February and May 1969,[79] to promote security co-operation with Saudi Arabia, the Saudi government pushed ahead with promoting its own understanding with Iran. At the time of the Saudi-Iranian talks in April 1970 there was speculation that the two countries were planning a defence pact,[80] and indications that such a pact was under discussion continued to emerge over the three years which followed.[81] While no formal pact was ever concluded, there could be little doubt that Saudi Arabia saw Gulf security as resting more safely in Iranian hands than Iraqi hands. The Iraqi government became steadily more sharply critical of Saudi complicity in 'the United States' and Iran's plans to carve out spheres of influence in the Gulf'.[82]

The new Iraqi government which came to power in July 1968 soon made clear its desire to establish closer relations with Kuwait. Kuwait was, in fact, the first state to extend recognition to the new regime, and by the end of 1969 the two states had concluded an agreement co-ordinating information media (as part of a programme to preserve the Arab character of the Gulf);[83] held a series of talks on military co-operation;[84] agreed terms for the compensation of nationalised Kuwaiti property in Iraq;[85] and reached an agreement on co-operation in the oil sector.[86] In February 1970 the two states re-started talks on the demarcation of their common border,[87] and in February 1971 a new customs agreement was concluded – continuing the free trade provisions of the 1964 agreement but providing also for an increase in the quantities of goods traded.[88] Kuwait and Iraq co-ordinated their policy closely over Iran's claims to Abu Musa and the Tunb islands,[89] and in June 1972 the Kuwait government gave support to the Iraq government's nationalisation of the Iraq Petroleum Company.[90]

The developing co-operation between Kuwait and Iraq was brought to an abrupt end in December 1972. Reports circulated of an Iraqi military build-up on the Kuwait border,[91] and it became apparent that Iraq was strongly pressing its claims to Warba and Bubiyan islands. A border incident at al-Sameta in March added to the tension.[92] The re-emergence of the border issue appears to have been directly related to the escalating crisis between Iraq and Iran: deprived of effective sovereignty over the Shatt al-Arab and therefore of secure access into the Gulf through the Shatt, Iraq's pursuit of a Gulf role required control over the sea-lanes into and out of Umm Qasr. The low point reached in Iraq-Kuwait relations after December 1972, therefore, was not an effect of anything intrinsic to the relationship but rather of the Iraqi-Iranian confrontation.

As with the case of Kuwait, Iraq's relations with the states and shaikhdoms of the Lower Gulf expanded rapidly in the years immediately following July 1968. The new regime extended support to the process of forming a federal entity in the Lower Gulf, and governmental visits were exchanged with Bahrain,[93] Qatar[94] and Abu Dhabi.[95] Iraqi trade centres were opened in the area and agreements on economic co-operation were concluded with Bahrain[96] and Qatar.[97] An agreement was made with the government of the UAE for Iraq to provide the new federation with Iraqi personnel.[98] Between 1972 and 1975 little development occurred in Iraq's relationship with the states of the Lower Gulf; it seems that the problems encompassing Iraq's relations with Iran, Kuwait and Saudi Arabia exerted an influence on the Lower Gulf states' relationships with Iraq.

A further aspect of intra-Gulf relations over at least part of this period was the suspicion harboured by the governments of the other Arab states in the Gulf that Iraq was encouraging movements hostile to and subversive of the existing monarchical regimes. In one respect this sprang from the nature of the regime which had come to power in Iraq: the Ba'th Party's objective spread beyond the concerns of Iraq to the wider Arab world, and the Ba'th Party was certainly eager to build up a following in the Gulf states. The prominent part played by non-Arab powers in the Gulf, moreover, jarred with the Ba'th's Arabist rhetoric and provided a clear incentive for the Ba'th to expand its activity. Whereas before July 1968 the Ba'th had only a limited basis for attracting a following in the Gulf states, after July 1968 the resources of the Iraqi state could be used to support this objective. The newly established Iraqi trade centres in the Gulf appear at times to have been more significant in the political sphere (as channels for Ba'thist influence) than the economic.[99]

No doubt the concern of Gulf governments over Ba'thist activity provides one explanation why, despite the apparent desire of the new Iraqi regime in July 1968 for closer relations with the Arab states of the Gulf, these relations failed to develop significantly between 1972 and 1975. Of greater importance, however, were the differences over Iran's role in the Gulf, and the direct and indirect effects of the Iraqi-Iranian conflict. The Iranian dimension determined the souring of Iraqi-Saudi relations after an initially encouraging start, as also the disruption which occurred in Iraqi-Kuwaiti relations. The same factor, together with influences spreading from the Saudi and Kuwaiti experiences, seems to have been prominent in affecting Iraqi relations with the remaining Arab Gulf states.

The Ba'th's 'subversive role', in fact, may have been more the effect than the cause of the problems in Iraq's relations with the Arab states of the Gulf. While the party maintained some activity in the Gulf states throughout this period (and after, also), the activity seems to have increased with the Ba'th's concern at Iran's expanding role and at the preparedness of some Gulf governments to accept Iranian leadership in the protection of Gulf security.[100] Moreover, the Ba'th reserved its more overt or significant activity for those states where the regime was deemed to have 'betrayed the Arab nation'. In Oman, where the Sultan maintained a continuing British and latterly also Iranian military presence, Iraqi financial and military assistance flowed to the Popular Front for the Liberation of Oman. In Sharjah, following Shaikh Khalid's cession of part of Abu Musa island to Iran in November 1971, weapons supplied by Iraqi sources appear to have been used in Shaikh Khalid's subsequent assassination.[101]

Concluding Perspective: 1975-81

The development of Iraq's relations with its Arab neighbours on the Gulf since 1975 is covered in Naomi Sakr's contribution to this book (Chapter 11). No details on that topic, therefore, need to be given here. The 1975-81 period witnessed a steady increase in co-operation and co-ordination between Iraq and these states. The co-operation and co-ordination involved the conclusion of bilateral free trade agreements, the establishment of joint committees to recommend measures of economic co-operation, the participation of Iraq in functional organisations geared to satisfy particular Gulf needs and the pursuit of compatible policies in oil pricing and production.

Most of this co-operation has been in the economic sphere rather than the political. Iraq has, it would seem, not been encouraged to participate in meetings with a political flavour which the remaining Arab states of the Gulf have held. No Iraqi delegation was invited to the Taiz summit meeting of April 1980, nor was Iraq invited to take part in the meetings leading up to the establishment of the Gulf Co-operation Council in February 1981. Nevertheless, some of the bilateral agreements reached between Iraq and its Arab neighbours on the Gulf have had a political dimension, as with the Saudi-Iraqi security agreement of February 1979.

The establishment of closer relations (at least on the economic and functional levels) between Iraq and the Arab states of the Gulf after 1975 did not follow from any change in Ba'thist policy towards the traditional structures of power in these states. On the contrary, the Ba'th remained intent on putting across its own very different ideological perspectives to the populations of the area, and continued to provide support for groups which shared these perspectives. Only with respect to Oman was there a discernible change: following the establishment of diplomatic relations between Iraq and the Sultan's government in January 1976, Iraq appears to have stopped providing military assistance to the Popular Front for the Liberation of Oman. General contacts with the PFLO, nevertheless, were maintained.

The crucial factor which did change around 1975 was in the wider international context. Iraq and the Arab states of the Gulf were no longer sharply divided on issues of Gulf and international politics. On the one hand, domestic factors had impelled Iraq to establish a workable relationship with Iran, embodied in the March 1975 agreement. Iraq was less likely, therefore, to conceive of Iran's links with the remaining Arab states of the Gulf as directly threatening to her own interests. The Iranian-Saudi relationship, besides, had not developed into the formal defence structure which Iraq had feared in the early 1970s.

On the other hand, the October 1973 Arab-Israeli war had brought Iraq and the other Arab states of the Gulf together in the collective imposition of an oil boycott on the United States and some of its Western allies. Saudi Arabia and the smaller Gulf states could, therefore, play a role in defence of Arab interests, at least when the issue and the overall environment were appropriate. It was clear that a hostile relationship between Iraq and its Arab neighbours on the Gulf could undermine the very objectives which the Iraqi government sought to pursue – driving these states into closer relations with the West and with Iran, rather than encouraging them to take an independent line.

The fall of the Shah in February 1979 complemented the degree of compatibility between the international policies pursued by Iraq and those pursued by the other Arab states of the Gulf. There was a shared apprehension of the new Iranian regime, and therefore a common concern to avoid unnecessary divisions among the Arab states in the region.

In conclusion, the strains so frequently evident in Iraq's relations with the other Arab states of the Gulf have not been caused primarily by 'radical Iraq' seeking to undermine the 'conservative monarchies'. A more prominent factor has been different perspectives in the international sphere – most crucially regarding the role of non-Arab powers in the Gulf region. In the early 1970s the willingness of some of the Arab states to accept a security system dominated by non-Arab powers (whether by the Western powers directly or by a Western-supported Iran) met with severe disfavour in Iraqi governmental circles. This in turn led Iraq into actions which disrupted its relationships with other Gulf states. Paradoxically, therefore, the West's attempts to create a security system capable of maintaining stability in the Gulf appear, in this context, to have been the major source of instability.

Notes

1. In addition to the ports of Basra and Umm Qasr there was also the port of Fao. The disadvantages of developing Fao as Iraq's major point of access into the Gulf were not only that it lay in an exposed position (as became evident in the early stages of the Iran-Iraq war) but also that it lay upstream of the mouth of the Shatt al-Arab such that it could be reached only by ships of under 35 feet draught.

Iraq has only some 40 miles of coastline on the Gulf, with mainly shallow waters. The port of Basra lies some 60 miles up the Shatt.

2. The 'conservative monarchies' referred to here are specifically those on the Arab side of the Gulf. Iraqi policies may have posed some threat to Iran, just as Iranian policies posed a threat to Iraq. As Iran has been quite capable of defending itself, however, the Iraqi threat to Iran has scarcely constituted justification for Western involvement in maintaining Gulf security. The scale of Western military sales to Iran – and the consequent imbalance in the military strength of the two countries – in fact seems to have been the central factor leading Iraq to conclude a Treaty of Friendship with the Soviet Union in April 1972.

3. A. Humaidan, *Les Princes de l'Or Noir* (SEOEIS, Paris, 1968), p. 121.

4. Ibid.

5. Sir M. Peterson, *Both Sides of the Curtain* (Allen and Unwin, London, 1950), p. 38.

6. Ibid.

7. M. Khadduri, *Socialist Iraq* (The Middle East Institute, Washington, 1978), pp. 153-4.

8. This is the contention in W. Gallman, *Iraq under General Nouri* (Johns Hopkins Press, Washington, 1964), p. 148.

9. Khadduri, *Socialist Iraq*, p. 154.

10. Ibid.

11. Ibid.

12. Ibid.

13. See W. Moubarak, 'Kuwait's Quest for Security, 1961-73', unpublished PhD thesis, Indiana University, 1979, p. 52.

14. Ibid., p. 63.

15. Khadduri, *Socialist Iraq*, p. 154.

16. Moubarak, 'Kuwait's Quest', p. 64.

17. M. Khadduri, *Independent Iraq, 1932-58* (Oxford University Press, London, 1960), p. 323.

18. Ibid., p. 330.

19. See A. Fawzi, *Qasim wa al-Kuwait* (Qasim and Kuwait) (Dar al-Manar, Cairo, 1961), pp. 46-7.

20. Moubarak, 'Kuwait's Quest', p. 58.

21. M. Khadduri, *Republican Iraq* (Oxford University Press, London, 1969), p. 169.

22. Ibid., p. 169, n. 53.

23. The account given here of the 1959-60 conflict is taken from R.D. McLaurin, M. Mughisuddin and A. Wagner, *Foreign Policy Making in the Middle East* (Praeger, New York, 1977), pp. 142-3.

24. Moubarak, 'Kuwait's Quest', p. 58.

25. *Daily Telegraph*, 19 Feb. 1963.

26. *Le Commerce du Levant*, 6 Apr. 1963.

27. *Observer*, 2 June 1963.

28. *Daily Telegraph*, 27 Sept. 1963.

29. *Financial Times*, 3 Oct. 1963.

30. *New York Times*, 5 Oct. 1963.

31. *Financial Times*, 22 Oct. 1963. Further details of the overall Kuwait-Iraq agreement can be found in Dawood, *Al-Khalij al-'Arabi wa al-'Amal al-'Arabi al-Mushtirik* (The Arab Gulf and Joint Arab Action) (Centre for Arab Gulf Studies Publications, Basra University, 1980), p. 135.

32. *Egyptian Gazette*, 26 Oct. 1964.

33. *Middle East Economic Digest*, 15-28 Jan. 1967.

34. *Le Commerce du Levant*, 12 Feb. 1964.

35. *Le Commerce du Levant*, 1 Jan. 1964.

36. *Dawn*, 14 Jan. 1964.

37. *Middle East Economic Digest*, 1-15 Oct. 1966; *Middle East Economic Digest*, 1-15 Oct. 1967.

38. *Middle East Economic Digest*, 1-15 Jan. 1968.

39. *Middle East Economic Digest*, 16-31 Mar. 1968.

40. *Middle East Economic Digest*, 1-15 June, 1966.

41. *Middle East Economic Digest*, 15-28 Jan. 1967.

42. *New York Times*, 27 April 1967.

43. *Middle East Economic Digest*, 15-28 Feb. 1966.

44. *Middle East Economic Digest*, 1-15 Jan. 1967.

45. *Middle East Economic Digest*, 16-29 Feb. 1968.

46. Details given here of the mission's tour are taken from Dawood, *Al-Khalij al-'Arabi*, pp. 122-3.

47. *Egyptian Mail*, 3 Oct. 1964.

48. *Financial Times*, 27 Oct. 1964.

49. Ibid.

50. *Egyptian Gazette*, 29 June 1965.

51. *Middle East Economic Digest*, 16-30 Apr. 1966.

52. *Egyptian Gazette*, 13 Aug. 1967.

53. *Middle East Economic Digest*, 16-31 July 1967.

54. *Middle East Economic Digest*, 16-31 Mar. 1967.

55. *Middle East Economic Digest*, 16-29 Feb. 1968.

56. *Middle East Economic Digest*, 15-28 Feb. 1966.

57. *Le Commerce du Levant*, 3 July 1968.

58. *The Times*, 15 Aug. 1963.

59. *Dawn*, 18 Mar. 1964.

60. *Guardian*, 17 Dec. 1965.

61. *The Times*, 28 Dec. 1965.

62. *Egyptian Gazette*, 31 Dec. 1965.

63. *The Times*, 13 Jan. 1966.

64. *Egyptian Gazette*, 28 May 1966.

65. *The Times*, 20 Mar. 1967.

66. *Egyptian Gazette*, 30 Apr. 1967.

67. *Egyptian Mail*, 29 June 1968.

68. *New York Times*, 9 Feb. 1970.

69. *Christian Science Monitor*, 4 Feb. 1972.

70. *Christian Science Monitor*, 27 July 1973.

71. *Financial Times*, 31 May 1973.

72. *Christian Science Monitor*, 27 July 1973.

73. *Egyptian Gazette*, 12 Dec. 1968.

74. *Le Commerce du Levant*, 18 Jan. 1969.

75. The account of this incident given here is taken from McLaurin, Mughisuddin and Wagner, *Foreign Policy Making*, p. 143.

76. Taken from Khadduri, *Socialist Iraq*, p. 150.

77. *Egyptian Gazette*, 26 Sept. 1968.

78. *The Times*, 13 Nov. 1968.

79. *Egyptian Gazette*, 3 Feb. 1969; *Egyptian Gazette*, 19 May 1969.

80. *Dawn*, 15 Apr. 1970.

81. *Egyptian Gazette*, 15 July 1970; *The Times*, 17 July 1970; *Egyptian Gazette*, 27 Dec. 1972; *The Times*, 13 Dec. 1972; *Egyptian Gazette*, 27 Mar. 1973.

82. *Christian Science Monitor*, 24 Jan. 1970.

83. *Middle East Economic Digest*, 1-15 Sept. 1968.

84. *Egyptian Gazette*, 29 Apr. 1969.

85. *Neue Zurcher Zeitung*, 8 Oct. 1969.

86. *Le Commerce du Levant*, 8 Nov. 1969.

87. *Middle East Economic Digest*, 15-28 Feb. 1970.

88. *Middle East Economic Digest*, 15-28 Feb. 1971.

89. *Middle East Economic Digest*. 16-30 Nov. 1971.

90. *Middle East Economic Digest*, 1-15 June 1972.

91. *Financial Times*, 22 Dec. 1972.

92. *Middle East Economic Digest*, 16-31 Mar. 1973.

93. *Egyptian Gazette*, 25 Feb. 1969.

94. *Egyptian Gazette*, 9 Apr. 1969.

95. *Egyptian Gazette*, 28 July 1969.

96. *Egyptian Gazette*, 8 Apr. 1969.

97. *Middle East Economic Digest*, 1-15 Aug. 1970.

98. *Middle East Economic Digest*, 1-15 Dec. 1973.

99. It is difficult to provide any firm evidence on this topic. For the suspicions of Western circles in this regard, however, see *Le Monde*, 3 Mar. 1973.

100. For the growth of Ba'thist activity see *Le Monde*, 3 Mar. 1973.

101. Reported in *Middle East Economic Digest*, 16-31 Jan. 1972.

11 ECONOMIC RELATIONS BETWEEN IRAQ AND OTHER ARAB GULF STATES

Naomi Sakr

Introduction

Iraq's economic relations with other Arab Gulf states improved dramatically during the first half of 1981. By the summer of that year Iraq had received the promise of extensive financial assistance from Kuwait and Saudi Arabia and had announced plans to build oil pipelines through these states.

The first clear indication that funds would be forthcoming from the Gulf came at the end of April, when Kuwait's National Assembly approved a $2,000 million interest-free loan to help Iraq repair damage caused during the war with Iran. The first $500 million instalment of this was to be paid immediately, with the remainder to be paid in monthly instalments of $300 million each. Confirmation of the loan gave added credence to reports that other Gulf states were also providing Iraq with finance. According to one Kuwaiti newspaper in mid-April, Saudi Arabia had pledged $6,000 million, the United Arab Emirates (UAE) $3,000 million and Qatar $1,000 million, half of which had already been disbursed.[1] Saudi Arabia subsequently declared its readiness to assist Iraq when, in mid-July, its Information Minister, Mohammad Abdu Yamani, announced that King Khaled had given instructions that his government should release credits to cover the reconstruction of Iraq's nuclear reactor at Tammuz, destroyed by Israel the previous month. Two weeks after that the Iraqi Oil Minister, Tayeh Abd al-Karim, revealed that feasibility studies were under way regarding the construction of an oil pipeline, or pipelines, to the Red Sea via Saudi Arabia or to the Gulf via Kuwait. According to Abd al-Karim both countries had already consented to the plan, which was intended to reduce Iraq's dependence on its existing Gulf terminals (out of action because of the war with Iran) and on outlets through Syria and Turkey. That Iraq and Saudi Arabia had reached some form of special understanding was apparent from the start of the war with Iran. Well-informed sources in Saudi Arabia even claimed that the Saudi government was fully behind the Iraqi offensive (or

150

counterattack[2]) because of fears that Iranian militants were planning to use the annual pilgrimage to Mecca in October 1980 as a means of entering the kingdom and leading a rebellion – perhaps along the lines of the Mecca siege of 1979. The Saudi Interior Minister Prince Naif admitted in a television broadcast on 10 October that security forces had discovered pilgrims distributing subversive literature. In fact, some reports suggested that arms were discovered as well, carried by Iranian 'pilgrims' whose age and financial status did not point to their having paid for their journey to Saudi Arabia out of their life savings. If, as a result of these developments, the Saudis supported Iraq politically in its war with Iran, it followed that they would be ready to support it practically as well. Indeed, Western intelligence reports in February 1981 said that about a hundred T55 tanks had been sent to Iraq from Poland via Saudi Arabia in a series of shipments starting in mid-December 1980.[3] The tanks were said to have been refused passage through the Jordanian port of Aqaba, which, according to eyewitness accounts, seems to have been used only for the transit of non-military supplies to Iraq.[4]

Iraq's relations with Kuwait, Saudi Arabia, the UAE, Qatar and Bahrain have also been reinforced over the past year or so by its active membership in a number of economic institutions grouping some or all of these states. These institutions will be discussed in greater detail later, but it is worth mentioning briefly here that Iraq belongs to the Doha-based Gulf Organisation for Industrial Consulting, the Riyadh-based Conference of Ministers of Agriculture of the Gulf States and Arabian Peninsula, the Kuwait-based Arab Maritime Petroleum Transport Company, the United Arab Shipping Company, the Gulf International Bank and the Arab War Risks Insurance Syndicate, as well as a good number of other companies that have emerged as offshoots of these bodies.

It is all the more interesting, then, that Iraq does not currently belong to the Gulf states' latest joint creation, the Gulf Co-operation Council. Foreign ministers representing the six member-states of the Council initialled its constitution in Muscat in March 1981 and this was duly ratified by the heads of state in Abu Dhabi at the end of May. The constitution refers specifically to the 'special relations and similarities' existing among the Council's members and to the 'importance of establishing close co-ordination in economic and social spheres'. It states that the Council will 'draw up regulations covering the economy, finance, education, culture, social affairs, health, communications, information, passports and nationality, travel,

transport, trade, customs, haulage and legal and legislative affairs'.
Various explanations have been offered for Iraq's exclusion from the
Gulf Co-operation Council. In the initial stages official comment from
the Iraqi leadership was limited; it was not until July, several weeks
after the Gulf summit had taken place in Abu Dhabi, that President
Saddam Husain made his first deliberate — and somewhat critical —
allusion to it in public. The official Iraqi stance was that any formal
co-operation pact among Arab states should be signed within the
framework of the Arab League. Iraq, in fact, sponsored the Arab
National Charter, a set of eight principles put forward in February
1980. This was designed to remove any foreign military presence from
the area, to promote non-alignment and to foster Arab economic
integration and collaboration in matters of defence. The perspective
of the other Arab Gulf states in this regard has been rather different:
they see their own area as a sub-region of the Arab world which —
given time — could become increasingly capable of fending for itself
economically without always having to take part in unwieldy schemes
intended to encompass the entire Arab world.[5] Furthermore the Gulf
Co-operation Council's six members are anxious not to be seen to be
'ganging up' on Iran. A combination of these six states plus Iraq could
be interpreted as tilting what was at one time a delicate balance
between three local 'powers' — Iraq, Saudi Arabia and Iran.

It is, however, possible to argue that Iraq really is a member of the
new Council in all but name. First, some regard the current war with
Iran as being fought by Iraq on behalf of other Arab Gulf governments,
with the common objective of ensuring that Iran's brand of revolutionary fervour should not spill over on to the Arab side of the waterway.
Second, Iraq does appear to be included in at least some of the
Council's practical plans. UAE Oil Minister Mana Said al-Otaiba has
been quoted as saying that the Council members are planning to build
strategic oil pipelines to bypass the Straits of Hormuz. This would be
a major network, running

> all the way from southern Iraq, through Kuwait, Saudi Arabia,
> Qatar and Abu Dhabi and heading out to the Gulf of Oman. When
> not carrying oil the same network could be used to pipe fresh water
> from the Shatt al-Arab to desert areas further south.[6]

Third, there is reason to believe that Iraq is contemplating co-operation
with other Gulf states in the field of military industries. Foreign
companies have been invited to Iraq for discussion on the subject of

local production of jet engines, and Iraqi officials visited Britain in July 1981 to explore the possibility of British involvement in setting up an aircraft industry in Iraq. This apparently represents only the start of a wide-ranging programme of armaments manufacture – a programme in which other Gulf countries may play a role similar to that which they played in the Arab Industrialisation Organisation (established in Egypt in 1975 but dissolved after Egypt signed the Camp David agreement with Israel in 1979). Fourth, as the rest of this chapter will attempt to show, Iraq's economic links with Gulf Co-operation Council members are steadily gaining in importance. This has been the result of deliberate Iraqi policy and suggests that Iraq's co-operation with other Gulf states will outlive the present war.

Developing Contacts

Iraq's interest in the Gulf is relatively recent. Except for the occasional call for unity with Kuwait made in the 1930s, and actively revived by Qasim in the early 1960s, Iraq's attention has traditionally focused primarily on the Fertile Crescent. Interest in the Gulf first began to grow with the development of two new oilfields at Zubair and Rumaila in the south of Iraq in the late 1940s and with the opening of the terminal at Fao on the Gulf in 1951. It was, however, not until the post-1958 revolutionary government put pressure on the Iraq Petroleum Company (IPC) in a bid to increase oil revenues that southern Iraq began to play a significant part in oil development plans.[7] The IPC, having finally promised in 1962 to double its oil production, started building new transport, loading and storage facilities, most of which were located in the south in an attempt to avoid a repetition of the difficulties incurred in conveying oil through Syria in the 1950s. Iraq's unsettled internal situation, however, continued to preclude the formation of a coherent Gulf policy; such a policy only emerged after the coup of 1968 which restored the Ba'thists to power. A stretch of political stability, combined with the oil price explosion of 1973-4 (which suddenly pushed the Gulf to the forefront of international affairs), and a period of bitter feuding with Syria gave rise to a series of Iraqi diplomatic initiatives designed to put Iraq's relations with other Gulf states on a new footing.

The watershed in these relations came in 1975. Under the famous Algiers Agreement of March 1975 Iraq made border concessions to Iran, in return for which Iran undertook to end support for Kurdish rebels in Iraq, thereby virtually ending the Kurdish war. The border deal with Iran was followed almost immediately by another with Saudi Arabia. In April 1975 Baghdad and Riyadh announced their decision to reach a settlement on the disputed diamond-shaped 'neutral zone' and to rebuild the 1,280-kilometre road from Najaf to Medina. Iraq accepted Saudi mediation in its dispute with Syria over the sharing of Euphrates waters and, in June of that year, Crown Prince Fahd visited Baghdad. July 1975 saw the Iraqi-Saudi border agreement signed, and in August it was agreed that air services between the two countries should be stepped up. At the same time reports began to circulate that Iraq had asked Saudi Arabia for a $200 million loan. These reports, though never confirmed, were credible because they coincided with news that Iraq had raised its first $500 million Eurodollar loan and was planning to borrow heavily to finance its 1975-80 investment programme.[8]

Relations with Kuwait underwent a similar change during 1975. As recently as December 1974 Iraqi troops had apparently set up military installations more than a mile inside Kuwaiti territory, but in 1975 the two countries suddenly appeared to be on the brink of settling their long-standing land border dispute. The Arab League had recommended in 1963 that their common border should be redrawn 350 metres south of the existing line, but this revision was never ratified by either side. In 1975 Iraq seemed prepared to make concessions on the land border in return for concessions from Kuwait regarding access to the two islands of Bubiyan and Warba (needed for the development of Iraq's commercial and naval ports). In the event, the agreement did not materialise. In August 1975 nevertheless, bilateral relations were good enough for Iraqi Industry Minister Taha Jazrawi to announce that he had asked Kuwait to join Iraq in setting up a petrochemical complex. Subsequent clashes between the two countries over the border issue were quickly contained. Indeed, Iraq's troop movements over the frontier in September 1976 and Kuwait's resumption of drilling at the oil well at Jirfan in disputed territory in early 1977 may be interpreted, with hindsight, as forms of bargaining over the border issue.

After the March 1975 Iran-Iraq agreement, Iraq appears to have sought a degree of military co-ordination with some of the states of the Gulf. There was speculation in April-May 1975 that the three local powers, Iraq, Iran and Saudi Arabia, would soon come together in a mutual non-aggression treaty. Iraq, however, let it be known that it was not seeking a military pact. The main issue, Foreign Minister Sa'adoun

Hammadi said, was the removal of foreign military bases from the area. To this end the Iraqi government engaged in intensive diplomatic activity to co-ordinate the attitudes of Arab Gulf states. This was reflected in a series of visits to Iraq of high-ranking military officials from lower down the Gulf. Bahrain's Crown Prince and Minister of Defence paid a four-day visit in May and, in the same month, the Chiefs of Staff of the UAE, Qatar and Bahrain attended a military parade in Baghdad. In December, following talks with the UAE Minister of Defence, it was reported that Iraq had offered the federation military and technical assistance. The beginning of 1976 was marked by an upgrading of Iraqi-Omani relations and the exchange of ambassadors between Muscat and Baghdad.

Significantly, the initiative at military level was accompanied by a spurt of activity on the economic front. When the Ruler of Qatar visited Baghdad in July 1975 the Iraqis offered his government technical assistance in the fields of housing and water supply. During 1976 commercial centres for the promotion of Iraqi exports were established in Kuwait, Bahrain, Abu Dhabi and Dubai. Also, in 1977, when Saddam Husain embarked on his Gulf tour (a similar tour planned for April 1976 had to be postponed, apparently due to the discovery of an assassination plot), he was accompanied by the Ministers of Agriculture and Trade and the Governor of the Central Bank of Iraq. Iraq has in recent years given economic co-operation high priority in its relations with Arab Gulf states. The question arises, however, as to whether these regional links have special significance or whether they are simply part of Iraq's wider policy aimed at strengthening economic relations among all Arab states. Some analysis of Iraq's economic interests and policies in the Gulf is required before this question can be answered.

Agricultural Co-operation

Iraq makes no secret of its aim to achieve self-sufficiency in food and develop its agricultural potential to the point where it will have significant export capacity. Agriculture is described as the country's 'permanent oil', and large-scale irrigation and land-reclamation schemes have been under way since before the dramatic increase in oil revenues that followed the 1973 oil price rises. Irrigation contracts have continued to be awarded despite the war with Iran — one notable example being the $1,500 million contract for the Mosul dam signed in January 1981.

An official at the Ministry of Planning pointed out to the writer that the ancient land of Mesopotamia was able in history to feed 40 million people.[9] The implication is that, even though it cannot feed 13 million people now, it is only a matter of time until technology makes the country truly productive again. The potential for expanding the area under cultivation is great, whichever estimate of the total cultivable area is accepted. At present some 6 million hectares are farmed and the Ministry of Agriculture and Agrarian Reform calculates that this could be quadrupled to 24 million hectares. A British consultant familiar with the terrain and water resources puts the potential total more conservatively at 12 million hectares.[10] Production can, of course, be expanded vertically (through better yields and land use) as well as horizontally.

Although the achievement of Iraq's agricultural goals may still be distant (wheat imports are currently equal to production), planners in Baghdad are already clear on the uses to which eventual food surpluses will be put. Exports will be destined first and foremost for the Gulf area, then other Arab states and then what spokesmen in Baghdad call 'some of our friends'. Ultimately, Iraqi officials maintain, food will become a more strategic product than oil is now; they point out that food is already being used as a strategic commodity in trade with developing states.[11] Iraq's own readiness to use its exports for political purposes has already been demonstrated. During 1980, for example, Iraq sought to use oil credits to persuade the Somali and Kenyan governments to refuse US requests for military facilities. The same tool was used in an attempt to persuade Djibouti and the Malagasy Republic to reduce the number of foreign troops on their soil.[12] However, even supposing that a time does come when the Gulf states are not able to obtain food supplies from traditional sources, Iraq will not be in a position to plug the gap – and thereby influence Gulf policies – for many years to come. In the meantime the Iraqi government is seeking other forms of agricultural co-operation with Arab Gulf states.

First, the Iraqi government has liberalised its legislation so as to enable private Gulf investors to participate in agricultural projects in Iraq. Iraqi officials would themselves not necessarily describe the legal changes as 'liberalisation'; they prefer to use the term 'clarification', stressing that the changes were prompted by the greater availability of private capital both inside and outside Iraq. Whatever term is preferred, it is now possible in practice for the private sector to hold a 20 per cent share in agricultural projects, with agricultural co-operatives gaining a 29 per cent share and the state holding standing at 51 per cent. How far this arrangement will suit private Gulf investors remains to be seen, but it is known that requests have been lodged with the appropriate authorities in Iraq for participation by Gulf companies and individuals in agribusiness projects – especially poultry farming and livestock rearing. In April 1981 these latter requests, relating to the establishment of completely new projects, were awaiting the Iraqi government's final approval. According to Planning Ministry sources, Kuwaiti interests are most active in seeking to invest in Iraq, encouraged both by their proximity and their family links, since many Kuwaiti families have branches in the Basra area.

Second, besides considering private agricultural investment from Gulf sources, Iraq is also playing an active part in the Conference of Ministers of Agriculture of the Gulf States and Arabian Peninsula (CMAGSAP). This organisation, based in Riyadh and headed by the Saudi Minister of Agriculture and Water Muhammad Ali Mekki as Secretary-General, has been meeting regularly once a year since 1976. But it was not until 1978, amid growing concern over food security throughout the Arab world, that CMAGSAP's discussions began to move from a theoretical to a practical level, with the proposal for actual projects to be jointly implemented by the organisation's member states – Bahrain, Iraq, Kuwait, Oman, Qatar, Saudi Arabia, the UAE and North and South Yemen. The Conference's fourth session in Kuwait in March 1979 called on a committee of experts to look into possible joint ventures in the production, storage and marketing of cereals and fodder. That committee then met in Riyadh and formed a team which, after touring member states, identified a number of projects that it considered to be financially rewarding, three of them in Iraq.[13]

Two of the projects which the CMAGSAP committee commended were subsequently approved by Gulf ministers as being suitable for regional participation. Both were already under implementation at the time of the initiative. One of them, a $70 million scheme to develop 20,000 hectares of irrigated land at Delmaj in central Iraq, envisaged producing wheat, barley, corn, potatoes, onions, peas and fodder. The annual return on investment in this enterprise was estimated by the CMAGSAP committee at 13 per cent. The second project, costing $30 million, involved the production of a total of 83,000 tons of certified seeds a year from six centres in Iraq, Saudi Arabia and North Yemen. This amount of seed, initially including wheat, barley, sorghum, maize, alfalfa and clover but also including vegetable seeds at a later stage, was sufficient to cover one-third of the region's needs in certified seeds. It would give a return on investment of 14 per cent a year. As for financing arrangements for these and other CMAGSAP projects, the special committee envisaged in its report that the host country would put up 32 per cent of the capital, with a further 32 per cent being contributed by a specially established Gulf Authority for Food and Agriculture. An additional 16 per cent would come in the form of private investment, with the remaining 20 per cent being obtained in the form of commercial loans.

The channels for agricultural co-operation between Iraq and other Gulf states are therefore open. Indeed, without the grain-producing potential of Iraq and North Yemen, CMAGSAP members would have little hope of ever meeting a significant proportion of their internal cereal demand through local resources. One field on which CMAGSAP is expected to focus in the future is co-operation in irrigation – where Iraq has greater experience than other Gulf states. A delegation of Iraqi agricultural experts visiting the UAE recently discussed the application of Iraqi expertise in irrigation and land reclamation with the Deputy Ruler of Ras al-Khaimah.[14]

As for the reasons for Iraq's interest in the forms of agricultural co-operation discussed above, Iraqi officials look ahead to the post-oil era. Dr Sabah Kachachi of the Planning Ministry puts it as follows:

You can see it from a historical point of view. What did the people of the Gulf do 1,000, 2,000, 3,000 years ago? They went to Mesopotamia and the Nile. What will they do in the future when the oil runs out? They will migrate again – only this time the Nile will be fully booked. By the time the oil runs out the millionaires will already have left (I doubt whether even Switzerland would be good enough for them) and those who stay will want food and jobs. We have to help to stabilise the population. That is why Iraq is expanding its agricultural sector, to feed Iraqis and make food available to Gulf states.[15]

Industrial Co-operation

Whatever view is taken of Iraq's industrial performance in the past five years or so, it is clear that Iraq has not embarked on industrial projects likely to lead to surplus capacity in the region. Plans for an aluminium smelter and drydock, for example, drawn up in the mid-1970s, were postponed – at a time when Dubai was incurring some criticism for going ahead with its own smelter and drydock, both of which duplicated facilities already existing in Bahrain. Not all of the Iraq government's reasons for postponing its own projected development, however, stemmed from altruism. The drop in purchasing power of oil revenues in the 1976-8 period, supply bottlenecks and port congestion in the Gulf, combined with a fear of inflation, can all help to explain Iraq's hesitation in implementing large-scale industrial ventures. Projects such as a motor industry complex, which would have been completely new to the area, were postponed for similar reasons. Nevertheless, Iraqi officials often do choose, when discussing industrial development, to highlight their concern for the Gulf region as a whole. They imply that Iraq, with its ability to assess overall Gulf requirements and having the Gulf's best economic interests at heart, deliberately refrains from competing with neighbouring states for a share in an already limited market.[16]

While Iraqi officials are sometimes critical of the tendency for other Gulf governments to start new projects without due planning and without studying the market potential, they also recognise that Gulf oil producers have little choice in terms of industrial development. States with oil and gas reserves have no alternative but to go in for industries such as petrochemicals, fertilisers and steel, and if this results in a world surplus of petrochemicals and other products, then 'it is the West which should worry about it, not the Gulf'. Until recently there was a basic difference in the field of manpower policy, in that Iraq used to reject the notion of employing non-Arabs to implement its industrialisation programme. But even this policy now seems to have undergone some modifications, bringing Iraq more in line with other Gulf states. In 1980, for example, Chiyoda Chemical Engineering became the first Japanese company to arrange to employ Chinese workers on a project in Iraq, and in 1981 a Manila-based firm, NGV, brought in several hundred Filipino workers to prepare the ground for an important irrigation project. South Korean firms now have $500 million worth of contracts in Iraq, which seems to indicate growing dependence on Korean construction workers.

Now that Gulf states have started to co-operate in the industrial sector through the Doha-based Gulf Organisation for Industrial Consulting, Iraq says it 'definitely will' take part in all GOIC-sponsored ventures.[17] GOIC, founded in 1976 and comprising Iraq, Bahrain, Oman, Kuwait, Qatar, Saudi Arabia and the UAE, was set up primarily to carry out feasibility studies. Lately it has followed up such studies by actively promoting projects at ministerial level. The latter policy has led to the launching of an aluminium rolling mill in Bahrain, which is being jointly financed by all the Organisation's members except the UAE. The Bahrain mill will be the second in the region – the first, located at Nasiriya in Iraq, currently meets most of Iraq's own needs in rolled aluminium products. Despite already having an aluminium rolling mill, Iraq has taken a 20 per cent stake in the Gulf Aluminium Rolling Mill Company (GARMCO) in Bahrain.

GOIC's second project, under discussion at the time of writing, is a factory to produce sheet glass. This is to be sited in Iraq, probably near the site of the country's sizeable silica deposits in the west which already supply an existing glass factory at Ramadi. The projected expansion of the Ramadi plant has been taken into account in the feasibility study for the new joint venture factory, which is expected to satisfy the region's needs in sheet glass for construction purposes for the next 10 years. As with the aluminium rolling mill, Iraq is expected to take a 20 per cent share, or thereabouts, in the Gulf glass plant. Beyond this, GOIC is promoting a joint aromatics plant, the location of which has yet to be decided. In the meantime Iraq has become involved in another joint industrial project – a $300 million iron-pelletising plant in Bahrain, which is due to start producing by the end of 1983. Besides the Iraqi government, other shareholders in this project are the Kuwait Foreign Trading, Contracting and Investment Company, Kuwait Metal Pipe Industries, the Amman-based Arab Mining Company and private investors from Bahrain and other Gulf states.

In addition to these largely government-to-government schemes, there is some private Gulf involvement in a few small-to-medium-sized manufacturing projects in Iraq and, Iraqi officials say, scope for more in the mixed sector, in which factories producing radios, air conditioners and other household items are in some cases 60 per cent owned by private interests. At the same time contractors from Iraq and other Gulf states are working more and more in each other's territory. The government in Baghdad provides assistance for Iraqi consulting engineers and others involved in projects in the Gulf region; a large number are thought to be working in Abu Dhabi. Similarly, several Kuwaiti contractors, having won contracts in Iraq, have opened branch offices in Baghdad, and four Kuwaiti suppliers of building materials were last year reported to be doing the same.[18] These firms appear to be attracted to Iraq by the size of the market, laws against middlemen and commission-taking and, according to some Kuwaiti managers, Iraq's preference for Arab, as opposed to non-Arab contractors.

Trade

Kuwait has consistently been Iraq's leading trading partner in the Gulf, in terms both of its exports to and imports from Iraq. This, however, is not particularly remarkable since Iraq's trade with other Gulf states over the past 15 years has been almost negligible and, in some cases, has actually declined in absolute, as well as real, terms. This decline took place even before the oil price revolution of 1973, which radically altered the relative values of oil and non-oil trade and which increased Iraq's domestic capacity to absorb commodities that were previously exported to the Gulf. Whereas Iraq's exports to its six Arab Gulf neighbours reached a peak of 27.7 per cent of total non-oil exports in 1968, they had dropped to 17.3 per cent by 1970 and were only marginally up, to 19.3 per cent, in 1973.[19] Some diversification did take place during this period. In the mid-1960s items exported to the area were mainly agricultural, including grain, dates, vegetables, fruit and live animals. The only industrial raw material of any consequence was cement, destined mainly for Kuwait and Bahrain. By the early 1970s the overall list had grown to include tobacco and tobacco products, milk and milk products, sugar products, edible oils, asbestos, fertilisers, liquid propane gas, clothing and shoes. The increase in the variety of exports, however, was not accompanied by a consistent increase in the real value of exports to all the countries concerned. Iraqi commentators attribute this phenomenon to three main factors. First, trade relations were not planned, they were simply a function of Iraq's own exportable surpluses. Second, Iraqi goods were (it is claimed) at a disadvantage in some Gulf states because of competition from the Far East and Iran. Cement from Pakistan and Singapore was reportedly cheaper for Gulf buyers than cement from Iraq, while the market for foodstuffs was 'monopolised' by Iranian merchants. According to one estimate,[20] only 700 shops out of a total of 5,500 in Qatar in this period were run by native Qatari Arabs. The rest were owned by Iranians (3,500 shops), Indians (1,000 shops) and Arabs from other countries (300 shops). Iranian, or Iranian-born, merchants were said to have been equally active in Bahrain and the UAE. Third, an increase in construction activity in Iraq led to a decline in the availability of cement for export. As for Iraqi imports from Gulf states, other than goods transiting Kuwaiti ports, these were extremely limited.

There is some evidence that the imbalance in Iraq-Gulf trade is now being reversed, i.e. that imports from the Gulf are growing and exports to the Gulf are declining. The statistics, however, are not yet available

Table 11.1: Iraqi Trade with the Gulf States, 1966-78 ($million)

Exports to	1966	1969	1972	1975	1978[a]
Kuwait	6.0	8.3	13.0	5.6	9.7
Saudi Arabia	4.4	1.7	1.8	1.8	1.4
Bahrain	1.7	1.6	1.4	0.3	5.8
UAE	−[b]	0.8	0.8	0.6	1.5
Qatar	1.1	0.9	0.1	0.7	0.9
Oman	0.1	0.2	0.1	−	−
Imports from	1966	1969	1972	1975	1978[a]
Kuwait	0.9	1.2	4.9	298.2[c]	87.6
Saudi Arabia	−	−	−	1.7	1.7
Bahrain	1.9	−	−	−[b]	0.3
UAE	−	−	−	−	3.9
Qatar	0.2	0.2	−	−	n.a.
Oman	−[b]	0.4	0.2	−	−

Notes: a. No later figures are available for Iraq.
   b. Less than 0.1.
   c. Including re-exports.
Sources: Gulf Organisation for Industrial Consulting (figures submitted to author);
and Central Statistical Organisation, *Iraq Statistical Abstract 1977* (Ministry of
Planning, Baghdad, 1978), p. 21.

to prove this. Some observers would say that Iraq's failure to make
substantial progress in the non-oil sector is beginning to make itself
felt.[21] Internal consumption of foods that were previously exported is
now reaching unprecedented levels. One aspect of this is that food
shortages have been almost totally eliminated since the start of the war
with Iran in September 1980. Demand for cement, meanwhile, has
increased so rapidly that the Ministry of Industry expects its 20-million-
ton annual production target set for 1983 to meet local requirements
only. Conversely, industrial imports are now arriving in Iraq from
Kuwait, Bahrain and the UAE. Kuwait, as mentioned above, is
supplying construction materials, while Bahrain, under a free trade
agreement signed last year, is providing aluminium in return for which
Bahraini importers will be entitled to duty-free purchases of Iraqi rice,
ghee and vegetables. A similar agreement, involving Dubai aluminium,
has been negotiated with the UAE, while trade talks of a more general
nature have also been held with Saudi Arabia. There is a problem here,
in that Iraqi officials, besides having doubts about their cement exports,

are also uncertain as to how soon food exports can resume at any significant level. Nevertheless, it is worth noting that it has been Iraqi policy in recent years to foster trade with Gulf partners, while the growth of non-oil trading contacts with Arab countries such as Syria and Egypt (members with Iraq in the lifeless Arab Common Market) appears to have been impeded by political differences.

Transport and Tourism

Iraq's increased reliance on Gulf ports, though brought to world attention by the Iraq-Iran war, in fact predated it by several months. The ports of Basra and Umm Qasr have proved to be incapable of coping with import requirements even in normal circumstances. As long ago as April 1975 Iraq made an agreement with Jordan to import 0.3 million tons of goods through Aqaba, in return for which it provided Jordan with soft loans to finance expansion of the port and construction of roads from Aqaba to Iraq. In the spring of 1980 this agreement was renewed to allow for 1.5 million tons of Iraq-bound goods to pass through Aqaba by mid-1981, increasing to a ceiling of 2 million tons a year by 1982. Access to Aqaba alone, however, was not enough. Unwilling to rely on transit through Syria (which had blocked the route to Iraq-bound goods at the beginning of 1978) the obvious alternatives were ports in Kuwait and the UAE. In the early summer of 1980 Kuwait allocated a combined total of four berths in the ports of Shuwaikh and Shuwaiba for the exclusive use of vessels carrying cargo to Iraq. This agreement, made when 185 ships were waiting to enter Basra, was expected to make possible the transit of 2 million tons a year. It was soon followed by a similar deal with the Sharjah Port Authority, allowing for the transhipment of an unspecified volume of goods (mainly timber and steel) through Port Khalid. By the time the war started in September, transit agreements were also under negotiation with Abu Dhabi and Dubai.

The Kuwaiti and Iraqi governments have agreed to build a railway line linking their two countries as the first step in the construction of a railway network linking all the Gulf states. The feasibility study for this project was completed in 1980 and the go-ahead was finally given early in 1981. The two sides will reportedly pay construction costs inside their respective territories for a double-track railway which will handle high-speed passenger trains and some 5 million tons of freight a year. This line will continue northwards to the Iraqi border with

Syria—the Baghdad-Hussaiba stretch having already gone ahead because of the need to transport phosphates from the newly opened mines at Akashat. Iraq signed the necessary transit agreements relating to a railway link with Kuwait and Saudi Arabia in 1978. The project itself, having now been agreed with Kuwait, will be presented to Saudi Arabia and other Gulf states at a later stage.

Finally, tourism is an area in which the Iraqi government has encouraged contacts with other Gulf states. While its ancient monuments could have considerable attraction for Western tourists, Iraq has so far shown little or no interest in accommodating them. Hotel-construction programmes to date have been intended mainly to serve foreign businessmen and official delegations. There is some question as to whether the hotel capacity required for the non-aligned summit meeting which Baghdad is due to host in September 1982 will serve the international tourist market once the summit is over. For its own nationals, however, and for other Arabs, Iraq is building holiday resorts geared not to sightseeing but to enjoyment of riverside and lakeside leisure pursuits. Iraqi and other Arab private interests are being offered investment incentives in the form of low-interest loans covering up to 60 per cent, or sometimes even 80 per cent, of the capital cost of a tourist project. These incentives, announced in mid-1979, also include income tax relief for five years after the start of the scheme and further tax concessions after that.

It is fairly clear that the Iraqi government intends the measures promoting investment in tourist projects to attract Gulf investors, since entrepreneurs from other parts of the Arab world are likely to have potential tourist attractions nearer home. Iraq has, in fact, signed an automatically renewable five-year tourism co-operation agreement with Bahrain, designed to promote tourism in both countries by means of joint festivals, joint hotel training schemes and co-ordination of tour operators' planning and marketing. Iraqi officials explain their overall objective in the area as being to 'break down barriers; to get Gulf people to visit Iraq, mix with each other and exchange ideas'. The Planning Ministry confirmed to the writer that applications have been received from Gulf nationals who want to invest in tourist resorts in the north and in the marshes.

Conclusion

The economic links being forged between Iraq and other Arab Gulf states are, in most cases, less than five years old. Despite this they appear at present to be stronger, more diverse and more considered than links with any of Iraq's other Arab neighbours (Jordan and Syria) or indeed countries elsewhere in the Arab world. Iraq does have special relations with some Arab countries outside the Gulf (e.g. refinery investments in Tunisia and Somalia, oil supplies to Morocco, extensive aid to Jordan and North Yemen) but these are not on the same regionally institutionalised basis as ties with the Gulf. Iraq's relations with Gulf states are not those of aid-giver and aid-receiver but of countries which share the same dependence on oil and the same fears about security, within and without. In its links with Gulf states, the Baghdad government has shown that it is ready to sweep ideological differences aside. Officials questioned about these differences are fond of explaining: 'We concentrate on the things we can agree on', or 'The Gulf countries know the Iranian risk is theirs too'.

Among the few people in Baghdad who have the authority to make pronouncements about such important issues as the Gulf Co-operation Council, there seems to be a complete lack of concern that Iraq is not a founder-member. This is matched by a similar indifference regarding the Council's ideological bias. The stock response in this context is:

I think any aggregation of two or more Arab states is good, whatever direction it takes. The Arab world was a bigger entity that has been fragmented; it's good to start putting the pieces of the jigsaw back together, even if it's only two or three countries at a time.

Besides its economic and security links with the Council's members, Iraq is also taking part with them in regional media and cultural co-operation, covering everything from joint television broadcasts to poetry festivals. When the formation of the Gulf Co-operation Council was announced, Iraq's Information Minister was taking part with his Gulf colleagues in an annual meeting in Oman.

Iraqi officials know that there is not a complete coincidence of views within the Council itself. Kuwait, for example, does not see eye-to-eye with Saudi Arabia on all issues and, on some of these, it agrees with Iraq. Kuwaiti Oil Minister Shaikh Ali Khalifah al-Sabah has spoken out recently against large-scale participation by major international companies in Gulf refining and petrochemical ventures, warning that the majors will 'expend all possible efforts to delay co-operation between Gulf countries in product pricing and marketing'.[22] Likewise the Kuwaiti government pays more than lip-service to non-alignment, as was evident in the Foreign Minister's April visit to Moscow and the government's rejection of an Omani formula for Gulf security which would have entailed extensive Western participation. Iraqi officials also know that they have the only credible army in the Gulf and by far the greatest agricultural potential — assets of considerable importance to their southern neighbours. It is fair to assume that Kuwait, and possibly Bahrain and the UAE, would, in the long run, favour Iraqi participation in the Council as a counterweight to Saudi Arabia.

These factors, combined with the economic co-operation efforts outlined in this chapter, suggest that Iraq — at least in its own eyes — is now a fully paid-up member of a budding Arab Gulf community. As such it is a serious candidate for regional leadership.

Notes

1. *Al-Rai al-Aam* (Kuwait), 16 Apr. 1981.
2. Iraq claims the war began on 4 September not 22 September, and that it was started by Iran.
3. *Financial Times*, 6 Feb. 1981.
4. G. Benton, 'Iraq's Port of Call Abroad', *The Middle East*, Dec. 1980, p. 64.
5. Bahrain's influential Minister of Development, Yousif al-Shirawi, is known to think along these lines.
6. Interview with Patrick Seale in *Observer*, 15 Feb. 1981.
7. See E. Ghareeb, 'Iraq: Emergent Gulf Power', in H. Amirsadeghi, *The Security of the Persian Gulf* (Croom Helm, London, 1981), pp. 197-230.
8. Information for this and following paragraphs comes from successive issues of *Middle East Economic Digest*, 1975.
9. Dr Sabah Kachachi, Adviser for Industrial Affairs Planning, made this remark to the writer in 1978. Dr Kachachi made the same remark, more recently, to Peter Mansfield in a BBC Radio 4 broadcast entitled 'Saddam's Babylon', 15 Mar. 1981.
10. R. Smythe, 'Agriculture and Consultancy', in 'Arab British Chamber of Commerce', *Focus on Iraq*, July 1980, p. 21.
11. N. Sakr, 'Food Seen as Future Defence Weapon', *The Middle East*, Feb. 1979, p. 117.
12. C. Wright, 'Secrets of Iraq's Oil Sale Surge', *The Middle East*, Aug. 1980, p. 54.
13. Food and Agriculture Organisation, *Joint Programme for the Production of Cereals and Fodder in the Gulf and Arabian Peninsula* (FAO, Rome, Dec. 1979), part IV.
14. A description of other ways (e.g. nuclear food research, water supply, stockpiling, etc.) in which Iraq is equipped to contribute to a Gulf food programme is given in N. Sakr, 'The Potential for an Iraqi Contribution to Gulf Food Security', Paper presented to the Fourth International Symposium of the Centre for Arab Gulf Studies, University of Basra, Mar. 1981.
15. Interview with the writer, Baghdad, 2 Apr. 1981.
16. Dr Saadoun Qassab, Director of Follow-up at the Ministry of Industry, told the writer in December 1978: 'We finished the studies for the aluminium

smelter almost two years ago but we revised our plans because by then some of our brothers had entered the same field. You see, we are trying to take others' plans into account, even if they don't do the same for us.'

17. Statement made by Iraq's representative to GOIC, Akram Mohieddin Kumait, to the writer, Baghdad, 2 Apr. 1981.

18. *Mideast Markets*, 30 June 1980.

19. Figures and some information for this section are taken from Medhat al-Hayyali, *An Analysis of Economic Relations between the Republic of Iraq and the Arab Gulf Countries* (Centre for Arab Gulf Studies, Basra, 1978).

20. Ibid.

21. Economist Intelligence Unit, 'Iraq: A New Market in a Region of Turmoil', EIU Special Report no. 88, 1980, pp. 80-2.

22. *Middle East Economic Survey*, 11 May 1981.

12 IRAQI OIL POLICY: 1961-1976

Paul Stevens

Introduction

There are numerous problems which arise when attempting to divine policy objectives and the use of policy tools with respect to an oil producer.[1] In the case of Iraq, moreover, the general problems are compounded by the excessive secrecy which cloaks the actual workings of the oil sector. Many of the conventional information sources, such as the annual *OPEC Statistical Bulletin*, have severe gaps on the Iraqi pages.[2] This adds considerably to the amount of detective work required, and also increases the risk of misinterpretation of developments in the oil sector. Both the figures and the analysis in this chapter, therefore, should be treated with care.

The period covered begins in 1961, with the enactment of Law 80 which sequestered virtually all of the concession area of the Iraq Petroleum Company (IPC)—except for the fields actually in production. In Iraq, however, there can be no convenient starting-date since it is impossible to begin to understand the issues in Iraqi oil policy unless the pre-1961 period is considered. It was from the earlier period that so many of the problems and constraints stemmed. Fortunately, there has been considerable documentation of this earlier period[3] and so reference to it can be limited to some broad conclusions, with quotations for the sceptic who wishes to examine the proof underlying the conclusions. The end of the period also presents problems. In one sense it ends with the enactment of Law 101 in October 1976 which reorganised the administration of the oil sector. Some of the narrative, however, continues into more recent times. How far the conclusions drawn for the period between 1961 and 1976 carry on into this later period is far from clear and is a matter of some heated debate. Unfortunately, the dearth of adequate information makes it virtually impossible to be certain.

There are four sections to the chapter. The first section examines the main targets of policy associated with the oil sector in very broad terms. The targets are identified as independent oil development and the use of the oil sector as the engine for economic development. The second section examines what policy tools were available to the government of Iraq and what constraints acted upon the use of those tools. The third section concerns itself with an evaluation of the successes of the policy, given the original policy objectives. These three sections deal in very broad terms. The fourth section takes a case study – the 1968 ERAP agreement – to examine one issue in some detail, based on fieldwork carried out by the author in London, Beirut and Baghdad in 1971. The reason for this particular case study is that in many ways it epitomises in specific terms many of the generalities discussed in the earlier sections.

It may be helpful at this stage to indicate the basic hypothesis which the chapter is seeking to justify. It is contended that during the period under consideration, Iraqi oil policy was relatively unsuccessful. The basic cause of the lack of success was the politicisation of the oil sector. The politicisation interacted with another factor – the legacy of the past – and made it impossible for political leaders to solve the problems of the oil industry. The failure of the oil policy, however, did not result in lasting damage, if only because oil in the ground is a non-perishable item. Future generations of Iraqis may well be grateful for these earlier failures of policy.

Oil Sector Targets

There have been many official statements regarding the objectives of Iraqi oil policy. The targets consistently emphasised have been to develop the oil sector on an independent basis and to use oil as an engine of development. For example, '[the] foremost objectives [are] the establishment of a national oil industry free from world monopoly and capable to support national economy [*sic*] through oil exploitation and export by the INOC'.[4] (The INOC is the state-owned Iraq National Oil Company, established in 1958.) In the latter half of the 1970s greater public emphasis was placed on such aspects as 'the consolidation of relationships between oil producers and the Third World' (Sa'adoun Hammadi, Foreign Minister)[5] and 'to help establish a fair new international economic order' (Tayeh Abd al-Karim, Oil Minister).[6] How far such concepts have really affected policy is not clear, but it is only fair to point out that Iraq's record on aid-giving appears good[7] and she has pressed hard for the development of institutional arrangements to assist Third World countries.[8] While in recent years a greater degree of pragmatism in policy orientation has been suggested, it is nevertheless the first two objectives mentioned which can be regarded as providing the principal motivation. In mid-1975, Saddam Husain – the then vice-president – was quoted as saying in a closed session at the OPEC summit that 'Arab states were obliged to develop their policies strictly in line with what was practicable and what would serve their development goals'.[9]

Independent Oil Development

The issue of Iraqi involvement in its oil industry began with the first concession in 1925[10] and has been a consistent theme ever since. At the Eighth Regional Conference of the Ba'th Party in January 1974, for example, President Bakr declared that 'the total liberation of Iraq's economy and resources from any foreign control has been and will remain at the base of our development strategy'.[11] The most specific and detailed exposition of this conception was given in 1968 when Khair al-Din Hasib developed the theme in an article published in the May issue of *Dirasat 'Arabiyyah*.[12] This was in the context of a dispute between two schools of thought then prevalent in the administration. The first held the view that the way forward lay through an accommodation with the oil companies since, given Iraq's dependence on oil, it was not possible to confront the companies. The second school of thought was that it was precisely because of this dependence on oil revenues, which put Iraq 'at the mercy of the oil companies', that Iraq should 'end the foreign control of this vital sector'. This school advocated that Iraq's oil policy should pass through two phases. In the first phase, covering three to five years, the government should establish and develop a national oil sector independent of the companies,[13] gain access to crude markets, diversify Iraq's sources of income and accumulate currency reserves. In the second, longer-term stage the government would acquire full control of the foreign companies, using the success of stage one to provide the muscle to fight and the experience to capitalise on the victory.[14]

   That independent development was a key goal – if not the key goal – can be seen from actions as well as words. The whole programme of building crude-oil pipelines in the 1970s was geared to this aim. Both the Haditha-Rumaila strategic pipeline[15] and the Kirkuk-Dortyol line[16] were designed to break out of the dependence of Iraqi crude exports on other countries or companies. Similarly, there has been a great reluctance to use foreign companies in all sectors of Iraq's economy.[17] Where companies have been used, turnkey projects have been strongly favoured – despite the growing evidence of the unsuitability of such projects in Third World countries. As will become apparent throughout the rest of this chapter, there are numerous other examples which confirm the supremacy of independent development as an objective in the oil sector.

Oil as an Engine for Development

That oil development is seen as the key to wider economic development is evident from the scale of Iraq's development programmes, and the extent to which those programmes depend on oil production to provide the necessary finance – or, perhaps, a raw material input. Since the very early days the function of oil revenues has been seen as that of financing development. For example, the Iraq Development Board which was created in 1950 was to receive all the government's oil revenues, although in 1952 this was reduced to 70 per cent of the revenues and in 1958 to 50 per cent.[18] All of the development plans produced by the Ministry of Planning have had the same objectives – namely industrialisation, diversification, reduced dependence on crude oil exports and greater oil-processing capacity. In the last ten years the emphasis on costly schemes of industrialisation has probably increased. For example, in the 1976-80 plan the output of manufacturing industry was planned to grow by 32.9 per cent compared with the overall growth target of 16.8 per cent. This confirms the fact that 'industry apparently holds a favoured position within the development objectives of the Ba'th Government'.[19] Given the factor endowment of Iraq, this means that 'petrochemicals are emerging as the principal area of state investment'.[20]

The critical importance of oil revenues to the wider developmental effort is indicated by the effects which financial constraints – caused by disputes with the oil companies impairing revenues – have had on the development programmes. The conventional wisdom is that the lack of financial stability had been a major factor in slowing development. Thus 'the timing and pace of construction of the petrochemical industry have been erratic, with projects adopted or postponed depending on the availability of finance for the plan'.[21] Similarly, in a discussion of the causes of delays in projects, one trade paper suggested that 'it is far more likely . . . that it is finance . . . which is behind the delay'.[22] This view appears to be supported by the extent to which Iraq has borrowed abroad. In mid-1975, for example, Iraq borrowed $500 million on the Eurocurrency markets, and in the same year it was widely rumoured in Beirut that Iraq had obtained a $200 million loan from Saudi Arabia.[23] Also in 1975, Iraq undertook a series of legislative acts to attract Arab capital, including the provision of free movement of funds and affording Arab capital the same privileges and exemptions as Iraqi capital.[24]

In all probability, the extent of the real barrier to development presented by revenue constraints has been overstated, especially when one considers the other very considerable problems associated with development. Thus of the 1.25 billion Iraqi Dinars (ID) allocated for expenditure on development during the 1951-64 period only 46 per cent was actually spent, and of the 2.256 billion ID allocated between 1965 and 1975 only 60 per cent was spent.[25] Some of this shortfall, of course, may have been caused by revenue shortages, particularly during periods of maximum dispute with the IPC, but it is likely that other factors were more responsible. There can nevertheless be little doubt that the view of a financial constraint on development has become a central pillar in Iraqi thinking, both official and unofficial. Thus an official government publication in 1974, discussing the background to Law 80, talks about the companies being determined to 'exert pressure on Iraq and deny it the additional revenues required for the growth of its economy'.[26]

The importance of this in the argument is as follows. It is a central theme of this chapter that one of the key signals of the failure of Iraqi oil policy was the failure to develop oil-producing capital and use it. The development of capacity needed to be sufficient to cover the financing of the country's development programmes. It may be argued that at least since 1973 finance has been broadly sufficient and that Iraq has not wanted to acquire large financial surpluses. But this view ignores the fact that revenues were only 'sufficient' because of exogenous price rises in 1973 and again in 1978-9. Thus the availability of revenues owes little or nothing to Iraqi oil policy since these price increases could not have been reasonably foreseen. Had the price rises not occurred then the failure of the policy would have been very apparent. As it turned out, exogenous changes disguised the failure. Alternatively, if and when revenues were insufficient, the policy clearly had failed.

Oil Policy Tools and their Constraints

In general terms the policy tools available stem from the ability of the Iraqi government to take administrative decisions. We will now examine, therefore, the administrative structure through which decisions on oil are made, together with two crucially important areas of administrative decision – namely production and pricing.

Administrative Decisions

Since 1968 the Revolutionary Command Council (RCC), representing the ultimate authority in the administrative structure, has held overall responsibility for decision-making on oil. Given the nature of the RCC's coverage, however, it can only deal in terms of broad generalities, and the specifics of the oil sector have therefore been vested in a committee responsible to the RCC: the Follow-up Committee for Oil Affairs and the Implementation of Agreements. The Ministry of Oil works under the general direction of the Follow-up Committee. The broad strategy of the Follow-up Committee was outlined in the ten-year sectoral development plan for the oil industry, which emerged in 1971. This envisaged:

(1) The increase of the capacity of the Iraq-Mediterranean (Banias and Tripoli) pipeline network from 60 to 70 million tons annually.

(2) The construction of a new Iraq-Turkey pipeline with an initial annual capacity of 25 million tons, to be raised later to 35 million tons.

(3) The construction of the Haditha-Fao 'strategic pipeline'. (According to INOC's programme this pipeline can be utilised in 'normal times' to carry 44 million tons annually from the southern fields to Haditha then to the Mediterranean and, in 'emergency cases', to carry 50 million tons annually from the northern fields to the Gulf. The 'emergency cases' refer to possible interruptions of Iraqi oil-pumping to the Mediterranean.)

(4) The increase of the capacity of the pipelines connecting the southern fields to Fao terminal to 120 million tons annually.

(5) The construction of a deep-water terminal at Khor al-Khafja in the Gulf with an 80 million-ton per year capacity, which could be raised to 120 million tons per year.

(6) The enlargement of Fao terminal to raise its loading capacity to 15-18 million tons per year.

(7) The increase of the loading capacity of Khor al-Amaya terminal to 80 million tons per year.

(8) The exploitation of associated gas produced in Iraq's southern and northern fields.

(9) The construction of new refineries in Iraq and in 'the

Arab and friendly countries'.
(10) The development of the tanker fleet so as to be able to carry at least 10 per cent of the national production.[27]

The plan also contained the production targets which will be discussed below.

In January 1973, the Follow-up Committee took over direct responsibility for INOC, with powers of veto over any INOC decision. In January 1974 the Committee also took over responsibility for marketing crude oil[28] and in mid-1975 took on the job of reviewing all agreements, oil or otherwise, before conclusion.[29] Attached to the Committee there was an Advisory Council for Oil Affairs, which effectively served as the secretariat of the Committee.[30] During the period before 1976 when the Committee was taking on more detailed responsibility, the Council became particularly influential – in part because the nine members consisted largely of technical experts who knew the oil industry well. Clearly in 1973-4 the Oil Ministry experienced a substantial diminution of power. Several explanations have been offered for this. The current official Iraqi explanation is that it was due to the reorganisation of the IPC in 1972. Alternative explanations concern internal political wrangling.[31]

In November 1974 the oil portfolio went to Tayeh Abd al-Karim in a cabinet reshuffle. This seems to have ushered in a new phase in Iraq's oil administration. Under Law 101 (1976) many of the responsibilities of the Follow-up Committee reverted to the Oil Ministry, and in 1976 the Ministry also regained direct control of INOC. Specifically, the Ministry

shall be responsible for the management of the oil sector which involves carrying out operations for oil and gas exploration, drilling and production, as well as refining and gas processing in addition to the transportation and marketing of oil and gas and their products, the execution of oil projects and the importation of the sector's specialized requirements.[32]

All implementing bodies reverted to the control of the Ministry. The Follow-up Committee, however, did continue to provide guidelines for the Ministry and to monitor developments. The change was intended merely to relieve the Committee of the pressure of minor details and to allow it to concentrate on the key areas of policy. There was no diminution of the Committee's power.

Since Law 101, several additions have been made to the structure such as the Energy Affairs Planning Administration[33] and a Supreme Technical Authority responsible for the development of new fields.[34] This structure – the working problems of which will be discussed below – has the power to take decisions in order to implement policy.

The administrative structure of the Iraqi oil sector has probably been one of the main causes of the relative failure of Iraqi oil policy. The central constraint on the successful operation of the oil sector in the period under consideration is that officials have been unwilling to take critical decisions, and that a large number of experienced, highly skilled technocrats have left (or been expelled from) the oil industry. Both of these factors, as will be expounded on below, stem from the fact that 'political conflict . . . [in Iraq] . . . is resolved by violence, revolt and coercion'.[35] With this background we can turn to examine two specific areas of administrative decision which can be viewed as policy tools – production and pricing.

Production

Since the very early days, the issue of production has been a central point of contention in Iraqi oil affairs. Before 1939, there was consider-able dissatisfaction by the Iraqi government with the offtake levels of IPC.[36] This was compounded after 1945 as the world moved into a situation of relative oil glut and Iraq – due to the structure of the IPC group[37] – was effectively used as an oil stockpile by the major oil companies.[38] After the issuing of Law 80 in 1961 the situation reached its nadir when the IPC group added a recriminatory element to its 'stockpiling' behaviour.

With this background it is hardly surprising that the main thrust of the production policy was to expand capacity and output as rapidly as possible. Before the 1970s, the ability of the Iraqi government to achieve an expansion was strictly limited. IPC still retained control over the bulk of production and INOC had failed to generate very much output. In the 1971 ten-year plan for the oil sector, the original production target for 1980-1 was a production capacity of 242 million tons per year (mty). In 1972 this figure was increased to 325 mty, but in June 1975 it was reduced to 200 mty.[39] In a statement in mid-1980, Oil Minister Tayeh Abd al-Karim stated that capacity had reached 200 mty, with production varying between 160 and 185 mty 'depending on demand and financial needs'.[40] While the 1980 target (as redefined in 1975) does appear to have been reached, however, the interim figures were well below target. In February 1974, for example, it was announced that Iraq's production was to reach 3.5 million barrels per day (mbd) by 1975,[41] but the actual figure for 1975 was only 2.26 mbd.[42]

As well as productive capacity, great emphasis was laid upon exploration. In 1974 reserves of crude were estimated at 35 billion barrels, but in March 1975 an official spokesman claimed that the real figure was closer to 75 billion barrels. In June 1975 the exploration priority was formalised with the inauguration of a five-year exploration programme costing some $1.5 billion.[43]

The final strand to the use of production as a policy tool concerned trying to secure markets for the anticipated increased output. There was in Iraq a very strong feeling that production levels had fallen well below the levels they ought to be at, largely as a penalty for the moves taken by Iraq against the IPC—from which it was claimed the other Arab oil-producers gained.[44] Therefore it was felt only reasonable that other oil-producers should, if necessary, reduce their production in order to make way for a rapid expansion of Iraqi output. It is this factor which has been behind the continual calls by Iraq for 'pro-rationing' in OPEC. The first such call was made in 1973[45] and the most recent was in mid-1980 when Tayeh Abd al-Karim called for pro-rationing to 'minimise harmful competition'.[46]

The constraints on the use of the production tool are of two types—voluntarily incurred restraints and exogenous constraints. The first type derives from decisions taken by the Iraqi government. Thus one official statement listed the factors which would influence the production decision as including the financial needs of Iraq and the size of the oil reserves.[47] Narrowing this down even further in December 1973, Oil Minister Sa'adoun Hammadi indicated that 'it is now the requirements of the economic development plans which decide the level of oil production and the size of our oil reserves'.[48] Constraints of a non-voluntary nature are probably more numerous. The first concerns the geographic location of Iraq and the oil fields within Iraq. In 1973, for example, Sa'adoun Hammadi stated that 'the production of the INOC is restricted not because of the productive capacity of the fields but because of the limited capacity of the port installations. The same is true of the productivity capacity of the northern fields'.[49] These problems of getting the oil out are clearly reflected in many of the projects undertaken in the 1971 ten-year plan. The completion of many of these projects, noticeably the two pipe-lines, considerably eased the problem.

A second problem concerns access to technology. For reasons to be

described below Western oil companies provided very little techno-
logical assistance before 1972 and much of the technology had to be
imported from the Soviet bloc. While Soviet technology in a Third
World context has the advantages of being less sophisticated than its
Western counterpart and therefore more amenable to a 'learning by
doing process', it also tends to be less effective. Among the more recent
technical assistance agreements with the Soviet Union was one in
December 1979, which committed the Soviet Union to assisting Iraq
to increase the production of the North Rumaila field to 42 mty.[50]
Interestingly enough, this figure had originally been targeted to be
reached in the early 1970s; recent estimates suggest that production is
only around 18 mty, and that with considerable technical problems.[51]
Finally, there is the problem of being able to dispose of the crude —
which brings us to the second area of policy tools, namely price.

Price

Price as a policy tool is the obverse of the production tool. In its use,
Iraq has always tended to be lumped in with the so-called OPEC
'hawks'. While there were clear signs of Iraq's delight over the 1973-4
price increases, however, Iraq also expressed concern over the impact
which the rapid increases in price would have on the oil-consumers. It
would be easy to reject this concern as mere political rhetoric, but Iraq
did have good reason for concern: she was about to embark on a very
large production expansion. This expansion would inevitably create
marketing problems in the aftermath of the price increases. When the
market firmed up in the latter part of 1976, however, Iraq was clearly
on the side of the 'hawks' calling for price increases of 15 per cent
rising by the end of the year to 26 per cent.[52] Broadly speaking, Iraqi
policy had been to charge whatever the market would take. If this
meant cutting the price, then the price was cut. Thus in July 1974 the
price of Kirkuk crude on the Mediterranean was reduced from $12.20
to $11.50 per barrel, and in January 1975 to $11.20. Apart from these
official cuts, moreover, Iraq was consistently accused by other OPEC
members of secret price-cutting, an accusation vehemently denied by
the Iraqis.[53]

   Iraq's official policy has always been to eschew the accumulation of
large official reserves. Thus, in 1979, the Director-General of the
Foreign Relations Department in the Ministry of Oil stated that 'Iraq
is not producing more than it needs . . . revenues [from oil] are only
50 per cent of the national income and the proportion has been progressively lowered'.[54] This is, however, not incompatible with charging the

highest price possible since the equation can always be balanced by reducing output.

The Effectiveness of Iraqi Oil Policy

Given that production levels had been at the heart of the disputes with the IPC, and given the innumerable references to the aim of expanding productive capacity in the context of an 'independent oil policy', it is in terms of this production criterion that the success or failure of Iraqi policy can largely be judged. On this basis, at least up to the mid-1970s the policy had failed. In order to justify such a conclusion it is necessary to place it in the context of the dispute with the oil companies. Although the dispute effectively began with the bitterness over the very first concession,[55] it escalated largely as the consequence of the structure of the IPC. Crude-surplus companies had been linked with crude-deficit companies, which meant that complex and cumbersome agreements had to be drawn up in order to provide an operational whole.[56] The consequence was that Iraqi production became victim to the whims of the general world supply picture, and the diversity of ownership of the IPC meant that any negotiations with the Iraqi government always fell foul of the fact that a concession to the Iraqi government endangered —from the companies' point of view—a very large number of agreements elsewhere.

The watershed, and the opportunity, came with Law 80 of 1961, which sequestered virtually all of the IPC concession area except for the fields actually in production. This injected the administrative system with its first constraint. As a result of Law 80 there could be no co-operation with the companies. The IPC companies appeared willing to reach an accommodation, as witnessed by the attempted agreement of 1965,[57] but it had become politically impossible for the Iraqi government to accept the IPC's terms. Given the world oversupply situation, the IPC could afford to be intransigent on terms. In a sense the Iraqi government had become victim of its own rhetoric against the companies. While non-IPC companies were very willing to involve themselves in Iraq, most of them were unwilling to do so until the IPC withdrew its objections to Law 80.[58] In such a situation independent development was the only possible path, but for a very long time Iraq had neither the political will nor the expertise to follow such a path.

While difficulties with a still-independent IPC explain the failure of Iraq's oil industry to expand in the 1960s, it was problems inherent in

Iraq's own management of its oil resources which account for the
failure to expand productive capacity in the 1970s. After the nationalisation of the IPC's assets in Iraq in 1972, oil production did increase,
but the productive capacity does not seem to have expanded
significantly. Due to the dearth of public information on Iraqi oil
production, this point is difficult to substantiate definitively. The
problem is in knowing what the IPC capacity was in 1972 at the time
of nationalisation. OPEC figures suggest that the daily average production
in 1973 was 2.02 million barrels per day (mbd) and by 1978 this had
risen to 2.6 mbd. Unless the IPC capacity is known, however, it is
impossible to tell how far this increase and subsequent increases were
the result of Iraqi efforts and how far it was inherited capacity which
merely needed the turning of a tap to bring onstream.

There is, in fact, one clue to the IPC capacity given by an official
Iraqi source.[59] During the negotiations in May 1972 the final offer
submitted by the companies before nationalisation offered to increase
production to some 3 mbd by 1977. Given past history, it would appear
unlikely that such an offer would have been made if any large amount
of investment in capacity was required. Given the Iraqi production of
2.6 mbd in 1978, and assuming the IPC offer was genuine,[60] this
suggests that much of the increase in production after 1972 was the
result of inheriting excess capacity rather than developing new
capacity.

This evidence is not conclusive but it does tend to point in favour
of the argument that Iraq failed to develop her oil capacity satisfactorily.
The failure of the policy was a result of a general paralysis during the
1960s which appears to have spilled over into the following decade.
Behind this paralysis, three main factors can be identified which
impinged heavily on the operation of oil policy: the use of political
criteria to operate tactical policy (as opposed to political criteria to
determine strategic objectives, which is usual); bureaucratic paralysis;
and a phobic distrust of the oil companies. Each of these will now be
examined.

The Use of Political Criteria

Examples of the domination of the use of political criteria abound
throughout the period. Two more recent examples will serve to illustrate.
In mid-1979 Iraq approved the development of the Majnoon field with
the Brazilian company Braspetro; Brazilian sources indicated that the
decision of the Iraqi government was conditional upon acceptance by
Brazil of 'Iraqi political conditions'.[61] Around the same period, Iraq

announced that it was to maintain 100,000 barrels a day of extra crude supplies to France in 1980; French sources described this as 'a political response to a political request'.[62] Examples from earlier periods are also apparent in the case study given below.

The problem with political criteria is that, in practice, as the basis for tactical (as opposed to strategic) decisions it tends to mean no criteria at all. This is because identifying the gains and losses is very imprecise. Given the political in-fighting which has dominated Iraqi politics, and the often very bloody consequences, it is hardly surprising that decision-takers would be reluctant to take decisions on such a basis. This is compounded in the oil sector, moreover, by the high level of risk involved and the high level of complexity. In such a context it is very easy to attack a decision on the grounds of 'corruption' or 'treachery'. Therefore risk-averters will simply seek to take no decision or, if forced to, delegate the decision elsewhere.

The creators of the INOC were, of course, well aware of the problems of operating in an Iraqi political environment. When the INOC was set up in 1964 by Law 11 the company was structured in such a way as to minimise the impact of this political in-fighting. Thus the company was to be administered by a board of nine members, only three of whom were to be 'senior government officials', i.e. political appointees. The remainder were to be specialists whose function was – presumably – to take action using economic and technical criteria. Such a 'non-political' grouping, however, was bound to be left out in the wilderness in the politically orientated government structure. When this point is coupled with the very limited resources given to the INOC at its creation, it is not surprising that the company was ineffective in its first few years. In September 1967, the INOC was completely restructured by Law 123. The President and Chairman of the Board – a political appointment – was given much greater powers to operate, which resulted in the ousting of the technocrats. As a result, the INOC could become an effective body in the government, but its politicisation meant that decision-taking was now slowed down by risk-averters concerned that any decision made by them could be dragged up later and used in evidence against them.

There were signs by the mid-1970s that other criteria were being increasingly applied at project level in an attempt to order the development of the oil sector along more clearly defined lines. One source, for example, suggested that 'Iraq's investment programme [for 1976] . . . already shows signs that projects are being rigorously appraised for their profitability'.[63]

Bureaucratic Paralysis

Part of the reason for the bureaucratic paralysis lies in the effects of using political criteria as described above. This was compounded by the very rapid turnover in staff. The latter aspect stemmed on the one hand from the constant reordering of the administrative structure described above, and on the other from the political in-fighting which so often led to purges of ministers and officials. One source points out that between 1964 and 1968 there were eight ministers of industry, seven ministers of public works, six agriculture ministers and six planning ministers.[64] Such changes in personnel are hardly likely to create an efficient team. The experience of the oil sector was no different. Up to 1967, there existed a deep-rooted conflict between the Nasserist group in the cabinet and the INOC technocrats.[65] In 1967 the technocrats were ousted from the INOC and a group took over which had a much harder attitude towards the IPC. As a result, legislation was passed which forbade the return of the Rumaila fields to the IPC.[66] Thus for the first time the scene was set for Iraq to pursue a policy of independent development in the oil sector—a move which Law 80 of 1961 had in any case made inevitable. Yet, in the military *coup* of July 1968, the main architects of this new policy were 'swept away' with the rest.[67] Thus, as one writer puts it, the decade after 1958 was characterised by 'conspiracies and bureaucratic manoeuvring'.[68] After the Ba'th Party came to power in 1968, the various departments of state—including those in the oil sector—were the 'exclusive province of Ba'th party members'.[69] In February 1975 a further major shake-out occurred at the highest level,[70] which was the precursor to Law 101 (1976). More recently, in the second half of the 1970s, the situation seemed more settled—perhaps reflecting the greater security of the Ba'th government and thus something of a decline in the extent of political in-fighting.

Attitudes to the Foreign Companies

The attitude of Iraq towards the Western oil companies can best be described as a deep distrust and hatred, bordering on the psychotic. On the other hand, it must be admitted that an examination of the history of the oil companies in Iraq provides innumerable examples to justify such attitudes. In particular, the Iraqis objected to what they saw as the role of the home governments of the members of the IPC, particularly the United States and Britain. There were the initial problems over the original concession and the feeling at the time and subsequently that the unfavourable terms received by Iraq were the result of other governments' pressures, emanating in particular from Britain, which was the mandatory power. Subsequent research has shown the reality to be less damning to the British government than had been generally supposed.[71] However, truth, like beauty, lies in the eyes of the beholder, and the victimisation of Iraq has entered Iraqi folklore. Subsequent events reinforced these views. In 1958, for example, during the US-British intervention in the Middle East at the time of Qasim's coup it was reported in Washington that 'intervention will not be extended to Iraq *as long as* the revolutionary government respects [*sic*] western oil interests'.[72] It was widely believed in Iraq, moreover, that the oil companies were behind the attempted assassination of Qasim in October 1959.

This suspicion of the companies carried many ramifications during the period under consideration, not least of which was the great reluctance of the Iraqi government to enter into contact with any of the Western companies. This emerges quite clearly in the ERAP Agreement, outlined below. Iraq's experience with the companies, moreover, had significant effects on the relations with other Arab states. Specifically, as Iraq had taken the lead in confronting the companies from 1959 onwards, the Iraqi government felt entitled to support from the other Arab oil-producers and from OPEC after its formation. The failure of the other Arab producers to support Iraq — and their tendency to draw benefit from Iraq's discomfiture by increasing production — embittered Iraqi governments. Indeed, during 1961 Iraq actually withdrew from OPEC and refused to attend meetings. The Iraqi government's stand on this matter ultimately led Iraq into not giving full support to the Arab oil embargo in 1973. Although Iraq boycotted the United States and Holland, production was not cut and was, in fact, increased. While a variety of excuses were offered, the real reason was indicated by Oil Minister Hammadi when he described Iraq's action as constituting 'only partial compensation for the accumulated adverse effects stemming from the production policy followed by the oil companies'.[73]

Iraq generally felt that she had acted as pathfinder for the rest and paid the price while other producers gained the benefit. Edith Penrose disputes this view, arguing that the other countries did not actually follow Iraq and gained much more at much less cost in the early 1970s.[7] While this is true on the issue of control it is more doubtful as far as relinquishment of concession areas is concerned. After Iraq's Law 80 in 1961 a number of Arab governments seem to have been able to exert

pressure on oil companies to relinquish concession areas which they
were not exploiting. In early 1962 the Kuwait Oil Company relinquished some 50 per cent of its acreage; in early 1963 the Arabian American
Oil Company in Saudi Arabia relinquished all but 20 per cent of its
concession area; and in 1966 the Iran consortium gave up 25 per cent
of its acreage.[75] It is always dangerous to assume *post hoc ergo propter
hoc*, but in this case it seems probable that the experience of the IPC
in Iraq may have gone some way to persuading the companies of the
'equity' of relinquishing some areas. On this basis, some of Iraq's
objections were justified.

The Iraqi government's attitudes to the oil companies certainly
placed serious constraints on the development of the oil sector, at least
up until the mid-1970s. The use of political criteria and the existence
of bureaucratic paralysis meant Iraq was incapable of successfully
developing her own oil sector at the rate required, while the attitude
to the companies meant that no-one else was allowed to step in and fill
the gap.

In order to justify some of these generalities the chapter now turns
to examine a specific case study in detail. The material gathered in this
section comes mainly from discussions with the participants undertaken
in London, Beirut and Baghdad in 1971. While many of the sources had
no objection to their names being cited, some preferred to remain
anonymous. In order to respect the anonymity of the latter it seems
fairer that no sources should be cited unless they be published sources.

The ERAP Agreement

Between 1961 and 1967 several independent oil companies had enquired
after acreage but 'the attitude of these . . . companies amounted to a
candid admission that they were not prepared to develop oil whose
ownership had been unilaterally expropriated from the major
companies'.[76] Ente Nazionale Idrocarburi (ENI) was much less
concerned about such niceties, mainly because previous constraint at
the time of the Iranian nationalisation had gone unrewarded by the
major oil companies.[77] Nevertheless, every time ENI began discussions
with the Iraqis, the Italian government — ENI was state-owned — received
a flurry of diplomatic notes from the IPC participants' governments.

It became apparent that for any agreement with an oil company to
work, the home government of the company would have to be able to
withstand considerable pressure. This held true for French companies,

such as Enterprise de Recherches et d'Activités Petrolières (ERAP), as de Gaulle in the 1960s was seeking to pursue an independent foreign policy to allow 'the development of a third force . . . to influence significantly the behaviour of the big powers'.[78] France's opportunity came after the June War of 1967; ENI was now deemed politically unacceptable due to the stance taken by the Italian government in the United Nations. Negotiations with ERAP began. Following the visit of a French delegation to Baghdad led by the head of the French hydro-carbon office (a political appointment), the INOC received official instructions to 'co-operate and reach an agreement'. The French government confirmed its willingness to ignore pressure from other IPC participants' governments, showing the Iraqis secret diplomatic notes from the British government protesting about the negotiations. In February 1968, President Aref himself went to Paris to ratify the agreement.

The agreement[79] designated an area of 10,800 square kilometres in four blocks, some of which had already been explored seismically by the Basra Petroleum Company. Exploration was to last for six years, with an obligation by ERAP to spend at least $12 million. After three years, 50 per cent of the area was to be relinquished, after five years a further 25 per cent and after six years all non-producing fields were to be returned. ERAP would act as the financier of the project. If no commercial oil was found then ERAP was to bear all the costs. In the event of commercial discovery, the INOC had to repay the exploration cost — interest free — within fifteen years or at the rate of 10 US cents per barrel, whichever repaid the debt fastest. The development and production costs were also to be borne by ERAP until the INOC had a net cash flow. These costs were to be treated as an interest-bearing loan, at a rate not exceeding 6 per cent and amortised as a cost of production. Finally, ERAP was to pay a non-recoverable bonus of $15 million over the production life of the contract, which was to be twenty years after the date of commercial discovery.

After five years of commercial production the INOC was to take over management of the project, but the INOC could take no major decision without consulting ERAP. A major decision was defined as that which 'could provoke any major change in the costs and/or the volume of production'.[80] The nature and scope of the consultation, however, was left curiously undefined. Before the take-over date the operation was to be controlled by an operating committee composed of representatives of both sides. At the end of the agreement all operating assets became the property of the INOC.

The marketing side of the agreement saw several innovations.[81] Of all the oil discovered, one-half was to be set aside as a 'national reserve' for the INOC. This clause was highly unrealistic – it could not possibly have any operational meaning – and well-illustrates the fact that both sides of negotiators were under enormous pressure to reach an agreement. It was to lead to severe complications later. ERAP's reward for all this was to have access to 30 per cent of the offtake; 40 per cent of ERAP's share was to be at a special 'bargain price' of costs plus royalty, on which there would be no 50 per cent profits tax. ERAP had a commitment to sell the INOC's share of the offtake at a commission of 1 cent per barrel.

The agreement was greeted in the official press as 'a great step forward which breaks the monopoly of the foreign companies over Iraq's national resources'.[82] Very soon after, however, doubts began to be raised. The Iraqi economist, Zayid Muhammad, claimed that the agreement was simply a disguised concession.[83] More detailed criticisms were forthcoming from T. Shafiq and G. al-Uqaili, both of whom were part of the INOC technocrat group ousted in 1967.[84] Using a static model, assuming a posted price of $1.72 per barrel, costs of 20 cents per barrel and a realised price of $1.35 per barrel, they calculated an annual return to ERAP on the non-returnable capital of more than 200 per cent per year, compared with an average return on investment by the major companies in the producing phase of five other Middle Eastern countries estimated at 66 per cent per year. They then asked what INOC was to receive in return for this substantial reward. They pointed out that although ERAP was providing technical, financial and marketing services, it was – apart from the interest-free exploration loan – being paid for these services. Moreover, ERAP's provision of risk capital for exploration was not of great significance as the acreage was so promising that there was virtually no risk. Finally, they concluded that such large returns must be a reward to ERAP for defying the IPC.

This critical view received further support from analysis by Tom Stauffer[85] who pointed out that static analysis grossly underestimated the return to ERAP and if discounted cash flow techniques (DCF) were used with a realised price of $1.30 then the profitability ratio for ERAP lay between 200 and 550 per cent. The Iraqi government's response to such criticism was to ignore it and claim the agreement as a great victory. In particular, constant comparison was made between the ERAP agreements and the abortive 1965 agreement with the IPC. There can, however, be little doubt that the government (and the INOC) knew that the terms were highly advantageous to ERAP. It knew that 'the risk of not finding commercial oil was virtually nil', based upon existing work done by the Basra Petroleum Company on the acreage. Also, they had carried out DCF analysis on the agreement coming up with figures remarkably similar to those of Stauffer. Apart from political considerations, which were considerable in terms of the negotiators' brief, two factors account for the Iraqi negotiators' preparedness to offer favourable terms. First, any crude discovered would be deemed 'proscribed crude' by the IPC, which would take legal steps to block its sale. Only a state company like ERAP, from a state which was in the process of objecting to Anglo-Saxon domination of the world, could effectively overcome the legal niceties. Second, the oil market was in a situation of excess supply (a situation which most of the experts expected to continue for some time).[86] If Iraq wanted to expand production quickly, therefore, ERAP needed an arrangement which could enable the company to obtain the oil at less cost than that of other existing supplies. Thus, in the words of one of the negotiators, 'while the general terms of the agreement were set by essentially political criteria handed down from above, the actual mechanics of the agreement were set by people with a view to technical and economic considerations'. Such a multiplicity of criteria makes the agreement difficult to evaluate, and it also made it difficult to operate.

ERAP spudded its first wildcat well at the end of 1968. The acreage proved to be as good as everyone had said it would be, with virtually no dry wells being drilled. The Buzurgan field needed only one wildcat and two appraisal wells before ERAP declared it commercial. It was, however, not until early 1970 that the field was formally declared commercial and not until June 1971 that talks began on its development. In the light of the urgency with which Iraq was seeking to develop its independent capacity these delays are inexplicable unless account is taken of the factors discussed earlier. When the discussions on development did begin, moreover, they were to drag on over two years and the resultant production agreement was not ratified until February 1974.[87] The discussions were bedevilled by disagreements over the 'national reserve' concept, and over the repayment of the exploration expenses. The INOC argued that as the risks had been so low, ERAP should itself bear some of the exploration expenses.

Production eventually began in the last part of 1976, eight years after the first wildcat well. In July 1977 the INOC took over the operations—earlier than intended—with the consent of all parties.[88] Production was scheduled to average some 100,000 barrels per day in 1977 and rise progressively to 200,000 barrels per day by 1980.[89] No data have been released to indicate whether these targets have been reached. The whole case highlights the problems inherent in Iraq's management of its oil resources: there was a reluctance to allow the foreign company to perform and there was a reluctance to go ahead alone. The mixing of political criteria with economic and technical criteria at both the strategic and tactical levels created a situation of paralysis.

Conclusions

In general, between 1961 and 1976 Iraq oil policy failed in terms of the criteria set by the Iraqis themselves. This failure must be regarded in many ways as a disappointment, as the Iraqi government had had the courage to confront the companies and to demand more equitable treatment. Iraq, moreover, probably did have the talent and the skilled manpower to break out of the constraints imposed by the companies. The opportunities, however, were squandered in a sea of internal squabbles and general paralysis.

The effects of the failure, nevertheless, were minimal. The rise in oil prices disguised the failure, and indeed future generations of Iraqis will almost certainly benefit since more oil has remained in the ground. However, there was one present cost, stemming from the tendency to blame the poor production record on the machinations of the foreign companies. While much of this blame had previously been well placed, during the period examined by this chapter domestic factors became more significant. The legacy of blaming someone else tended to divert attention away from the very real and considerable barriers to development which were generated.

Since the mid-1970s there have been signs of improvement. Many, if not all, of the aims of the ten-year sectoral plan mentioned earlier have been achieved. Whether or not the basic weakness of productive capacity was solved is not clear, because the price-rises of 1978-9 would again have disguised any such failure. Data on the oil sector still remain very sparse and without more information it is impossible to evaluate more recent developments.

Notes

1. For an outline of the methodology see P. Stevens, 'The Interaction between Oil Policy and Industrial Policy in Saudi Arabia', *Proceedings of the First*

International Area Conference on Saudi Arabia (International Research Centre for Energy and Development, Colorado, 1981).

2. Between 1973 and 1975, for example, there is no information on export destinations in the *OPEC Statistical Bulletin*, while for 1972 (for which there are figures) nearly one quarter goes to 'unspecified destinations'.

3. E. and E.F. Penrose, *Iraq: International Relations and National Development* (Ernest Benn, London, 1978); G. Stocking, *Middle East Oil* (Vanderbilt University Press, Vanderbilt, 1970); J. Stork, 'Oil and the Penetration of Capitalism in Iraq', in P. Nore and T. Turner (eds.), *Oil and Class Struggle* (Zed Press, London, 1980); D. Hirst, *Oil and Public Opinion in the Middle East* (Praeger, New York, 1966); J. Blair, *The Control of Oil* (Macmillan, London, 1976); and J. Hartshorn, *Oil Companies and Governments* (Faber and Faber, London, 1967).

4. Iraq National Oil Company (INOC), *Direct and National Exploitation of Iraqi Crude Oil* (al-Thawrah Publications, Baghdad, 1972).

5. *Middle East Economic Survey* (*MEES*), vol. XXII, no. 51.

6. *Middle East Money* (*MEMO*), vol. 3, no. 5.

7. From 1974 to the start of 1978 Iraqi aid totalled $2.2 billion (*MEES*, vol. XXIII, no. 10), while in 1979 $1 billion was disbursed in grants and soft loans (*MEES*, vol. XXIII, no. 11).

8. *MEES*, vol. XXII, no. 33.

9. *MEMO*, vol. 2, no. 1.

10. Penrose, *Iraq*, p. 56.

11. *Arab Oil and Gas*, vol. III, no. 60.

12. Translation in *MEES*, vol. XI, no. 28, supplement.

13. Although the INOC had been set up in 1964, by 1968 little or nothing had been achieved.

14. This plan was actually implemented after the IPC was nationalised in June 1972. It would be difficult to argue, however, that phase I was successfully completed.

15. For details see *MEES*, vol. XVII, no. 1.

16. For details of this and other pipeline plans see *MEES*, vol. XVII, no. 9.

17. As applied to the oil sector, see below.

18. F. Jalal, *The Role of Government in the Industrialization of Iraq 1950-65* (Frank Cass, London, 1971).

19. K. McLachlan, 'Iraq, Problems of Regional Development', in Kelidar, *Modern Iraq*, p. 319.

20. Ibid., p. 140.

21. McLachlan, 'Iraq', p. 140.

22. *MEED*, 1 Oct. 1976.

23. *An Nahar Arab Report*, vol. 6, no. 26.

24. *MEES*, vol. XVIII, no. 40.

25. Penrose, 'Industrial Policy'.

26. Iraqi Ministry of Oil and Minerals, *The Nationalization of IPC's Operations in Iraq: the Facts and the Causes* (INOC Publications, Baghdad, 1974), p. 6.

27. Taken from *Arab Oil and Gas*. In mitigation of the accusations in this chapter of policy failure by Iraq, it is only fair to point out that by the end of the decade of the 1970s most of these objectives had, in fact, been achieved. Whether this also applies to the crude production targets remains to be seen.

28. *MEES*, vol. XVII, no. 29.

29. *MEES*, vol. XVIII, no. 28.

30. Some Iraqi officials have disputed the existence of this Advisory Council.

31. One source – *An Nahar Arab Report*, vol. 5, no. 33 – suggests it was because the Minister of Oil at the time (Sa'adoun Hammadi) was one of the few Shi'a at high government level and this was resented by the Sunni majority. To balance

this argument is the fact that subsequently Dr Hammadi became Foreign Minister.

32. Law 101, 1976. Translation in *MEES*, vol. XX, no. 1.

33. *MEES*, vol. XIX, no. 18.

34. *MEES*, vol. XXIII, no. 38.

35. A. Kelidar, 'Iraq: The Search for Stability', *Conflict Studies*, July 1975, no. 59, p. 3.

36. Penrose, *Iraq*, p. 144.

37. See below.

38. Blair, *Control of Oil*, Ch. 5.

39. *MEES*, vol. XVII, no. 30.

40. *MEES*, vol. XXIII, no. 39.

41. *MEES*, vol. XVII, no. 17.

42. *BP Statistical Review* (1980), p. 19.

43. *MEES*, vol. XVIII, no. 35.

44. See above.

45. *MEES*, vol. XVIII, no. 35.

46. *MEES*, vol. XXIII, no. 39.

47. *MEES*, vol. XVIII, no. 35.

48. *MEES*, vol. XVII, no. 9.

49. Ibid.

50. *MEES*, vol. XXIII, no. 7.

51. Ibid.

52. *MEES*, vol. XIX, no. 40.

53. *MEES*, vol. XVIII, no. 30.

54. *MEES*, vol. XXII, no. 34.

55. Penrose, *Iraq*, p. 137.

56. For the general analytical problems associated with this situation see E. Penrose, 'Vertical Integration with Joint Control of Raw Material Production: Crude Oil in the Middle East', *Journal of Development Studies*, vol. 1, no. 3, April 1965.

57. Penrose, *Iraq*, p. 387.

58. B. Itayim, 'The Cost of Law 80', unpublished MSc thesis, University of London, 1970.

59. Ministry of Oil and Minerals, *The Nationalisation of IPC's Operations in Iraq* (INOC Publications, Baghdad, 1974), p. 6.

60. Official Iraqi sources have claimed that this last-minute offer was merely stalling on the part of the companies and was never intended to be taken up.

61. *MEES*, vol. XXII, no. 31.

62. *MEES*, vol. XXII, no. 39.

63. *MEED*, 1 Oct. 1976.

64. Penrose, 'Industrial Policy'.

65. *MEES*, vol. X, no. 46.

66. Law 97, August 1967.

67. Penrose, *Iraq*, p. 397.

68. Stork, 'Oil and the Penetration of Capitalism', p. 181.

69. *An Nahar Arab Report*, vol. 5, no. 8.

70. *MEES*, vol. XVIII, no. 16.

71. C. Davies, 'British Oil Policy in the Middle East 1919-1932', unpublished PhD thesis, University of Edinburgh, 1973.

72. H. O'Connor, *World Crisis in Oil* (Monthly Review Press, New York, 1962), p. 312.

73. *MEES*, vol. XVII, no. 9, supplement, p. 2.

74. Penrose, *Iraq*, p. 268.

75. Stocking, *Middle East Oil*, pp. 131, 193 and 326.

76. Khair al-Din Hasib, text from *Dirasat Arabiyyah* translated in *MEES*, vol. XI, no. 28. See also similar reports in *Financial Times*, 31 Mar. 1964, and *Sunday Times*, 28 Aug. 1964.

77. E. Penrose, *The Large International Firm in Developing Countries* (Allen and Unwin, London, 1968).

78. N. Anuri and N. Hevener, 'France and the Middle East 1967-68', in *Middle East Journal*, vol. 23, no. 3, Autumn 1969.

79. Published in G.M. Butros, *The Second Oil Monograph* (Bureau of Lebanese and Arab Documentation, Beirut, 1969).

80. Law 5 (1968), article 13, section 1a.

81. For the terms of similar agreements elsewhere see P. Stevens, *Joint Ventures in Middle East Oil 1957-1974* (Middle East Economic Consultants, London, 1976).

82. *Al-Thawrah al-Arabiyyah*, 24 Nov. 1967.

83. *An Nasr*, 30 Nov. 1967.

84. The criticisms were published in *MEES*, vol. XI, no. 25.

85. *MEES*, vol. XI, no. 25.

86. See M. Adelman, *The World Oil Market* (Johns Hopkins University Press, Washington, 1971).

87. *MEES*, vol. XVII, no. 18.

88. *MEES*, vol. XX, no. 38.

89. *MEES*, vol. XX, no. 5.

13 PROBLEMS OF RURAL DEVELOPMENT IN AN OIL-RICH ECONOMY: IRAQ 1958-1975[1]

Robin Theobald and Sa'ad Jawad

Introduction

For most of the countries of Africa, Asia and Latin America rural development, the eradication of poverty and of low levels of living generally in rural areas, has for some considerable time been a primary goal of government policy. Yet despite prodigious efforts and the allocation of considerable resources to the agricultural sector, the goal remains elusive. In fact it is not an exaggeration to portray agriculture throughout most of the underdeveloped world as being in a state of stagnation, with low levels of productivity, poor if not the poorest living conditions and a continued exodus of rural inhabitants to cities already bursting at the seams.[2]

It is not easy to situate the Republic of Iraq on a development-underdevelopment continuum. In terms of *per capita* income Iraq is probably on a par with the countries of the European periphery: Greece, Turkey, Spain. But a high overall level of *per capita* income masks substantial internal inequalities, particularly between urban and rural areas. Such inequalities manifest themselves not only in terms of differences between urban and rural incomes[3] but more generally in the continued existence of a backward peasantry, that is, an under-developed stratum of the population which is poorly educated, traditional in its outlook and basically unresponsive to sustained exhortations to adopt modern methods of production.

The existence of such a state of affairs in the mid-1970s is somewhat surprising given Iraq's apparently favourable resource-endowment. First, Iraq does not suffer from population pressure on land. On the contrary, with an estimated 20 million acres of cultivable land and a total rural population of just less than 4 million[4] Iraq has an average cultivable area *per capita* of about five acres – or 25 acres per family, which is about the same as that of France, twice as much as Italy, fifteen times that of Japan and twenty times that of Egypt.[5]

Perhaps even more important than Iraq's relatively low population-density are its massive oil revenues which have given the country that crucial advantage denied to most countries of the Third World: the ability to generate internally the capital necessary for the establishment of an agricultural infrastructure. Furthermore, since the revolution of 1958, successive governments in Iraq have pledged themselves to a radical programme of land reform, which has involved, *inter alia*, the allocation of very considerable funds to the agricultural sector. Yet despite these advantages the level of agricultural production, although showing a trend to increasing yields, is alleged not to have kept pace with the increasing demands of a growing population, and is still subject to substantial seasonal fluctuations. Whereas before 1958 Iraq was in good years able to export cereals, during the first half of the 1970s over $100 million per annum was spent on grain imports.[6] Even more serious is that land, for reasons which we shall examine, continues to go out of cultivation and there is a serious shortage of agricultural labour as migration to the cities continues unabated.

As Doreen Warriner has pointed out, Iraq's experience is particularly fascinating because 'it demonstrates what money can and cannot do'.[7] With such an apparently favourable resource base and with a high degree of commitment to reforming agriculture – the present government recently affirmed its belief that 'agriculture is everlasting oil'[8] – how do we explain the ostensible failure of Iraq's agrarian reform programme? The aim of this chapter is to identify the major impediments to rural development[9] in Iraq over the last two decades. Since the problem of rural development, in fact any development problem, can be adequately understood only in its historical perspective, we begin by providing a necessarily brief background to the land question in Iraq.

Although the chapter draws upon data collected in Iraq, mainly from interviews with government personnel, it is not based upon a systematic field study of the impact of development programmes in rural areas. The chapter is, rather, primarily a review of related literature both in European languages and in Arabic. Some of this literature is not easily available in the United Kingdom, so the writers hope that some purpose will be served by bringing it together in this context. The contents of the chapter are intended to form the background for a comprehensive study of the training of specialised personnel for agriculture in Iraq.

Traditional Agriculture in Iraq: Some Basic Characteristics

Climatically, Iraq may be divided into a rainfall zone in the north and north-east, an irrigated zone in the centre-south and a desert zone in the south and south-west. Dry farming occupies around 48 per cent of the cultivable land in Iraq, with wheat and barley as the principal winter crops. Rainfall is inadequate in the north for the cultivation of summer crops; small quantities of cotton, rice and tobacco, however, are grown using water from springs and streams. In the mountainous north-east the semi-nomadic Kurdish population traditionally raised cattle, sheep and goats.

Wheat and barley are also grown as winter crops in the irrigated zone, with barley predominating, as it is better-suited to the arid climate and to saline soils. The principal summer crops in the centre-south are rice and cotton, with smaller quantities of sesame, millet and sorghum also being grown. Citrus fruits are grown particularly in the Diyala, and the area around the Shatt el-Arab near Basra is the world's foremost date-producing area.

The desert zone in the south and south-west occupies about 40 per cent of the land area of Iraq and is sparsely inhabited by nomads raising camels, sheep and goats. In the middle of the last century just over a third of Iraq's population was reported to be nomadic, but with the rapid expansion of settled agriculture, especially during this century, and the promotion of sedentarisation policies by successive regimes, the nomadic population is now probably less than one per cent.[10]

For centuries agricultural techniques in Iraq were primitive. Agricultural implements were simple, the majority of cultivators working with the traditional nail plough, the hoe, the digging stick and the sickle. The scythe – at least five times more efficient than the sickle – was unknown. Little animal manure was used for fertilisation and crop rotation was not practised. The response to the inevitable decline in the fertility of the land was to leave it fallow, usually for a year. Thus under the traditional *niren-niren* system only half of the cultivable land would be in production at any one time.[11]

The hazards of primitive methods of cultivation were augmented by the instability of the natural habitat, especially in the south by the perversity of those 'gifts of nature', the Tigris and the Euphrates. It needs to be appreciated that the waters of the twin rivers do not provide a regular natural renewal of the fertility of the soil as does the Nile. Whereas the Nile rises to deposit a fertile layer of silt just at the right time in the growing season, the spring flooding of the Tigris and Euphrates was often severe enough to wash out the winter's crops. Until the inauguration of major flood-control schemes in 1956 the danger of serious flooding was always present in the centre-south. In 1954 severe Tigris floods threatened Baghdad itself and destroyed crops in about one quarter of the irrigation zone.[12] Ironically, too much water in the spring was combined with too little water during the summer, due to inadequate storage facilities. This meant that, before the introduction of pump irrigation in the last decades of the nineteenth century, summer crops could be grown only in those areas where natural 'flow' irrigation was possible. But even there an additional hazard presented itself in the form of soil-salinisation.

Since the irrigation zone was in the distant past a marine delta, the subsoil is saline. Continuous irrigation and flooding has raised the water table so that subsoil water is drawn to the surface through capillary action and then evaporates leaving the salt behind. The only solution to this problem is to provide adequate drainage so that the water table is lowered. In the past, cultivators attempted to deal with the problem of salinity by trying to 'wash out' the salt through using still more water. Since this tactic simply exacerbates the problem by raising the water table still further, the land must eventually be abandoned and cultivation moved elsewhere. Thus Iraq traditionally exhibited the unusual feature of irrigation associated with *extensive* cultivation whereas elsewhere, in Egypt for example, irrigation has usually been linked with the *intensive* use of land, with higher yields and double-cropping.

Given such adverse conditions it is probably not surprising that permanent settled agriculture is a relatively recent socio-economic activity in Iraq. In fact, Warriner suggests that as much as three-quarters of the land under cultivation in the 1960s had been brought into production since 1918, and one third since 1945.[13] It has already been noted that at least a third of the population was nomadic in the middle of the last century. The remaining rural population consisted primarily of part-time farmers who supplemented their meagre income from agriculture by herding, some of them fluctuating between a settled and a nomadic existence.[14]

Natural hazards apart, the appeal of settled agriculture was not enhanced by overall conditions of insecurity and lawlessness. Prior to World War I the area now known as 'Iraq' had been part of the Ottoman Empire from the sixteenth century. Since 'Iraq' was maintained primarily as a buffer area by the Ottomans against Persia, administration was fairly minimal and barely extended beyond the principal towns. The Ottomans accepted a *modus vivendi* with tribal shaikhs who were given rights over large tracts of land in exchange for collecting taxes and supplying the authorities with manpower for military purposes when necessary. This situation gave rise to what is sometimes referred to as a 'feudal' or 'semi-feudal' system.

The application of the term 'feudal' here is, in the writers' view, a little confusing. Although the system was obviously characterised by the exchange of rights in land for military service, a factor which many scholars would consider to be an equally significant feature of feudal systems – the appropriation of various forms of rent by a superior stratum of landholders from an unfree peasantry – was absent. This aspect of feudal practice could not really be claimed to have existed in 'Iraq' before the middle of the nineteenth century. Although the tribal shaikhs[15] were clearly set apart from their tribesmen, their position did not approximate to that of feudal landholders. Rather the shaikh was the custodian of tribal lands (the *dirah*), allocating and re-allocating land for pasture or cultivation to individual tribesmen. The shaikh also performed certain judicial and ceremonial functions, as well as leading his tribe in war. However, there were to occur, during the second half of the nineteenth and the first decade of the twentieth centuries, certain important politico-economic changes which acted precisely to transform the tribal shaikh into a feudal landowner.

The first series of changes were associated with the attempt by the Ottomans, from 1839 on, to modernise the administration of their empire. The various reforms associated with the period of *tanzimat* barely touched 'Iraq' until 1869, when Midhat Pasha arrived in Baghdad as governor of the province. Midhat was an extremely capable and liberal-minded reformer who strove energetically to bring to an end the acute instability and administrative chaos which characterised this part of the Empire. Central to the problem of instability, Midhat believed, was the question of land. Hitherto all land in Iraq was regarded as belonging to the state, with the tribes granted usufruct (but not possession) through their shaikhs. Given the predominance of shifting cultivation and pastoralism, this state of affairs had resulted in endless disputes and inter-tribal wars. Midhat hoped to remedy this situation, as well as to stimulate the agricultural economy, by granting legal tenure to individual cultivators. Although some progress was achieved in this direction, such gains as were made during Midhat's three-year period of office were quickly dissipated by his successors. Agreements that Midhat had made with the tribes were broken, the policy of divide and rule was re-adopted, bribes were taken and, most serious of all, holdings were registered in the names not of individual tribesmen, as Midhat intended, but in those of shaikhs, town notables and city merchants.[16]

It is important to understand that these 'reforms' coincided with the penetration of market forces into 'Iraq'. The rising European demand for foodstuffs and raw materials, together with improvements in transportation – the opening of the Suez Canal in 1869 and the introduction of steam navigation on the Tigris in 1861 – stimulated the export of agricultural products, mainly cereals, wool and dates from Iraq.[17] Along with the expansion of trade went the penetration of commercial conceptions of land. In this situation the minority of merchants and shaikhs who were involved in trade soon grasped the implications of the Ottoman attempts at land registration and used the process to have vast tracts of land registered in their names. The tribesmen, on the other hand, were generally uninterested in the registration process, partly because of a long-standing reluctance to deal with any representatives of government but also because they could not see why they should pay a fee to acquire rights to land which they already enjoyed.[18]

When the British came into occupation of Iraq at the end of World War I the land situation was, to say the least, confused. Serious attempts were made by the British to establish what was accepted practice in relation to land, but the British unfortunately came to believe that the prevailing chaos could be attributed to the erosion of the shaikh's authority as a result of Ottoman interference with the tribal system. In other words, the British concluded that the shaikhs had at some point exerted firm control over their tribesmen but that their position had been undermined by attempts to impose the Ottoman Land Code. In fact the shaikh's authority *was* declining, but the decline stemmed from the dissolution of traditional bonds – a process brought about by the progressive monetisation of the rural economy and the consequent transformation of a relationship based upon mutual obligation to relationships based upon exploitation. However, the British chose to strengthen the authority of the shaikhs not simply out of some atavistic attachment to tribalism but primarily because the political support of the shaikhs was vital to their ability to assert control over the country.

The British reliance on the shaikhs was a vital component in the lengthy process whereby tribal sheikhs were transformed into feudal landowners, and free tribesmen were transformed into serfs. The seal of legality was put on this transformation by the Law of Settlement of Land Rights (1932). The Law was the outcome of the exhaustive investigations of Sir Ernest Dowson, an expert in land tenure systems, whose aid had been solicited by the British in 1929 in an attempt to resolve once and for all the vexed question of land. Whilst the Dowson Report and the law that it prompted certainly clarified the land situation and so helped to reduce inter-tribal disputes, it effectively led to the consolidation of land ownership in the hands of a small minority. This situation came about because the 1932 Law required all cultivators to register the lands they were currently farming. As might be expected in a society where over 95 per cent of rural inhabitants were illiterate and totally unused to dealing with government bureaucracies, the overwhelming majority of tribesmen remained ignorant of these stipulations whilst shaikhs and city merchants were, in many areas, able to make use of the occasion to register tribal lands as their own freehold tenures. The newly independent government of the day was well aware that land was being alienated in this way in many parts of the country but did nothing to stop the process, primarily because it was heavily dependent upon the political support of the shaikhs.

The end-result of this complex process was a highly inegalitarian pattern of landholding. Prior to the revolution of 1958 2 per cent of landowners possessed as much as 68 per cent of all cultivable land, whilst 70 per cent owned only 3.3 per cent. One third of the cultivators owned less than 2.5 acres.[19] The reality behind these figures was one of generally appalling living conditions for the mass of the rural population, particularly in the irrigation zone. With landlords taking from 30 to 80 per cent of crops whose yields were declining due to improvident farming,[20] the peasant was forced to resort to the money-lender for loans at exorbitant rates of interest. Debts were inherited and a law of 1933 which prevented indebted peasants from leaving their lands completed the condition of serfdom. Some idea of the generally low level of existence can be had from the following passage from Warriner:

> Increased production has not touched the poverty of the *fellahin*. They live on a bare subsistence margin, in windowless mud huts built up out of the earth. Health conditions are appalling: 'It is not exaggerating to state', says Professor Michael Critchley, 'that the average agricultural worker is a living pathological specimen, as he is probably a victim of anklystomiasis, ascariasis, malaria, bilharzia, trachoma, bejel, and possibly tuberculosis also'. The crude death rate is believed by medical authorities to be about 30 per thousand population. 'An overall average of 300 to 350 per thousand for the country as a whole is probably not far wrong for the infant mortality rate.'[21]

A direct consequence of rural misery was the large-scale migration of cultivators to the cities, especially from the irrigation zone where conditions were usually worse and the degree of exploitation greater than in the north.[22] By the 1950s Baghdad was ringed with shanty towns containing, according to one estimate, about 47,000 mud or reed huts.[23] It is not surprising, then, that disaffected urban elements were to play a significant role in the events which led to the overthrow of the Hashimite monarchy in July 1958 and the establishment of the republic of Iraq.

The 1958 Reform and its Consequences

First it should be pointed out that an attempt at a kind of land reform had been made before the upheaval of 1958. The Dujaila Land Development Law, which was passed by parliament in 1945, authorised the distribution of state-owned land to selected cultivators in parcels of 37-74 acres. The cultivation of these lands was to be under the ultimate supervision of the Ministry of Economics, and beneficiaries were expected to conform to certain requirements such as constructing a certain type of housing and growing specified crops. The settlers were to be assisted by a committee, set up by the Ministry, which would help to establish credit facilities and various forms of agricultural extension. From about 50,000 applicants the committee selected initially 1,200 settlers. At the end of the ten-year probationary period 1,300 settlers were farming approximately 50,000 acres of land. By 1955 there were 2,300 settlers on five projects covering 186,000 acres.[24]

This is not the place to embark upon a detailed assessment of these schemes. However, it does seem that on the whole they enjoyed very limited success. The original project at Dujaila achieved considerable gains at first with significant increases in crop yields and consequently in cultivators' incomes. But in the long term a number of serious problems presented themselves. A shortage of appropriate managerial skills proved to be a serious impediment; the expansion of irrigation facilities without adequate drainage created a severe problem of soil salinity. But perhaps most important of all in the light of subsequent events was the way in which landowners, merchants and other urban elements were able to subvert the schemes for their own ends, controlling such co-operatives as existed and actually employing cultivator-beneficiaries on lands over which they, non-cultivators, had acquired control.[25] The experience with these settlement schemes illustrates, *inter alia*, the major difficulties of pushing through even limited agrarian reform programmes whilst a traditional landholding oligarchy continues to exercise considerable influence over the political and administrative process.

It is thus not surprising that the primary political objective of the Agrarian Reform Law No. 30, promulgated on 29 September 1958, was 'to destroy the feudal class'. Other political objectives were: to destroy the influence of imperialists; to strengthen democratic forces in the country; and to create a class of small independent owner-cultivators who would form the basis of political support for the new regime under the leadership of Brigadier Abd al-Karim Qasim. The major economic objectives were: to move from economic stagnation to economic development; to increase efficiency by abolishing shifting cultivation and preventing the fragmentation of holdings; providing greater incentives for production; and directing existing capital into industrial and commercial activities by establishing a maximal limit for land ownership.[26]

The projected reform was to a considerable extent modelled on the Egyptian agrarian reform of 1952. Iraq's Law No. 30 called for the expropriation of privately owned land in holdings in excess of 625 acres of irrigated land and 1,250 acres of rain-fed land. The landowner had the right to choose the area to be expropriated from his holdings and he was to be compensated in the form of government bonds, redeemable after not more than twenty years.

Expropriated land was to be distributed to beneficiaries in holdings of between 18 and 36 acres in irrigated areas and 36 to 72 acres in rain-fed areas. In the distribution, priority was given to landless cultivators—who were to pay for the new holdings over a period of twenty years. Like the Egyptian reform, considerable emphasis was placed upon co-operatives, which the beneficiaries were required to join. The major activities of the co-operatives were to be those of providing their members with loans, seeds, machines, transport and storage facilities. They were also to supervise farming techniques, land utilisation, irrigation and drainage work, and provide marketing facilities as well as various agricultural extension services. Article 15 of the Law called for the establishment of a Higher Agrarian Reform Committee, which was to be the national administrative organ for dealing with the expropriation, compensation, distribution and temporary management of sequestered lands. The Agrarian Reform Committee, transformed subsequently into the Ministry of Agrarian Reform, was also to oversee the setting up of the co-operatives.

Other sections of the act sought to regulate the positions of tenant share-croppers and agricultural labourers. Section III laid down the maximum share of a crop which could be taken by landlords against the provision of land and services such as irrigation, ploughing, harvesting, seed and other management inputs. Section IV of the Law stipulated minimum wage rates payable to agricultural labourers who were now to be permitted, for the first time in Iraq's history, to form unions and to engage in collective bargaining. Wage rates were to be fixed by special local committees made up of representatives of the government, landlords and labourers.

The process of expropriation turned out to be extraordinarily complicated. The Ministry of Agrarian Reform prepared a list of landlords whose holdings exceeded the prescribed limits. The list then had to be verified for accuracy by the Title Registration Office, the Ministry of Finance and the Department of General Taxation. When this had been completed a memorandum containing all pertinent details of each case, including the political standing of the landlord, was submitted for approval to a Higher Committee chaired by General Qasim himself. If approved, the decision was published in the *Official Gazette*, enabling the landlord to petition the Court of Appeal for Agrarian Reform. Litigation in the Court could be lengthy – up to twelve months – and its decision had to be approved by the Higher Committee.

Despite the complexity of this process the rate of confiscation seems to have been relatively speedy. By the end of 1963 more than 2.8 million acres had been expropriated, and by the middle of 1968 the figure had reached 4.3 million acres.[27] The process of distribution, however, was much slower. By the end of 1968 only just over a third of sequestered land (1.08 million acres) had been distributed to around 55,000 beneficiaries.[28] The fundamental reason for the substantial delay in distribution was Iraq's underdeveloped administrative infrastructure. This meant that not only were there insufficient trained administrators to supervise the actual process of distribution but, probably more indispensable, the government was unable to provide important services such as irrigation, marketing and the provision of credit that had formerly been provided, albeit at a price, by the landlords. These services were supposed to have been provided by the co-operatives, but by 1968 only 443 co-operatives had been established, just over half the estimated 800 minimum needed to provide the necessary services for Iraq's cultivable land.[29] Furthermore, the supply of trained personnel – agronomists, engineers, supervisors and accountants – was totally inadequate to staff the co-operatives that had been established. As a consequence many cultivators who actually received holdings, not having the resources for cultivation, abandoned them and migrated to the cities, especially to Baghdad where, according to Qasim's propaganda machine, the *fellahin* (peasants; sing.: *fellah*) would be able to live in palaces.[30]

The upheavals brought about by the agrarian reform programme did, as would be expected, affect levels of agricultural production. Generally speaking, the first five years at least are considered to have been an economic failure. Warriner maintains that, if the pre- and post-reform levels of production of Iraq's main crops are compared, cereal production will be seen to have fallen by 17 per cent, rice production by 20 per cent and the production of cotton by at least 16 per cent. Simmons likewise concludes that the agrarian reform caused a 'serious decline' in agricultural production.[31] However, the conclusions drawn from available figures will be affected to a considerable extent by the time periods chosen for comparison. Warriner's conclusions are based upon a comparison of average levels of production for the periods 1954-8 and 1959-63.[32] If one looks at comparisons over a longer period the decline appears to be less serious than has been claimed. In fact, the decline seems to be concentrated in Iraq's major crop, barley, the production of which, as we see from Table 13.1, showed no signs of recovering to pre-reform levels even by 1968. The production of wheat[33] and rice by contrast exhibited a clear tendency to rise, whilst that of cotton revealed a decline on the immediate pre-reform period though not on the period 1950-4.

Table 13.1: Production of Iraq's Main Crops, 1950-68

	Average production of metric tons (000's)			
	Barley	Wheat	Rice	Cotton
1950-4	927	699	158	17
1955-9	953	732	·113	30
1960-4	850	765	125	24
1965-8	841	1,099	261	25

Sources: D. Dahiri, *Economics of the Agricultural Sector in Iraq* (al-Ani Press, Baghdad, 1976), pp. 197-200; and D. Dahiri, *The Introduction of Technology into Traditional Societies and Economies* (al-Ani Press, Baghdad, 1969), pp. 185-8.

The somewhat overly pessimistic view of the effects of the 1958 land reform on the part of certain commentators is probably attributable to their tendency to focus primarily upon the Qasim period of 1958-63. During these years there was undoubtedly a great deal of disruption not only in agriculture but in social and political life generally, reflecting a vicious struggle at the national level between Communists, Ba'th socialists and an assortment of Arab nationalists. The purging of government bureaucracies which was a consequence of this struggle, as Palmer and Simmons have pointed out, could not but be a major impediment to the redistribution of expropriated lands.

The approach of the Qasim government to the problem of sequestered but undistributed holdings was for the Ministry of Agrarian Reform to lease them out under temporary tenancies to former tenants and to other peasant cultivators. This tactic, however, proved quite unsatisfactory for, as we have seen, the cultivators seldom had the resources or the expertise to work these holdings. With the overthrow of Qasim and the accession of the much less radical regime of the Aref brothers (1963-8), the Law of 1958 was subject to certain amendments, one of the most significant of which stated that henceforth landlords, and not the Ministry of Agrarian Reform, should continue to make use of land earmarked for sequestration until such time as the government was able to take them over.[34] This decision was no doubt based primarily upon a recognition by the Aref regime that, since the resources needed to administer the reform were in extremely short supply, the pace of its full implementation must necessarily be slowed. The fact that this decision was taken, and the background to it, are extremely important when evaluating the extent to which the 1958 Reform succeeded in achieving the major goal of 'eliminating feudalism'. Interestingly, commentators such as Simmons and Warriner, whilst evaluating negatively the economic achievements of the Reform, seem to believe that it did go a considerable way towards eliminating exploitation in the countryside.[35] However, exploitation could have been eliminated only to the extent that the dependence of the *fellahin* on the landowners had been reduced. Since landlords were still in nominal control of around two-thirds of expropriated land in 1968, the degree to which this dependence had decreased must be questioned. We must also bear in mind that the ceilings laid down by the 1958 Law left a sizeable amount of land in the hands of the landlord class. According to the Iraq Communist Party, permitting landlords to retain up to 620 acres of irrigated or 1,240 acres of rain-fed land left almost half of cultivated land in Iraq in the hands of a small minority.[36] Although the 1958 Law attempted to regulate tenancy agreements as well as establish a minimum wage for agricultural labourers, given the administrative deficiencies to which we have already referred, it is extremely doubtful if these stipulations could have been enforced on any significant scale.

The Agrarian Reform Law of 1970

In 1969, with the primary aim of stimulating agricultural production, the new Ba'th government set out to remedy what it saw to be the major deficiencies of the 1958 Law. In an attempt to relieve previous beneficiaries of debt, compensation was abolished and repayments suspended. In May 1970 a new agrarian reform law was promulgated, incorporating many of the provisions of the previous law but in a form which had been able to benefit from twelve years of experience of land reform. Whereas the 1958 reform classified land only in terms of whether it was irrigated or rain-fed, its successor attempted a much more sophisticated system of land classification. Rain-fed land was sub-divided into four categories and irrigated land into eleven. The sub-categories were based primarily on the fertility of the land, location, type of crop, type of irrigation and proximity to markets. Each sub-category was given its own land ceiling, which now ranged from 1,240 acres of unfertile rain-fed land down to 25 acres of certain categories of irrigated land. Land above these ceilings was to be expropriated, with landowners now relieved of the right to choose from among their holdings which land was to be sequestered. In order to speed up the process of appropriation the Agrarian Reform Appeal Courts were abolished.

Expropriated land was to be distributed in plots varying from 4 to 40 acres of irrigated land, and 62 to 124 acres of rain-fed land per family. The 1970 Law, in addition, allowed for collective forms of ownership. The previous experience of the distribution of land in family plots had led to serious difficulties, particularly in the irrigation zone. By encouraging collective forms it was hoped that over-fragmentation would be avoided and the pooling of effort and resources encouraged. The provision for different sizes and types of holding in the 1970 Law was symptomatic of a realisation by the reformers that conditions in rural Iraq were extremely varied.

As under the previous law, beneficiaries were required to join co-operatives. The co-operatives were charged with organising production, supplying agricultural equipment, providing credit and market facilities, as well as raising social, educational and hygienic standards with the aim of diminishing 'the great distance between the country and the city'.[37] However, unlike the Qasim government, the Ba'th regime appreciated that the establishment of co-operatives must be closely linked to a programme which provided for the flow of resources, both inanimate and in the form of trained manpower, into the agricultural sector. Accordingly, the agrarian reform programme of 1970 was conceived within the broader context of the national economic plan of 1970-4. The general objectives of the agricultural section of this plan were as follows: the overall reform of rural society and the raising of the standard of living of rural workers through the transformation of agricultural ownership and rural social relations; the expansion of agricultural production, both of foodstuffs and raw materials for industry, in order not only to meet domestic needs but also to make available a surplus for export. The plan also envisaged the further development of flood control, irrigation and drainage facilities.

Agricultural production was to be raised by expanding agricultural extension organisations and supplying them with the necessary resources: seeds, fertilisers, mechanised equipment, information on agricultural techniques, animal husbandry, pest control, water control and storage, tree planting, etc. The agricultural bank was to be expanded in order to meet requests for loans, and suitable marketing systems were to be established. The co-operative movement, which would obviously play a crucial role in channelling these inputs to cultivators, was to be supported, and collectivised units encouraged. In addition the plan inaugurated the creation of a number of state farms which could be used for the refinement of agricultural techniques as well as for training personnel.

By the end of 1974, 3.7 million acres had been appropriated under the stipulations of the 1970 Law, bringing the total area of land appropriated since 1959 to 6.3 million acres. By the end of 1974 2.1 million acres of sequestered land had been distributed in permanent tenure, whilst the remaining land was under the temporary direction of the Ministry of Agrarian Reform and was leased to cultivators.[38] In addition to sequestered lands, however, 1.6 million acres of state land had also been distributed to cultivators between 1959 and the end of 1974, by which time a total of 160,109 families had received holdings from either source.[39]

Whilst there were only 17 agricultural co-operatives in 1961, by 1975 there were 1,635, with 237,109 members. In addition to these, 173 combined co-operatives[40] and 79 collective farms with a total membership of over 10,000 had been established.[41] There were also 103 centres of rural industries, 756 illiteracy combat centres, 234 social centres and 234 village libraries.[42] In order to meet the manpower needs of such establishments vocational education in agriculture was expanded. In 1974 there were 4,317 students in Iraq's five universities studying agricultural subjects compared with 170 in 1958. In addition to the universities there were 3,531 students receiving training in agricultural specialisms in 14 centres. There was also a Training Institute for Co-operatives and Extensionists as well as other institutions created specifically to train personnel for agriculture.[43]

One could continue endlessly to quote figures illustrating the expansion of Iraq's agricultural infrastructure since 1970. To give a general impression of the priority given to agriculture by the Ba'th government, however, we may note that on average 22 per cent of the total development budget was allocated to the agricultural sector during the 1970-5 period compared with 11 per cent during the 1961-5 period. Between 1970 and 1975 this allocation resulted in an expenditure amounting to ID308 million.[44] The crucial question, however, is: has this scale of investment had a beneficial effect upon levels of production? If we look again at the production of Iraq's main crops, we note first an increase in the production of wheat, from an average of 1,116,238 tons per annum for 1965-9 to an average of 1,395,838 tons for 1970-4. The 1970-4 figure was almost double pre-reform levels. However, if we turn to barley we discover an average for 1970-4 of 617,761 tons compared with 865,852 tons for 1965-9, and an average of 940,000 tons for the 1950s. A major factor in the decline of barley production seems to be a corresponding decline in the area under barley cultivation, which fell from 2.5 million acres in 1950-4 to 1.4 million acres in 1970-4.

Turning to the main summer crops, rice and cotton, although the area under rice cultivation fell from 280,000 acres in 1950-4 to 185,000 in 1970-4, production increased over the same period because of improved yields, from 159,000 to 196,000 tons. Again with cotton, the area under cultivation declined from 135,000 acres (1950-4) to 83,000 acres (1970-4), but production increased from an average of 17,367 tons to 44,125 tons.[45] Accordingly, the production of wheat, rice, cotton and some of the lesser crops such as peas and broad beans have shown a tendency to increase. The production of barley, lentils, vetch, maize, millet and green grams has either decreased (substantially in the case of barley and millet) or failed to show a sustained increase. In the case of all these latter crops the acreage given over to each has declined since the pre-reform period. However, the decline in the area under cultivation would not be a problem if yields had increased sufficiently to meet at least the country's domestic needs for food and raw materials. In fact, Iraq is unable to produce enough food to feed its growing population and, more significantly, its expanding urban population.[46] Again, although cotton yields more than tripled over the period 1950-74, output is still inadequate to meet the demands of local industry, so that raw cotton and other industrial crops continue to be imported.[47]

Given the high levels of investment in agriculture, not only under the Ba'th but under previous governments, why have production levels often failed to show a sustained improvement and, in some cases, even fallen below pre-reform levels? Why, with the expressed aim of achieving self-sufficiency in agricultural products, is land still going out of cultivation? Why have living conditions in the countryside failed to improve sufficiently to stem the flow of migrants to the cities? The answers to these questions are many and complex. However, in an attempt to achieve a coherent view of the situation we propose to identify what we perceive to be three main problem areas: planning, the peasantry and political instability.

Planning

Several commentators on the performance of the Iraqi economy have located the root cause of a lack of progress in deficiencies in the planning process. Simmons, writing in the mid-1960s, identified several weaknesses in Iraq's administrative structure: the over-centralisation of decision-making and a consequent inability to delegate authority; an obsession with formal qualifications, especially American PhD's, leading to the employment of highly qualified but managerially unsuitable individuals in positions of responsibility. These and other defects were exacerbated by a rapid turnover of personnel, itself a symptom of the instability of the Qasim period.[48]

Ten years later, in the ostensibly more stable atmosphere of the early 1970s, a paper published by the United Nations Economic and Social Office in Beirut suggested that most of the above defects, together with others, continued to bedevil decision- and policy-making processes in Iraq. The report, which was concerned with the management of public industrial enterprises, revealed that these were organised as part of the state bureaucracy and were given very little autonomy in decision-making. Most decisions had to go through several layers, with too many going right up to the relevant ministries, thereby involving high-level administrators in routine decisions. Middle-level officials, on the other hand, displayed a marked reluctance to assume responsibility. Lines of authority were unclear and little premium was attached to the value of time. There was little by way of proper evaluation of costs in state enterprises: the costs of capital, for example, were largely ignored and there were few safeguards against the inappropriate use of fixed assets. One not-uncharacteristic response to the labyrinthine decision-making process and the procurement difficulties that this produced was the holding of large inventories. The Report also criticised the deployment of labour, particularly tendencies to overmanning and the inflexibility produced by Iraq's labour laws.[49]

At a seminar held in September 1976 and attended by leading government spokesmen, heads of institutions and trade union leaders, the country's labour laws were cited as a principal factor behind the generally low levels of productivity in industry. A law which prevented management from giving a worker a job different from that mentioned in his contract made it extremely difficult to retrain workers according to the needs of industry. What was felt to be the generally poor quality of managers and administrators was also discussed.[50]

Although the above observations were made in relation to the state of the industrial sector, they were symptomatic of a more general scarcity of administrative and managerial resources in Iraq. This is perhaps not so surprising when we consider the country's historical evolution and the low base from which it started only half a century ago. When Iraq came under the British Mandate in 1921 administrative and public services were virtually non-existent outside the principal towns.[51] In addition, Iraq was agriculturally a backward society, in the sense that full-time sedentary cultivation did not permeate the rural economy until after World War I. Agricultural backwardness was further intensified by the policies of the colonial power, Great Britain, and during the period 1932-58 by Great Britain's client, the Hashimite monarchy. Onto this rural economy was imposed, in 1958, a land-reform programme which had been imported virtually *in toto* from a country, Egypt, which, in terms of the evolution of agricultural technique and practices, was in a sense over a century ahead of Iraq.[52]

That Qasim and his supporters grossly underestimated the difficulties of modernising Iraqi agriculture cannot be gainsaid. This is not to argue, however, that Qasim was somehow 'wrong' to insist upon a radical solution to stagnation and exploitation in the countryside. Qasim was, after all, borne to power on a wave of popular discontent which demanded radical solutions. The idea of piecemeal reform or an approach based upon the resettlement of cultivators on state-owned land[53] was a non-starter, given the power of the landholding class to block or to subvert changes which were not in their interests. In other words, the power of the landlords had to be broken but at the cost of considerable disruption to the agricultural economy.

In its attempt to deal with the heritage of years of disruption the present government has greatly expanded the proportion of national resources devoted to agriculture. Large financial allocations, however, do not of themselves solve developmental problems. The efficient disbursement alone of such allocations requires considerable planning and managerial expertise. Here it is noteworthy that during the period 1965-70 the agricultural sector received only 32.4 per cent of its projected allotment, whilst during 1970-5 actual expenditure in the agricultural sector was 53.8 per cent of allotted expenditure. The latter figure would seem to represent a substantial improvement over the one for the previous five years, but it is still low, and, in fact, agriculture seems generally to have fared worse than other sectors in terms of the relationship of actual to allotted expenditure.[54] The reality in the rural areas is of a continuing shortage of agronomists, engineers, mechanics, veterinary specialists, co-operative supervisors, accountants and the like. All-important credit facilities are unevenly distributed: in short supply in some areas whilst over-abundant in others.[55] The resulting vacuum left by the unavailability of services and advice has caused many peasants to abandon their holdings and migrate to the expanding industrial sector, or else has thrown them back into dependence for loans, marketing and irrigation facilities on merchants, moneylenders, wholesalers and the larger landowners.[56]

The process of planning has, in addition, not been helped by fluctuations in agricultural policy, particularly in relation to the preferred type of agricultural unit. We have seen that a professed aim of the 1958 law was to establish a new class of small independent cultivators. Despite pressure for collectivisation from the Iraq Communist Party, the overwhelming tendency in the first decade of reform was to distribute land in family holdings of up to 75 acres. After 1970, however, the agricultural collective was to become a major instrument through which a revolution in the countryside was to be effected. Whilst the arguments in favour of medium-to-large agricultural units, especially in the irrigated zone, are extremely persuasive,[57] one wonders whether Iraq will have any more success with this most difficult of agricultural units than has the Soviet Union or Cuba. Indeed, whereas 72 collective farms were established between 1971 and 1974, only seven were set up in the two years after that and the number of members of these farms appears to have declined.[58]

Interestingly, bearing in mind the pronounced trend from collectives to state farms in both the Soviet Union and Cuba, the Ba'th government is experimenting with this latter type of unit, having established forty-two all over Iraq by the end of 1976. It has been suggested that a move towards large capital-intensive state farms is in part a response to the shortage of agricultural labour, a shortage which has been aggravated by the growth of employment opportunities in the expanding industrial sector. There is, however, no clear indication as yet of a definite trend in favour of state farms in Iraq. No new state farms have been set up in Iraq since 1977, and the government's policy is currently to study the operation of those already in existence before establishing any more. Iraq's state farms have faced a number of difficulties, such as problems of irrigation and the habitual problem of shortages of skilled manpower.[59]

At this point we should emphasise that a major problem for Iraqi agriculture is not just a shortage of skilled manpower but of *motivated* skilled manpower. In Iraq, as elsewhere in the developing world, the shortage of trained personnel is exacerbated by the unwillingness of those with appropriate skills to reside in rural areas where the availability of educational, medical, recreational and other facilities is generally inferior to that in the cities. Here we may move on to the other side of the planning coin – the human material upon which all forms of planning, no matter how accurately conceived or efficiently executed, must ultimately depend. A major obstacle for planners in Iraq is that on the receiving end of planning decisions is a backward and generally unresponsive peasantry, and it is to a consideration of the significance of this that we now turn.

The Peasantry

The term 'peasant' is used here to refer to cultivators who derive their living from the land through the application of primitive techniques and family labour, and who are constrained to surrender part of their surplus to a superior landowning class.[60] Iraq offers an extremely interesting case study of the process of 'peasantisation',[61] for only during the last hundred years has the transformation from semi-nomadic 'free' tribesmen into sedentary serf-like peasant cultivators taken place. Even as late as the 1960s a social anthropologist working in southern Iraq could observe that the people of Daghghara were 'not enthusiastic farmers'.[62] The recency of this transition has at least three important consequences which are of fundamental relevance to the problem of agricultural modernisation.

First, agricultural techniques in peasant societies are, by definition, primitive, due primarily to a combination of poor technology and human ignorance. Because of the relatively late transition to settled agriculture in Iraq, techniques there are even more primitive than in many other peasant societies. It is important to understand that the primitive methods of cultivation described earlier in this chapter are still widespread in Iraq today.[63]

Second, although tribalism *qua* social system has virtually disintegrated, except perhaps in the desert zone, tribal values continue to retain their strength, albeit to varying degrees. On this point it is worth noting that tribalism was to some extent artificially preserved by the operation of the Tribal Disputes Regulation. Until it was abolished in 1958 the Regulation actively maintained tribal institutions and customary law, as well as restoring customs and practices that had fallen into disuse.[64] Tribal values manifest themselves in a variety of ways: a high evaluation of generosity, hospitality, honour and manliness (which still leads to outbreaks of violence and feuding); and a corresponding contempt for thrift, frugality and materialism. Certain agricultural occupations such as the cultivation of vegetables, the raising of poultry and dairying are regarded as demeaning. Most important for our purposes, tribalism involves a deep attachment to and dependence upon kinship and other close personal relations, a feature which is reinforced in Iraq's case by the country's pluralistic structure.[65]

With the transition to a peasant society the parochialism of tribalism has been complemented by the complex of attitudes and values which derive from the peasant condition. There is a good deal of evidence from a variety of peasant societies which indicates that the instability of peasant existence, and particularly their often gross exploitation by landowners, the state or outsiders in general, tend to breed attitudes of apathy, submissiveness, fatalism, conservatism and a deep mistrust of the outside world and its representatives.[66] The degree of exploitation in Iraq before 1958 varied a good deal but at its worst, usually in the south, it was comparable with the serfdom that existed in pre-reform Bolivia, Ecuador and Peru. With up to 80 per cent of the crop being taken by the landlord, the peremptory eviction of tenants, arbitrary imprisonment in the shaikhs' private gaol for non-payment of debt,

beatings and other acts of violence, the *fellahin* were regarded and
treated as 'non-people'.[67] The cumulative effect of such experiences
has been to bequeath to modern Iraq a stratum of cultivators who are
physically, socially and mentally cut off from urban society. Several
writers have commented upon the suspicion and hostility of Iraq's
fellahin, especially to officialdom. Treakle emphasises the poor relations
he encountered between officials on the one hand and peasants on the
other, with undisguised contempt from the former reciprocated with
sullen non-co-operation from the latter. Both Treakle and Warriner,
visiting (independently) rural Iraq in the late 1960s, mention that their
excursions to the villages were always accompanied by an armed
guard.[68]

It is certain that the unrestrained propaganda of the Qasim era,
together with the promises made by succeeding governments, have
intensified the disillusion of the peasantry by raising expectations that
have not been met. Even when the *fellah* has been given his own plot
he has not infrequently been unable to derive a satisfactory living from
it, either because he has no proper irrigation and other facilities or
because the continued application of traditional techniques to a fixed
area of land has led to a drastic decline in yields. In return for his
piece of land the peasant has been constrained to join a co-operative,
for reasons which he does not entirely understand and whose
universalistic principles of operation are at odds with the personalism
of village society. Again, the Ba'th's advocacy of collective forms of
agricultural ownership is unlikely to arouse the enthusiasm of peasants
who typically display a strong emotional attachment to the idea of
owning their own plot of land. One may add here that resistance to
collectivised agriculture will be increased on account of its co-existence
with a private sector and the consequent heightening of the tension
between socialist co-operation and petty-bourgeois individualism. To
be sure, the present government is well aware of the problems posed
by Iraq's peasantry and since 1970 has made serious attempts to reduce
rural-urban imbalances, not least by placing considerable emphasis on
the broader educational aim of widening the peasant's horizons. Such is
the degree of economic and social backwardness of Iraq's peasantry,
however, that these policies can be expected to have a significant impact
only in the long term.[69] The peasant problem in Iraq is aggravated, we
would suggest, by the fact that urban-rural discontinuities are overlaid by
other discontinuities which again need to be examined in a historical
perspective. Let us now look at these discontinuities and their relationship
to the question of political instability in Iraq.

Political Instability

It is important to appreciate that the nation-state of Iraq is a fairly
recent creation. Iraq is also an artificial creation in the sense that,
unlike the major European states, it did not enjoy a lengthy process
of evolution but, like Syria, Lebanon and Jordan, was rather the
outcome of the machinations of Britain and France following the
collapse of the Ottoman Empire. As is the case with its neighbours, the
new state of Iraq came to contain within its boundaries social and ethnic
groups who were divided from each other by primordial loyalties. This
is most apparent in the basic split between the Arab majority and the
Kurdish minority who comprise from 15 to 20 per cent of Iraq's
population and who form a majority in the northern governates of
Sulaimaniya, Arbil and, according to some sources, Kirkuk.[70]

The Kurds aside, there exists another basic split, within Iraq's
Arabic-speaking population, between 'orthodox' Sunni Muslims and
Shi'a Muslims – who constitute a majority 55 per cent of the population. Although the Ba'th has pursued a policy of secularisation
aiming to combat sectarianism through the dissemination of Arab
socialism, experience from other countries in both developed and
developing worlds would seem to suggest that primordial attachments
are extremely durable and are significantly eroded only in the rather
long term. The point is that a majority of Iraq's peasants, as well as
its newly urbanised working class, are Shi'a Muslims, while Baghdad
and the policies that emanate from it have historically stood as a
symbol of Sunni hegemony. It is certain that the basic split between
the two tendencies in Islam and its historic manifestation in Iraq
underlies *some* of the resistance to government policies. It would be
simplistic to explain current conflicts in Iraq entirely in terms of
primordial divisions.[71] The more fundamental point is that because of
the nature of its evolution as a state, Iraq continues to be riven by
deep internal cleavages. Accordingly, political groupings in Iraq, whether
they be Kurds, Arabs, Shi'a, Sunni, Ba'thists, Communists, Arab
nationalists, the army, students or the working class, tend to be highly,
if not excessively, politicised in a manner reminiscent of Huntington's
'praetorian' society.[72] Such deep internal divisions have tended towards,
at times, acute political instability, characterised by a politics of
conspiracy in which the *coup* and the plot become the normal means of
effecting change and political repression the only way of preventing it.
Between 1958 and 1968 there were four major changes of regime, seven
major attempts to topple one or other of the governments in power and

at least double that number of more minor efforts. Given the atmosphere of uncertainty that is engendered by such upheavals, both internal and external, and given the frequent changes of government and civil service personnel that is a consequence, it is not so surprising that the decision-making process is highly centralised and that middle-range administrators seek refuge behind a screen of bureaucratic ritualism rather than take the initiative. In this respect the planning deficiencies discussed above need to be located within a broader political context.

Conclusion

Iraq provides an extremely interesting case study, for it illustrates both the complexities of, and profound disabilities contained within, the condition of underdevelopment. Although relatively well-endowed with resources when compared with most other developing societies, sustained attempts to modernise Iraq's rural economy have nonetheless encountered serious difficulties. The sources of these difficulties are many and diverse but we have identified three principal problem areas: planning, the peasantry and political instability. We have further suggested that these and other problems need to be considered in the light of Iraq's historical development as a nation-state. Iraq shares a number of features with other countries in the Middle East and North and tropical Africa, the formation of whose state structures owed more to the politico-economic interests of the former colonial powers than to the needs of the citizens contained within their borders. A major consequence is that such states have been afflicted by internal tensions so profound as to amount periodically to a state of civil war. Internal conflicts have furthermore been greatly aggravated, and not infrequently deliberately exploited, in the cause of great power rivalry. The effects of such tensions and the resulting instability on the development effort of any country may be readily appreciated.

Leaving aside, in so far as one may, the great imponderable of long-term political instability in Iraq, what, then, are the prospects for rural development? The Ba'th government remains firmly committed to the goal of agricultural modernisation, and investment in this sector (particularly in the field of specialist education[73]) continues to be given priority. It is virtually impossible to predict when this scale of investment may be expected to lead to significant improvements both in agricultural production and in the general standard of living in the countryside. It is worth bearing in mind, however, that very marked advances have been made in the field of flood control and water storage and that the devastation to crops once caused by spring floods is now virtually a thing of the past. We also saw that the yields of certain crops have shown an often substantial increase over the past twenty years, an improvement which must indicate the gradual penetration of modern techniques of agricultural production. We must also not overlook the radical transformation in the pattern of landholding in Iraq during the past quarter of a century. Some indication of the extent of this transformation may be gathered from Table 13.2. Whereas holdings of 620 acres and above accounted for 68 per cent of land in individual tenure in 1958, by 1971, before the 1970 Act could have had a profound impact, this figure had fallen to 14.1 per cent. At the other end of the scale, holdings of under 62 acres occupied only 10 per cent of land in 1958 whereas in 1971 the figure was 53 per cent. In 1958 there were 168,346 agricultural holdings; by 1971 there were 539,040.[74] We have seen, of course, that simply receiving a plot of land by no means automatically leads to an increase in the cultivator's standard of living. We have also seen that the dependence of peasants on landowners, merchants and wholesalers was not entirely eliminated by the mid-1970s.

Table 13.2: Land Tenure in Iraq: 1958-9 compared with 1971

Size category (acres)[a]	1958-9[b]		1971[c]	
	No. of holdings in each category as % of all holdings	Area of holdings in each category as % of total area	No. of holdings in each category as % of all holdings	Area of holdings in each category as % of total area
Under 2.5	34.5	0.3	12.5	0.6
2.5-19	33.7	3.0	43.4	13.2
19-62	17.9	7.2	35.2	39.2
62-620	11.9	21.5	8.7	32.9
620 and above	2.0	68.0	0.2	14.1

	1958-9	1971
Total number of holdings:	168,346	539,040
Total area of holdings:	14,462,800	14,214,583

Notes a. The size of the categories derives from the original data which were in Iraqi *donums.* (One *donum* = 0.62 acres, 0.25 hectares.)
   b. Figures for 1958-9 taken from D. Warriner, *Land Reform in Principle and Practice* (Clarendon Press, Oxford, 1969), p. 90.
   c. Figures for 1971 adapted from Agricultural Census 1971, cited in D. Dahiri, *Economics of the Agricultural Sector in Iraq* (al-Ani Press, Baghdad, 1976), p. 106.

Nonetheless, it is not unreasonable to assume that a transformation in the pattern of landholding on this scale, and the elimination of rent which this entails, must have resulted in increases in income for a sizeable proportion of Iraq's *fellahin*.[75]

It should finally be pointed out to those, both inside and outside Iraq, who have bemoaned the country's slow progress with agrarian reform that the modernisation of the countryside is a complex and invariably protracted process, and we would remind them that a residual peasant economy, and all that that signifies, survived in certain countries in western Europe until well after World War II.

Notes

1. This chapter was originally produced as a research working paper for the Polytechnic of Central London.

2. See, for evidence of this, M. Todaro, *Economics for a Developing World* (Longman, London, 1977), Ch. 14.

3. S.M. Issa, 'The Distribution of Income in Iraq, 1971', in A. Kelidar (ed.), *The Integration of Modern Iraq* (Croom Helm, London, 1979), pp. 123-34.

4. D. Dahiri, *Economics of the Agricultural Sector in Iraq* (al-Ani Press, Baghdad, 1976), p. 47.

5. M. Yudelman, 'Some Issues in Agricultural Development in Iraq', *Journal of Farm Economics*, vol. XL (1958), p. 80.

6. E. and E.F. Penrose, *Iraq: International Relations and National Development* (Ernest Benn, London, 1978), Ch. 18.

7. D. Warriner, *Land Reform and Development in the Middle East – A Study of Egypt, Syria and Iraq*, 2nd edn (Oxford University Press, London, 1962), p. 113.

8. *Baghdad Observer*, 17 Mar. 1979.

9. We should perhaps clarify that by 'rural development' we mean not simply the expansion of agricultural production and the modernisation of agricultural techniques but the overall development of the rural sector. That is, the extension of health, education and other vital services to rural populations, and the progressive eradication of serious rural-urban differences. We further believe that since rural development is a multi-faceted process its analysis requires an inter-disciplinary rather than a single-disciplinary perspective.

10. R. Lawless, 'Iraq: Changing Population Patterns', in J. Clarke and W. Fisher (eds.), *Populations of the Middle East: a Geographical Approach* (University of London Press, London, 1972), p. 109.

11. See F. Baali, 'Relationships of Man to the Land in Iraq', *Rural Sociology*, vol. 31 (1966), p. 180; D. Dahiri, *The Introduction of Technology into Traditional Societies and Economies* (al-Ani Press, Baghdad, 1969), Ch. XV; and R. Fernea, *Sheikh and Effendi: Changing Patterns of Authority among the al-Shabana of Southern Iraq* (Harvard University Press, Cambridge, 1970), pp. 46-7.

12. Warriner, *Land Reform and Development*, p. 116.

13. Ibid. See also M. Hasan, 'The Role of Foreign Trade in the Economic Development of Iraq: a Study in the Growth of a Dependent Economy', in M. Cook (ed.), *Studies in the Economic History of the Middle East* (Oxford University Press, London, 1970), pp. 350-1.

14. Warriner, *Land Reform and Development*, p. 116; see also P. Sluglett, *Britain in Iraq, 1914-1932* (Ithaca Press, London, 1976), pp. 232-3.

15. A problem arises in the English-speaking world because of the popular connotations of the word 'shaikh', which is habitually associated with an extremely wealthy, invariably portly and licentious, eastern potentate. Whilst a shaikh in the Arab world may indeed be in possession of enormous political and economic power, he might equally be someone who simply has a claim to high status through piety, learning, descent or merely longevity.

16. A. Jwaideh, 'Midhat Pasha and the Land System of Lower Iraq', *St Antony's Papers (Middle Eastern Affairs)*, vol. 16, no. 3 (1963), pp. 124-34.

17. S. Haider, 'Land Problems of Iraq', unpublished PhD thesis, University of London, 1942, Ch. VI; and Hasan, 'Foreign Trade', pp. 349-53.

18. Jwaideh, 'Midhat Pasha', pp. 124-5.

19. A. al-Hadithi and A. al-Dujaili, 'Problems of Implementation of Agrarian Reform in Iraq', paper given at the Food and Agriculture Organisation conference held in Tripoli, Libya, October 1965. See also Warriner, *Land Reform and Development*, pp. 140-1.

20. Hasan, 'Foreign Trade', p. 52.

21. Warriner, *Land Reform and Development*, p. 119; see also M. Azeez, 'Geographical Aspects of Rural Migration from Amara Province, Iraq, 1955-1964', unpublished PhD thesis, University of Durham, 1968, pp. 56-7; M. Quint, 'The Idea of Progress in an Iraqi Village', *Middle East Journal*, vol. 2, no. 4 (1958), pp. 369-70; and H. Treakle, 'Land Reform in Iraq', *Agency for International Development, Spring Review*, June 1970, p. 25.

22. Warriner, *Land Reform and Development*, pp. 108-9; Treakle, 'Land Reform', p. 28.

23. Azeez, 'Geographical Aspects', pp. 266-7; see also Baali, 'Relationships', p. 361; and Lawless, 'Iraq', p. 121.

24. Dahiri, *Economics*, pp. 77-82.

25. Azeez, 'Geographical Aspects', pp. 71-3; Dahiri, *Economics*, pp. 77-82; and Warriner, *Land Reform*, pp. 162-9.

26. M. Palmer, 'Some Political Determinants of Economic Reform: Agrarian Reform in Iraq', *Journal of Asian and African Studies*, vol. 6 (July/October 1971), p. 170; and Azeez, 'Geographical Aspects', pp. 73-5.

27. See R. Gaby, *Communism and Agrarian Reform in Iraq* (Croom Helm, London, 1978), p. 114; and D. Warriner, *Land Reform in Principle and Practice* (Clarendon Press, Oxford, 1969), pp. 89-90.

28. Dahiri, *Economics*, p. 157; Gaby, *Communism*, p. 116.

29. Treakle, 'Land Reform', pp. 55-6.

30. J. Simmons, 'Agricultural Development in Iraq: Planning and Management Failures', *Middle East Journal*, vol. 19, no. 2 (Spring 1965), pp. 129-40; Palmer, 'Political Determinants', p. 176; Gaby, *Communism*, p. 116.

31. Warriner, *Principle and Practice*, pp. 94-5; Simmons, 'Agricultural Development', p. 140.

32. The period 1954-8 includes an exceptionally good year for all crops, 1954, whilst 1959-63 includes two years, 1959 and 1960, during which there was a serious drought in northern Iraq.

33. Wheat is grown largely in the rain-fed zone and would therefore have been subjected to less disruption than crops grown in the irrigation zone. Barley is the major cereal crop in the irrigation zone.

34. Gaby, *Communism*, p. 117.

35. Simmons, 'Agricultural Development', p. 140; Warriner, *Principle and Practice*, p. 91; see also A. Badre, 'Economic Development of Iraq', in L. Cooper and S. Alexander (eds.), *Economic Development and Population Growth in the Middle East* (Elsevier Publishing Company, New York, 1972), pp. 283-328.

36. Gaby, *Communism*, pp. 132-3.

37. Ministry of Agrarian Reform, *Agrarian Reform Law No. 117, 1970*, (Ministry of Agrarian Reform, Baghdad, 1970), p. 36.

38. Central Statistical Organisation, *Annual Abstract of Statistics 1974* (Ministry of Planning, Baghdad, 1975), pp. 106-9.

39. Ibid., p. 109.

40. The formation of joint co-operatives is encouraged in the 1970 Agrarian Reform Law (Article 42). They are the result of a union of two or more co-operatives within a given area. As with the collectives, the aim is to unify effort and consolidate resources.

41. Dahiri, *Economics*, p. 8.

42. Gaby, *Communism*, p. 212.

43. Central Statistical Organisation, *Annual Abstract of Statistics 1976* (Ministry of Planning, Baghdad, 1977), p. 349; see also Gaby, *Communism*, p. 181; and Dahiri, *Economics*, Ch. 8.

44. Central Statistical Organisation, *Abstract 1976*, p. 269; Gaby, *Communism*, p. 221.

       1 Iraq Dinar (ID) = US$2.80 until December 1971

                  US$3.04 until February 1973

                  US$3.37 until February 1975.

45. The figures are taken from Central Statistical Organisation, *Annual Abstract of Statistics*, versions for 1970-6 (Ministry of Planning, Baghdad).

46. In 1960 the population of Iraq was 6,885,000, 56% of which was located in rural areas. In 1975 the population was 11,124,000, 36% of which was in rural areas.

47. Dahiri, *Economics*, Ch. 1; K. McLachlan, 'Iraq' in R. Burrell, R. Hoyle and K. McLachlan, *The Developing Agriculture of the Middle East: Opportunities and Prospects* (Graham and Trotman, London, 1976), pp. 51-2.

48. Simmons, 'Agricultural Development'; see also N. Raphaeli, 'Agrarian Reform in Iraq: Some Political and Administrative Problems', *Journal of Administration Overseas*, vol. 5 (1966), pp. 102-11.

49. Report quoted in Penrose and Penrose, *Iraq*, pp. 470-6.

50. Reported in *al-Thawrah*, 8, 9 and 10 Sept. 1976. Quoted in Penrose and Penrose, *Iraq*, pp. 470-6.

51. F. Jalal, *The Role of Government in the Industrialisation of Iraq, 1950-65* (Frank Cass, London, 1972), Ch. 1.

52. C. Issawi, 'Economic Revolution in the Middle East', *The Listener*, 5 Sept. 1957, p. 334.

53. See, for example, Palmer, 'Political Determinants'.

54. McLachlan, 'Iraq', p. 45; Central Statistical Organisation, *Abstract 1976*, p. 269.

55. Dahiri, *Economics*, pp. 267-9.

56. Ibid.; see also S. al-Nowfel and M. Hamdoon, *New Attitudes in Agrarian Reform and Agricultural Cooperation in Iraq* (Ministry of Agrarian Reform, Baghdad, 1972), pp. 11-15.

57. See Fernea, *Sheikh and Effendi*; and A. Poyk, *Farm Studies in Iraq (An Agro-Economic Study of Agriculture in the Hill-Diwaniya Area in Iraq)* (Agricultural University, Wageningen, 1962).

58. Central Statistical Organisation, *Abstract 1976*, p. 120.

59. General Establishment of State Farms, *State Farms: the Fifth Report* (Ministry of Agriculture, Baghdad, 1980).

60. See T. Shanin, 'Peasantry: Delineation of a Sociological Concept and a Field of Study', *European Journal of Sociology*, vol. xii (1971), pp. 289-300; and E. Wolf, *Peasants* (Prentice-Hall, Englewood Cliffs, 1973).

61. L. Fallers, 'Are African Cultivators to be called "Peasants"?', *Current Anthropology*, vol. 12, no. 2 (April 1961).

62. R. Fernea, 'Land Reform and Ecology in Post-Revolutionary Iraq', *Economic Development and Cultural Change*, vol. 17 (1969), p. 365.

63. Baali, 'Relationships', p. 180; Dahiri, *Technology*, Ch. 15; and Fernea, *Sheikh and Effendi*, pp. 46-7.

64. I. al-Wahab, 'Tribal Customary Law and Modern Law in Iraq', *International Labour Review*, vol. 89, no. 1 (1963), pp. 19-27.

65. Dahiri, *Technology*, Ch. 5; Fernea, *Sheikh and Effendi*; and S. Salim, *Marsh-Dwellers of the Euphrates Delta* (The Athlone Press, London, 1962). On the persistence of tribal values and customs among migrants in Baghdad see Azeez, 'Geographical Aspects', pp. 280-4.

66. See, for example, F. Bailey, 'The Peasant View of the Bad Life', in T. Shanin (ed.), *Peasants and Peasant Societies* (Penguin, Harmondsworth, 1971).

67. See Gaby, *Communism*, pp. 185-7; and Warriner, *Land Reform and Development*, pp. 154-5.

68. Treakle, 'Land Reform', p. 60; Warriner, *Principle and Practice*, p. 101.

69. An insight into the kinds of difficulties these educational programmes encounter may be gained from an article which appeared on the front page of *al-Thawrah* in October 1977. The article, entitled 'A Good Programme of Farmer's Education; but . . . ?', describes a short course for farmers (i.e. peasant farmers), demonstrating modern agricultural techniques. The fact that the techniques were actually demonstrated was useful, the report tells us, since most of the farmers were illiterate and would not therefore be able to understand a blackboard-type lecture. However, some of the farmers could not complete the course because the demands of the agricultural cycle forced them to return to their villages. Others complained of serious transport problems, having had to walk long distances before they could catch the specially organised transport (*al-Thawrah*, 31 Oct. 1977).

70. Lawless, 'Iraq', pp. 103-4.

71. M. Farouk-Sluglett, 'Contemporary Iraq: Some Recent Writings Considered' *Review of Middle East Studies*, no. 3 (1978).

72. S. Huntington, *Political Order in Changing Societies* (Yale University Press, New Haven, 1968).

73. Very much aware of the deficiency in trained agricultural personnel the government in its 1976-80 plan envisaged an increase in the number of admissions to agricultural colleges from 5,986 in 1976 to 282,234 in 1981. The number of agricultural colleges was also expected to rise from eleven in 1975 to 50 by 1980.

74. Warriner, *Principle and Practice*, p. 90; Dahiri, *Economics*, p. 106; Gaby, *Communism*, pp. 178-9.

75. See especially Gaby, *Communism*, pp. 178-80; and D. Warriner, 'Employment and Income Aspects of Recent Agrarian Reforms in the Middle East', *International Labour Review*, vol. 101 (1970), pp. 605-25.

14 WESTERN, SOVIET AND EGYPTIAN INFLUENCES ON IRAQ'S DEVELOPMENT PLANNING

Rodney Wilson

Introduction

Most Third World governments today believe planning to be a necessity, and there is currently no Arab country without some sort of development plan and a planning ministry or authority. As Iraq has a longer experience of development planning than any other Arab country, dating back more than three decades, some review of its experience is clearly instructive, even if it must be admitted that the influence of Iraq's planners on other Arab states has so far been minimal. The Baghdad authorities have themselves been strongly influenced by outside ideas, initially in the pre-revolutionary period from the West, but later by Soviet ideas, both directly as a result of the Iraqi-Soviet agreement of 1959 and indirectly through the Soviet influence over planning in Nasser's Egypt. In the 1970s Soviet influence over Iraq's economic affairs lessened, and there are no indications of it reviving. Instead there has been an earnest attempt to discover planning methods which are best suited to Iraqi conditions, rather than trying to conform with either Western or Soviet planning models.

Those concerned with development economics in the West are, of course, in a rather invidious position if they recommend planning at all in countries such as Iraq, as few Western economies have ever been, or are, planned. France, with its system of indicative planning which involves setting targets for particular industrial sectors, was an exception, but the targets set by the government's plans were achieved largely by relying on price incentives and market forces generally rather than through state direction of resources – although the latter was practised to some extent. Britain's own attempt at planning under George Brown in the 1960s was short-lived, viewed as a disaster by general agreement and soon readily forgotten by most of those involved, who moved on to other concerns. Yet, despite Britain's reliance on the economics of the free market and *laissez-faire* for its own industrial revolution, planning was recommended for Iraq by

British administrators and visiting experts, who were far from being radical thinkers. It is interesting to seek an explanation for this, especially as many right-wing development theorists continue to reject development planning in any form. Admittedly, outspoken critics of state involvement in managing the economy (like Peter Bauer – who is extremely influential today), were only starting to make their voices heard in the 1950s, but nevertheless there were plenty of advocates of a minimal role for the state around even then.

The Start of Planning in Iraq

There are several reasons why, as early as the late 1940s, Western experts were urging Iraq to adopt planning, most being directly concerned with the country's transition to an oil-based economy. It was realised that, given the likely expansion of oil revenue, the government would have to play a major role in economic activity if the oil revenue was not to be wasted fruitlessly on current consumption. The emphasis was on creating a well-organised centralised authority for administering oil-revenue expenditure, and on ensuring that funds were dispensed in an orderly fashion so that economic stability would prevail. At the same time it was acknowledged that the private sector in Iraq was unlikely to be capable of modernising the economy, especially as it was so limited in size. Although in 1954 the first industrial census revealed that there were 2,460 industrial establishments in the country, only 294 employed more than 20 workers, and most of these were in the fields of construction, quarrying, water supply and workshops providing services for government departments.[1] There were only 79 true manufacturing establishments involved in food-processing, shoe-making and textiles. Nor was there any significant traditional workshop sector as in the huge bazaar economy of neighbouring Iran.

Iraq also lacked a modern infrastructure; to develop such an infrastructure was viewed as essential, not least for the continuing growth of the oil sector itself. Although much of the basic infrastructure in the United Kingdom, especially the railways, had been financed through private capital, there was no way the redistribution of oil income into private hands would have ensured similar developments in Iraq. Indeed, the experience of neighbouring Kuwait's land purchase programme suggests that, if a similar policy had been adopted in Iraq in the 1950s, it would merely have fuelled land speculation and resulted in an increased demand for imports of consumer durables and non-durables.[2]

A further factor leading Western advisers to favour planned economic development in Iraq was the prevalence of political instability – with forty-seven different governments over the 1921-50 period. The perpetual political strife and personal rivalries not only distracted attention from economic matters but also led to the complete absence of any continuity in government expenditure plans. To overcome this problem, then, an autonomous Development Board was established.[3] Legally the Board had a juristic personality, and could rent or purchase goods and services and issue bonds on its own account, but more crucially it had its own budget which was financed directly from the state's oil revenues. Initially the Development Board was to receive the entire oil revenues, but during its first year of operation (1950) the enormous increase in revenue as a consequence of a new oil agreement resulted in its share being reduced to 70 per cent, while the government received the remainder to augment its current expenditure. Under Law 23 of 1950 the Board was given responsibility for all capital expenditure, and was empowered to draw up a five-year plan for the country's development. With respect to long-term economic strategy, therefore, the Board was to be of more significance than the government itself; and although it was ultimately responsible to the Council of Ministers, its continuity *vis-à-vis* the constantly changing governments must have strengthened its power even further.

The creation of such a powerful planning body was without precedent in those countries still aligned to the Western world, as Iraq was before its revolution. Even in Turkey, the Middle Eastern state with the longest experience of planning, the planning authorities enjoyed much less autonomy. The Turkish experience, moreover, exerted little influence on Iraq. After the demise of the Ottoman Empire Turkey's influence on its former colonies, including Iraq, became minimal, and the Ankara government's attempts to plan the Turkish economy in the 1920s and 1930s had little effect on those making economic decisions in Baghdad.

The Development Board's autonomy was not, of course, complete. The Iraqi Prime Minister chaired the Board, and the Minister of Finance was amongst the eight members. Other government ministers, however, were not represented. The main membership of the Board was constituted by 'executive members' who were not allowed to have any government or legislative position; three of these were to be experts in the fields of economics, finance and irrigation. Given the continuity of service of the executive members, it was these technocrats who were to exercise the real authority. Inevitably tensions arose between the government and the Board, especially as the two governmental members on the Board felt that they in particular, and the government in general, were being forced to take responsibility for decisions which were outside their control. Pressure from the cabinet led to the creation of a Ministry of Development in 1953, with the minister represented on the Development Board, thus increasing the political membership of the Board to three. This perhaps inevitably created further problems, as tensions arose between the Board and the new Ministry. Although the Board decided expenditure allocation, it was the Ministry which implemented the development plans, and the latter could therefore delay any Board proposals of which it disapproved.

A further difficulty with planning in Iraq in this early period was that the plans were continually being revised and even redrafted before they reached the implementation stage; there was much wasted effort. Thus the first 1951/2-55/6 investment programme drawn up by the Development Board was almost immediately replaced by a second programme for the 1951/2-56/7 period, while the third plan for the 1955/6-59/60 period was superseded by the fourth one for the 1955/6-60/1 period.[4] One reason for this was that the oil revenues on which the planned expenditure were based were continually being revised upwards. Oil production rose, for example, from 4 million tons in 1949 to 7 million in 1950, and the revenue share changed with the 50 per cent profit-sharing agreement of February 1952, which was backdated to January 1951. A further reason for change was the presentation of reports by outside bodies or experts called in to study the country's development prospects, such as that of the World Bank Mission in 1952,[5] which resulted in the adjustment of planning targets, or the report of Lord Salter in 1955,[6] which resulted in a fourth plan being introduced to replace the third. Planners within the country lacked confidence, and outsiders had a receptive audience for their suggestions and criticisms.

Iraqi planning methods were, of course, fairly basic in the 1950s, the usual procedure adopted being to forecast the likely level of oil revenue first (never an easy task), and then to draw up a spending programme in the light of these projections. No attempt was made to formulate development objectives in the light of the country's needs; it was solely the anticipated oil resources which determined what was to be done. The emphasis was exclusively on spending, and it was thought that, provided the funds were available, economic progress would ensue.

There was little real debate about what was meant by economic progress, or even what Iraq's ultimate development goals should be. The increased spending was intended to raise living standards, but the plans gave no details of the mechanisms whereby this could be ensured. The authorities could not be held responsible for all these omissions, however, as development economics itself was in its infancy. Less excusable defects were the lack of attention paid to the issue of income distribution, and the convenient assumption that existing property rights were inalienable.

As a consequence of the emphasis on expenditure and the scant notice taken of other factors, actual spending consistently fell short of the funds allocated (see Table 14.1). The development plans were a mere listing of possible projects, but these needed more than just money for their implementation – they also required real resources, both physical and human. Some supervisory labour could, of course, be imported at a price, but local manpower was required for most of the less-skilled tasks; and despite underemployment, and perhaps unemployment, this could not simply be harnessed. The inadequate infrastructure also created difficulties. Projects in the construction sector had the best record of implementation, and those in the industrial and transportation sectors the weakest. The construction sector tends to be import-intensive, yet also intensive in its use of unskilled labour, which was available in reasonably abundant supply. The industrial and transportation sectors both tend to have high managerial and skilled manpower requirements. From Table 14.1 it is apparent that it was not until the 1970s that the implementation record for industry reached a consistently high level, indicating that the planners were on target. The record for agriculture, conversely, became noticeably worse during the 1960s in the aftermath of the poorly administered post-revolution land reform programmes.

In Iraq's first four plans drawn up prior to the revolution of 1958 the aim was to develop the country along the lines of its perceived comparative advantage, namely in agriculture. At that time the prevalent thinking amongst Western economists was that developing countries should specialise in what they were best at producing, usually primary commodities, and import manufactured goods from the Western industrialised nations which had established a clear lead in this field. This was, of course, before the Prebisch thesis on declining terms of trade for primary produce was publicised,[7] and before problems of price-instability for non-processed products were the subject of widespread debate. In Iraq there seems to have been little questioning

Table 14.1: Planning Allocations and Expenditure (in Iraqi dinars at current prices)

	Allocation (million dinars)	Total expenditure (million dinars)	Proportion of expenditure to allocation (%)				
			All sectors	Agriculture	Industry	Transport	Construction
1951	9.2	3.0	33.0	29.1	–	34.4	36.8
1952	20.0	7.6	38.0	33.1	2.7	48.1	65.8
1953	27.8	12.0	43.0	46.9	9.2	41.8	72.0
1954	31.0	20.6	66.5	66.9	34.1	83.2	86.5
1955	43.7	31.3	71.6	83.5	70.1	61.7	69.0
1956	81.2	42.4	53.3	46.5	29.6	54.7	85.2
1957	100.7	56.7	56.4	45.3	53.7	48.5	81.7
1958	98.7	51.5	52.2	43.4	108.0	28.0	73.3
1959	163.2	49.5	30.4	22.7	25.8	30.6	38.6
1960	136.9	47.6	34.7	59.8	45.2	22.3	32.8
1961	196.7	56.7	33.9	36.2	28.4	27.8	37.9
1962	108.1	58.8	54.4	31.2	41.9	48.7	85.7
1963	117.6	53.6	45.6	19.8	24.1	61.5	83.3
1964	119.6	72.7	60.8	27.3	38.4	67.6	127.4
1965	113.4	49.7	43.8	23.9	47.1	46.6	54.7
1966	119.6	64.9	54.3	28.7	68.8	64.0	58.4
1967	113.2	61.6	54.4	37.0	59.5	64.7	58.6
1968	123.7	54.3	43.9	33.0	46.1	47.8	55.3
1969	70.0	57.0	81.4	79.5	83.8	84.1	78.7
1970	84.3	61.6	73.1	56.4	95.4	55.6	81.5
1971	166.0	119.8	72.2	82.2	71.1	60.6	62.9
1972	89.2	98.1	110.0	126.1	79.3	124.2	76.0
1973	210.0	150.3	71.6	53.1	87.6	73.8	74.9

Source: J. Hashim, *Development Planning in Iraq: Historical Perspective and New Directions* (Planning Board, Baghdad, July 1975), Tables 7 and 8, pp. 75-80.

amongst decision-makers of the Western conventional wisdom, and therefore the plans concentrated on agricultural development and infrastructure construction. The latter was intended to facilitate the further integration of Iraq's primary producing economy into the Western economy as a whole, through strengthening trade links.

The breakdown of development expenditure by sector shown in Table 14.2 illustrates how closely Iraq followed the Western proposed

Table 14.2: Actual Expenditure under Development Plans (%)

	Agriculture	Industry	Transport	Building and services
1951	33	–	30	37
1952	37	1	30	32
1953	52	4	18	26
1954	47	10	24	19
1955	40	9	32	19
1956	31	12	26	31
1957	25	15	25	35
1958	26	23	19	32
1959	22	10	28	40
1960	23	12	17	48
1961	20	13	25	42
1962	11	17	27	45
1963	8	18	34	40
1964	9	23	26	42
1965	12	30	25	33
1966	13	45	23	19
1967	18	38	22	22
1968	24	34	18	24
1969	30	31	18	21
1970	26	43	14	17
1971	41	30	14	15
1972	40	23	20	17
1973	23	35	20	22

Source: As Table 14.1, with percentages computed by the author.

strategy for growth in the early years of planning, with between one-third and one-half of expenditure devoted to agriculture. Most of the remainder was for transport and construction work – to help the export of oil and the monetarisation of the rural economy, so that local agriculture would at least be harnessed for national, if not initially international, needs. Industry was largely neglected, except in so far as a few plants could be justified (on grounds of transport costs alone) to satisfy local consumption. Such plants included a small oil refinery for internal requirements, two cement factories, a bitumen refinery and a cotton and weaving mill. There were no plans to develop export capacity in any of these plants, and even the domestic market was hardly catered for. Items in all categories continued to be imported.

The three major teams of Western advisers brought in before the revolution, at the time of Nuri al-Said, all supported the concept of outward-orientated development based on comparative advantage. The World Bank Mission in 1952 suggested that projects should only be adopted if they used existing resources—an approach which would now be labelled as supply-side economics. There was no consideration of the possibilities of infant industrial development based on protectionist measures through either tariffs or administered controls on trade. The World Bank Mission's approach was broadly supported in the Plan for Action submitted by Lord Salter in April 1955, and in the report prepared by Arthur D. Little, the United States consultants, who presented their plan for industrial development in 1956.[8] Salter tended to concentrate on the widely recognised defects of Iraq's administrative machinery, while Arthur D. Little consultants concerned themselves with detail, which was, of course, what they were paid for, and not with strategy. The Arthur D. Little report nevertheless remains a valuable document, and, and, interestingly, many of the projects which it recommended, including the plants to produce rayon and paper and the complex to recover sulphur from natural gas, were still twenty years later being either considered or implemented. In many ways the report's emphasis on an integrated and well-balanced industrial programme, and its stress on the complementarity and linkages between industries, were ahead of its time, and certainly far advanced in relation to the level of thinking on development in Iraq back in the 1950s.

Post-Revolution Planning

With the revolution of 1958 which brought Abd al-Karim Qasim to power all the vestiges of the previous regime were swept away, including its development plans. There was a rejection of the Western approach to planning—in part because it was associated with capitalists or neo-colonialists, but in part also because anything favoured by Nuri al-Said and his associates was deemed suspect. To some extent, then, a new approach was favoured for its own sake, and there were undoubtedly some who believed that any change would be desirable so long as it was different to what had already been tried. Given that most of those who were associated with the revolution were more concerned with political than with economic matters, it remained an open question what direction economic policy should take, especially as the revolutionary leaders were pragmatists rather than theorists.

Immediate organisational changes were nevertheless made, and following a review of planning machinery the Executive Power Law was passed in 1959, abolishing the Development Board and the Ministry of Development and establishing an Economic Planning Board and a Ministry of Planning.[9] These changes were far from being merely cosmetic, as they were not only intended to remove the former senior personnel from the pre-revolutionary period (which could have been achieved without an administrative reform), but were also designed to strengthen the government's control of the development effort. The government was evidently seeking a more centralised direction, in economic matters as in other fields, not as a result of any socialist ideals but rather because the new regime felt far from secure and wanted to maintain control of economic as well as political developments. In the reorganised system of administration the ministries, under their political heads, were given the authority to execute the plans, while the Planning Board formulated long-term strategy, and the Ministry of Planning acted as a technical secretariat, but without powers of enforcement. The old system of concentrating both executive authority and powers of formulation in the hands of one body, the Development Board, with some degree of autonomy from the government, was therefore terminated.

Planning objectives could only be modified more slowly than procedures, and under the Provisional Economic Plan adopted for the 1959-62 period the emphasis was on completing the projects initiated under the previous regime. It was decided that more time would be needed to draw up a full economic plan aimed at changing the economy's direction, especially as there were few supporters of the new regime with any experience of planning. Nevertheless, given the desire to direct the economy in a different direction than hitherto it was inevitable that the planners should start to look at the methods and planning objectives of non-Western countries. As the Soviet bloc states had the longest history of planning, their experience was of considerable interest to many of the supporters of the new regime in Iraq.

There were three main factors that led to increased Soviet influence over Iraqi planning from the late 1950s onwards. It would be difficult to determine which was the most crucial. First, the Soviet Union itself responded to the revolution in Iraq in a typically opportunist fashion, seeing that a setback to the West could be put to its own advantage. Although oil revenues were not affected by the revolution, Soviet diplomats apparently raised the fear in Iraqi official minds that these revenues might be at risk—especially given the experience of neighbouring Iran in the early 1950s under Mossadeq. The Soviet Union therefore offered to help Iraq by providing a loan of 65 million Iraqi dinars to help finance the Provisional Economic Plan for 1959-62. A further loan of 12 million dinars was made available by Czechoslovakia.[10] These amounts were, of course, relatively small in relation to the actual expenditure envisaged under the plan (almost 400 million dinars), and from the point of view of the Soviet Union they were an extremely modest price to pay for winning some degree of favour with the new regime. Furthermore, given Iraq's poor record of actual expenditure of allocated funds, of which the Soviet Union was well aware, it was unlikely that much of the loan would ever be utilised. In the event, as Table 14.1 shows, actual expenditure fell from around one-half of allocated funding in 1958 to around one-third over the 1959-61 period, and as oil revenue remained buoyant Soviet resources were never actually required. This experience is typical of Soviet relations with developing countries elsewhere, then and subsequently. In terms of cost-effectiveness Soviet influence has almost always been secured for a much lower price than that of the United States or its Western allies.

The second factor which favoured increasing Soviet influence was that Iraq had a long-established and well-organised Communist Party of its own which, although small in number and representative of only a limited section of the urban population, was nevertheless extremely effective. The Communists overtly supported the revolution and the Qasim regime, mainly because they viewed the new order as a vehicle which would help them achieve their long-term objectives. Although relations between the Communist Party and Qasim were far from easy, Communists did gain a significant influence in planning affairs and played a major role in the formulation of the Detailed Economic Plan which was to cover the 1961-5 period. A number of Iraqi Communists had been in exile in the Soviet Union under the previous regime and had studied Soviet planning methods. Whereas other supporters of Qasim, then, had only scant knowledge of economic affairs and planning techniques (whether Western or Soviet),[11] there were Communists who could offer their expertise.

A third factor which indirectly favoured the infusion of Soviet ideas was the influence of Nasser's Egypt, both through inter-governmental relations and via local Nasserite factions within Iraq. There was considerable movement of personnel between Baghdad and Cairo after the 1958 revolution, not only by senior ministers, but even by junior administrative staff, including employees of the Ministry of Planning.[12] Egyptian economic policy in the early 1960s, after the sweeping nationalisation measures which transformed Egypt's economic structure, was based on centralised control and direction of economic activity along the lines followed by the Soviet Union. Although personalities were arguably more important than ideology in Nasser's Egypt as in most parts of the Arab world, the Planning Ministry and the Institute of National Planning in Cairo were strongly influenced by Eastern European ideas. Ali Sabry, who later became Planning Minister under Nasser, favoured Soviet planning methods and, sharing the Marxist conception of history as being moulded primarily by economic forces, saw planning as a necessity for long-term strategic reasons. Moreover, Soviet and East German advisers were brought into Egypt's Planning Ministry in the early 1960s, and there is little doubt that Iraq's new planners came into contact with these advisers, as well as Ali Sabry supporters within the Ministry and Institute of National Planning.

The results of Soviet influence on Iraqi development strategy were more apparent in the changed planning targets than in planning methods— which remained rather crude by Eastern European standards. As in the Soviet Union, development was conceived in terms of a programme for industrialisation; merely channelling funds into agriculture was not deemed valuable. The emphasis, therefore, swung away from specialisation according to comparative advantage (which favoured primary production) into the development of a manufacturing capability. It was recognised that dependence on oil would inevitably continue, but in the longer run it was hoped to use the oil revenues, and possibly financial assistance from Eastern Europe, to diversify the economy away from oil. The policy pursued was not one of balanced growth, such as Western development economists like R. Nurske[13] favoured, but rather one of deliberately creating imbalances, sometimes referred to as a 'big push' strategy similar to that attempted by Stalin in the 1930s.[14]

The decision by the planners to give less emphasis to agriculture not only resulted from the traditional Marxist contempt for the peasantry, but also from the view that structural transformation through land reform would have to be completed before resources were devoted to rural development. The development plans of the pre-revolutionary period were often criticised for the funding devoted to agriculture, as much of this found its way into the pockets of the landlords. Those who actually worked the land received little benefit from government expenditure in any case. If the peasants had been without reward from the growth of the oil economy for so long, it was contended, an additional wait would cause little resentment; only the landlords would suffer, many of whom were leaving the country in any case with the expropriation of their estates. The share of agriculture in actual development expenditure had, in fact, declined markedly even before the revolution, from over one-half of expenditure in 1952, to around a quarter in the 1957-8 period (see Table 14.2). The real squeeze, however, came after the revolution: by 1963 expenditure on agriculture amounted to only 8 per cent of the total. The shift from agriculture did not lead to an immediate rise in industrial development, as it was necessary to undertake construction work on infrastructure and improve transport generally first. By 1966, nevertheless, the share of industry had been pushed as high as 45 per cent of total development expenditure, as Table 14.2 shows, compared with around 10 to 13 per cent over the 1958-61 period.

The position of agriculture *vis-à-vis* industry was, in fact, even more adverse than the figures on development expenditure suggest, as agricultural prices were deliberately held down by administrative controls in order to keep food prices low and hence industrial wages at competitive levels. This internal method of trade manipulation, which also characterised economic policy in Nasser's Egypt and the Soviet Union, meant there were few incentives for agricultural producers to participate in the market economy, and many areas of Iraq reverted to a subsistence orientation. Unlike the Soviet Union, which built up elaborate mechanisms for forced procurement of agricultural products from the 1920s onwards, what happened in Iraq, as well as Egypt, was an immediate increase in the food-import bill. The Baghdad government, therefore, was obliged to use some of its oil-generated hard currency earnings to finance food imports, rather than imports of capital goods and equipment as the planners had intended.

Planning methods changed less than planning targets after the revolution, and the approach remained partial rather than comprehensive. Projects were selected which seemed likely to increase the country's self-reliance, and the latter was generally taken to mean that import-substitution industries should be encouraged. There was little attempt to define possible linkages between the various projects and no elaborate input-output analysis was carried out, even though by the 1960s the use of such techniques was becoming commonplace in the Soviet Union.[15] If the selection of projects seemed rather arbitrary, it could, of course, be argued that the planners had to start somewhere – it was only after the plants went into production that possible linkages would become apparent. In a sense the planners were still following a Western hit-or-miss approach, based on risk-taking. In Iraq, however, there was no market mechanism to ensure that mistakes could be corrected if they were made. Unlike the Soviet Union, moreover, statistical sources in Iraq were poor; hypothetical economic forecasting models could not be built or experimented with in the absence of a data base. After the 1954 industrial census no further detailed work on manufacturing data was carried out for over two decades, and in the early post-revolutionary period statistics collection deteriorated rather than improved. The planners had no criteria for judging success, and all they could do was to compare actual expenditure with targeted expenditure.

Soviet advisers argue, not without some justification, that concepts such as profit, or even returns on capital, are particularly inappropriate in capital-abundant states such as Iraq. If any constraints are to be fed into the planning models, labour would be a more appropriate variable to choose. In the Soviet Union the planners aim for, and achieve, a full utilisation of the labour force – in the sense that everyone is employed. The problem of underemployment (as distinct from unemployment) is tackled, often it must be admitted rather inadequately, by building success indicators such as labour productivity into the system. In Iraq, however, labour force data were (and remain) poor; the labour constraint, therefore, could not be fed into the planning model. Iraqi planners had only highly aggregated data on the existing labour force by occupation in enumerated employment, and no detailed breakdown by skills. There had been no attempt at manpower planning, and certainly in the 1960s it would have been impossible to anticipate probable labour constraints, or identify where bottlenecks would need to be overcome.

Under the Iraqi-Soviet agreement of 1959 the joint projects ratified for further study with an aim of eventual implementation included – predictably – a steel mill, an agricultural machinery plant, a stocking and underwear factory and other similar Russian favourites, which, because they were deemed desirable within the Soviet Union, were also thought to be appropriate projects for Iraq to emulate. No attempt was made to assess the Iraqi market for steel or even underwear, and the joint feasibility studies, which in practice were more Soviet than co-operative ventures, merely assessed the technical feasibility of the projects. The main debate was over how many Soviet technical personnel would be required, and what the implications would be for Soviet exports, so that the Soviet plans could be adjusted accordingly. While no attempt was made to assess the overall impact of the projects on the Iraqi economy, the Soviet planners were concerned with even very marginal effects on their own highly sophisticated plans.

Continuing Planning Debates

The Detailed Economic Plan for 1961-5 marked the high point of Soviet influence on Iraqi planning. By the time the 1965-9 Five-Year Plan came to be drawn up there was growing disillusionment both with Soviet recommendations and results. Although the proportion of expenditure to allocation was significantly higher than in the 1950s, indicating increased success with actual implementation of projects, criticism was levied at the performance and nature of some of the projects. The agricultural machinery plant, which had a capacity far in excess of local market needs, drew particular criticism. Given the depressed state of Iraq's agriculture, and the minimal prospects for exports of machinery of this type (in view of Western competition on world markets), the scale of the project seemed clearly unjustified. Nor was the Soviet Union, whose own market was saturated, prepared to absorb any surplus production. The Soviet steel mill project was never implemented, and metallurgy was confined to nail-manufacture, tank-making and the production of some aluminium consumer items, with the imported inputs coming from the Soviet Union. Given the Egyptian experience with Soviet technology in steel-making at Helwan, it was probably fortunate for Iraq that the more ambitious project was not implemented. The change of government in Iraq in 1963 no doubt delayed the implementation of Soviet-proposed projects. Officially the Detailed Economic Plan was replaced by transitional annual investment programmes, but in practice the plan continued until 1965.

The greatest industrial success of Iraq, the cement plants, owed little to the Soviet Union, as two were already far advanced before the 1958 revolution, and were functioning before the start of the Detailed Economic Plan.[16] Cement, in any case, is commonly regarded as a non-tradable good, although Iraq had exported limited quantities to Kuwait and Jordan, and the industry would have thrived due to transport cost factors alone without any infant industry protection. The only industries significantly aided by the policy of infant industry protection, through the virtual prohibition of Western imports as advocated by the Soviets, were in the textiles field, especially the cotton mills at Mosul and Baghdad, and the woollen mill also near the capital. There was, however, some consumer dissatisfaction with the quality of the cloth produced by the textile mills, and with the old-fashioned styles of garments made by the clothing factories. As in Egypt, Turkey and Iran, the traditional tailors and clothing establishments in the bazaars find it easier to adapt to changing fashions than supposedly modern factories with fixed machinery and inflexible working arrangements.

Some critics of Iraqi industry have argued that state control was the central element inhibiting coherent industrial development. Not only were all the projects included in the Detailed Economic Plan publicly owned but the nationalisation measures of 1964 brought most existing industries of any consequence within the state's ambit. A General Establishment for Industry was created to control and co-ordinate all state-owned industries, which were divided into six groupings: tobacco and matches, leather and shoes, food industries, building materials, textiles and clothing and new projects. In practice control was weak and co-ordination non-existent. Given that the planners lacked the resources or the ability to prepare any detailed economic strategy based on state direction of industrial outputs and inputs on Soviet lines, it was difficult to see what economic purpose nationalisation was meant to serve. Clearly the decisions had to be taken on political and perhaps ideological grounds; they were certainly without any immediate economic rationale as far as planning was concerned.

The plan for the 1965-9 period was a much more sophisticated document than the Detailed Economic Plan of the previous five years. The economic theories behind the new plan came predominantly from the West rather than from Soviet thinking. For the first time in Iraq's planning history, consistent and readily quantifiable criteria were used for project-appraisal, so that possible investment undertakings could be ranked in an order of priority. Two criteria were used, capital-output ratios and capital to foreign-exchange savings ratios.[17] Under the first criterion, projects with higher output in relation to capital investment were preferred over projects with a lower output. The second criterion gave priority to projects with higher rates of foreign exchange saving per unit of investment over those with a lower saving. These criteria were clearly much cruder than the labour-utilisation techniques used in the Soviet Union.

The employment targets in the Plan were merely a reflection of anticipated labour needs in the light of the projects selected; they bore no relation to labour supply availabilities. Moreover, by basing project appraisal on only two criteria (capital defined in money terms, and foreign exchange), the Iraqi planners ignored all the other inputs which Soviet planners take account of in their complex input-output matrices. The simplicity of Iraq's new planning system was its main merit, as at least the criteria decided upon could be used, whereas the more comprehensive Soviet approach was inoperable in Iraqi conditions. The problem, however, was that neither capital nor foreign exchange were scarce inputs in Iraq's economy, and it is therefore questionable whether they could constitute the most relevant criteria for project appraisal. It seemed that in returning to Western economic methods, the Baghdad authorities and their consultants had chosen the wrong approach.

The implementation of the 1965-9 Plan was not notably more successful than the implementation of the previous plans had been, and even taking the basic allocation to expenditure criterion as an indicator of success, there was little difference in performance from the early 1960s. Such improvement in implementation as there was, was largely an effect of the 1966 law broadening the authority of the Planning Board, with the Board henceforward being authorised to co-ordinate economic, fiscal, monetary and commercial policies to ensure improved execution of projects.[18] This administrative reform contributed to the remarkably high level of expenditure in relation to allocated funds for 1969. It is doubtful whether the new elements introduced into the planning process made any real contribution.

The 1970-4 Plan marked a major change over the previous plan, both in terms of planning methods and development strategy. It would nevertheless be misleading to describe the new plan as comprehensive, as some observers have done.[19] In general the planning authorities decided to adopt a macro-economic rather than a micro-economic approach (as hitherto), and defined the planning objectives in terms of what should happen to key aggregative economic variables. The partial input-output exercise of ranking projects according to capital intensity was abandoned. Instead, targets were given for growth, consumption, exports, prices and employment. Investment was taken as the main determinant of the other variables, the level of investment itself being determined essentially by the anticipated oil revenues—as in the previous plans. The main innovation was that instead of measuring success merely by comparing actual with allocated expenditure, the target variables could be compared with actual performance. This is broadly the indicative planning approach now favoured by many Western economists.

The approach taken in the 1970-4 plan was, of course, far removed from the practice in Communist states—where the main targets are expressed in terms of physical output, consumption is treated as a residual and price targets can be ignored as prices are administered (rather than being determined by market forces). In the economies of Communist states, moreover, the basic determinants are defined in terms of employment, or labour force availability, and investment is merely one of several variables, not the sole basic determinant as in Iraq. There were, however, some elements in the new Iraqi plan which corresponded to Soviet practice—such as linking the rewards for managers of state-owned industries to the achievement of planned production targets. The overall growth target for national income was set at 7.1 per cent per annum, while that for manufacturing was to be 12 per cent.[20] In practice Iraq's national income grew at a rate of 6.7 per cent over the plan period, almost on target, but much of this growth was accounted for by the rises in the price of petroleum towards the end of the period, and manufacturing, in fact, seriously under-performed.

There has been considerable disillusion in Iraq with the poor record of the import-substitution industries created within the state sector, and in both the 1970-4 plan and the 1976-80 plan a renewed emphasis has been given to the merits of export-orientated industries. It would be incorrect to interpret this as any desire to return to pre-1958 policies. Even in theoretical terms there is a difference between the policies of the 1950s and those of the 1970s: although both involve some concept of specialisation according to comparative advantage, the specialisation envisaged in the 1970s is based on inputs and not on factors of production. The standard Heckscher-Ohlin version of comparative advantage, which advocates that countries abundant in unskilled labour specialise in labour-intensive products and that land-abundant countries specialise in agriculture, is rejected. Instead, the Iraqi planners recognise that Iraq's sole abundant resources are petroleum and gas, and that the new export industries must harness this resource in some way.

One of the main resource-related projects is the fertiliser plant at Basra, for which an ammonium sulphate unit and a urea unit were constructed. This project was, in fact, originally suggested by the World Bank Mission in 1952, but contracts were only awarded in 1967, and completion only took place during the 1970-4 plan period. The plant uses gas from the Kirkuk oilfield, as also does an ethylene plant at Basra, which was built with Japanese assistance. These oil-related developments absorbed over one-half the industry budget in the 1970s, but although the motivation behind the investment was to stimulate export-led growth, the long gestation periods for these projects has resulted in their contribution to exports being minimal. Fertiliser from the Basra plant has been absorbed domestically, which has meant some import-saving, but the plastic products which were to result as spin-offs from the petrochemical projects have yet to appear—even though specific targets for them were set down in the 1976-80 plan. Given that Saudi Arabia and other Gulf states are also hoping to produce plastic bags, boxes and pipes, Iraqi production would need to commence soon if potential Arab export markets are not to be already saturated. Indeed, if export-promoted industrialisation was really the key goal, then it might have been better to concentrate on liquefied petroleum gas units, such as that built at Rumaila. Industrialisation which is aimed merely at harnessing gas for export does not, of course, create very substantial employment opportunities, but neither do petrochemical complexes (although they do admittedly increase domestic value-added).

Since the late 1960s there has been a renewed emphasis on agricultural investment. As Table 14.2 shows, agriculture's share in total expenditure reached around 40 per cent in 1971 and 1972. Table 14.3, which presents more recent information on allocation by sector, indicates that allocated expenditure has remained high; no figures on actual expenditure are currently available. Agriculture's share of total actual expenditure may well have fallen since 1972, but as aggregate expenditure on development increased so dramatically in the 1970s, in real terms it seems probable that there has been a rise of over 10 per cent per year in spending on agriculture—an impressive result. The main constraint on spending on agriculture would appear to be the limited absorptive capacity of the sector itself, rather than any unwillingness by the planners to devote resources in its direction. Evidence of the renewed interest in agriculture comes from the plan document itself for 1976-80, which actually gives targets for crop yields for 1980 in comparison with the actual or estimated yields for 1975. It was hoped, for example, that wheat yields would be raised by over 80 per cent over the period and rice yields by over 60 per cent.[21] There are few planners in Third World countries who are daring enough to commit themselves to this type of specific prediction in print, especially given the customary variability of agricultural production.

The major change in the late 1970s in planning has not been in methods or strategy but in the machinery for administration of the development effort. So much research and background work has gone

Table 14.3: Distribution of Allocated Investments (in million Iraqi dinars at current prices)

	1974	1975	1976	1977	1976-80 Public	1976-80 Private	1976-80 Total	% of total	1981
Agriculture	190	208	268	390	2,374	180	2,554	18.7	689
Industry	225	448	709	966	4,000	360	4,360	32.0	1,378
Transport	120	166	242	352	2,200	180	2,380	17.5	1,287
Construction	175	188	213	348	1,400	910	2,310	16.8	1,886
Other	459	66	61	302	2,026	–	2,026	14.8	1,496
Total	1,169	1,076	1,494	2,358	12,000	1,630	13,630	100.0	6,736

Sources: 1974-7   Central Statistical Organisation, Annual Abstract of Statistics, 1977 (Ministry of Planning, Baghdad, 1978).
1976-80   Ministry of Planning, The National Development Plan (Ministry of Planning, Baghdad, 1978), Unofficial translation issued by J. Conway Bureau, Baghdad, 1978.
1976-80   Fiche du Monde Arabe, Iraq – The Five Year Plan (FMA, Beirut, October and November 1979).
1981   Middle East Economic Digest, London, 13 March 1981, p. 19.
1981   The Arab Economist, Beirut, March 1981, pp. 29-30.

into the 1981-5 plan that there has not been time to publish a complete
document, and instead annual figures are being released rather than
projections for the five-year period. The same situation arose with the
1976-80 plan, which did not appear in complete form until 1978,
although by that time most of the data and projections had already
been released in separate documents. This situation can be rather
frustrating for outside analysts of Iraq's economy, but is perhaps
inevitable given the complexity of the planning organisation, the
unpredictability of future oil revenue levels and, more recently, the
uncertainty as a result of the conflict with Iran. The latter conflict
does not, in fact, appear to have adversely affected the development
effort so far and, given the magnitude of Iraq's foreign exchange
reserves, the country can manage for up to a year even if oil production
was to be halted completely.

The Planning Ministry of Iraq is now organised into six major
departments, four of which deal with particular economic sectors:
agriculture, industry, buildings and services, and transport and communications.[22] A fifth department, concerned with education and
social affairs, is allotted the task of estimating the labour force
implications of the expenditure plans of the other departments. Manpower planning remains at a rudimentary level, and there has been
little attempt to match the output of Iraq's universities and colleges
to labour-force requirements, although more specific targets have been
laid down for vocational training establishments. It is questionable,
however, whether more detailed manpower planning would be valuable.
Outside centrally planned economies such as those of Eastern Europe
manpower planning has been notably unsuccessful, partly because
training takes so long that, by the time trainees emerge with particular
skills, they may no longer be required. In an economy where economic
expansion is ultimately dependent on fluctuating and often unpredict-
able oil revenues the difficulties inherent in manpower planning are
particularly acute. It has without doubt been more sensible for the
education and social affairs department to concentrate its efforts on
examining labour productivity problems in textiles and other industries,
and on discovering how capital-utilisation can be increased and
manpower-underemployment reduced. Positive recommendations have
resulted from these studies, which have been successfully implemented.

The sixth department—the economics department—is also essentially
concerned with research, carrying out work on behalf of the other
sectoral departments. It does not act as a co-ordinator, or exercise
overall control, and is best viewed as a service subsidiary. Responsibility

for drafting the five-year plans rests with the long-term planning commission, established in 1971. This tries to take a twenty-year view of the economy, to ascertain how current development policies and annual budgetary expenditure will affect long-run national income growth and the sectoral distribution of the gross national product. The renewed emphasis on agriculture in the 1970s was partly due to the thinking of this commission, especially when it started to make quantitative projections of Iraq's likely food-import requirements if the trends of the 1960s and early 1970s continued. In 1971 a further institution was created: the regional planning commission, whose aim was to see how the fruits of development could be spread more evenly throughout the country.[23] Initially the work of the regional planning commission was confined to the Baghdad and Basra areas, but after completion of a study on immigration into Baghdad it started to look at ways in which industrial employment could be brought to the rural population to counter the urban drift. Much of its recent efforts have concerned bringing manufacturing to the Kurdish autonomous region, where a woollen textile factory, a dairying plant and a cigarette factory have been established at Arbil, while hand-made carpet industry centres are located at Koisanjaq, Rawanduz, Dohok and Amadiya, as well as at Arbil. The cement and the sugar factories in the Kurdish area have been operating since 1974.

Clearly, planning has advanced considerably in Iraq over the last thirty years, and the machinery itself is certainly adequate. Much useful research has been carried out within the Planning Ministry, and the projects successfully implemented are concrete examples of the achievements made. Productivity has improved considerably within the state sector, and the waste resulting from underutilised capacity has been significantly reduced. The regional planning effort, although modest, has brought some positive benefits. Overall the approach to planning remains partial, however, and, as already indicated, it would be erroneous to describe Iraqi planning as comprehensive. Planning is, of course, only a means, not a goal in itself, and comprehensive planning may be neither necessary nor desirable in the Iraqi context. A blanket application of Soviet ideas in the early 1960s proved impracticable, and the later use of one-time fashionable Western techniques was highly dubious. Iraq has needed in the final analysis to discover its own way forward. Planning experience shows that care is needed with both the selection and the implanting of new concepts.

Notes

1. Cited by K. McLachlan, 'The Planning and Development of Iraqi Industry', in M. Ziwar-Daftari (ed.), *Issues in Development: The Arab Gulf States* (MD Research and Services Limited, London, 1980), p. 88.

2. For an account of Kuwait's experience see Y.S.F. Al-Sabah, *The Oil Economy of Kuwait* (Kegan Paul International, London, 1980), pp. 55-7 and 88.

3. F. Jahal, *The Role of Government in the Industrialisation of Iraq 1950-1965* (Frank Cass, London, 1972), pp. 14-19.

4. F. Abdul Rasool, *Planning Development of Iraq* (Al Zahra Press, Baghdad, 1973), pp. 8-11.

5. International Bank for Reconstruction and Development, *The Economic Development of Iraq* (Johns Hopkins Press, Baltimore, 1952).

6. Lord Salter, *The Development of Iraq: A Plan of Action* (Iraq Development Board, Baghdad, 1955).

7. Named after the Argentinian economist who first put it forward, Raul Prebisch.

8. Arthur D. Little, Inc., *A Plan for Industrial Development in Iraq* (Cambridge, Massachusetts, 1956).

9. E. and E.F. Penrose, *Iraq: International Relations and National Development* (Ernest Benn, London, 1978), pp. 252-4.

10. K. Al-Eyd, *Oil Revenues and Accelerated Growth: Absorptive Capacity in Iraq* (Praeger, New York, 1979), p. 45.

11. For an account of the position of the Communist Party in Iraq see R. Gabb, *Communism and Agrarian Reform in Iraq* (Croom Helm, London, 1978), Chs. 2 and 5, pp. 46-74 and 123-51.

12. P. O'Brien, *The Revolution in Egypt's Economic System* (Oxford University Press, 1966), Ch. 5, p. 104.

13. R. Nurske, *Problems of Capital Formation in Undeveloped Countries* (Blackwell, London, 1952).

14. A. Hirschman, *The Strategy of Economic Development* (Yale University Press, Yale, 1958).

15. Sometimes referred to as planning by material balances. See A. Nove, *The Soviet Economy* (Allen and Unwin, London, 1968), p. 89.

16. For detailed information on cement production see G. Halaby, 'An Analysis of the Appropriateness of Management Control Systems in Iraq State Industry with Special Reference to the Iraq Public Cement Company', unpublished PhD thesis, University of Durham, 1978.

17. F. Jalal, *The Role of Government*, pp. 54-9.

18. Al-Eyd, *Oil Revenues*, pp. 47-8.

19. Al-Eyd even described the 1965-9 Plan as comprehensive.

20. J. Hashim, *Development Planning in Iraq: Historical Perspective and New Directions* (Planning Board, Baghdad, July 1975), pp. 65-6.

21. Ministry of Planning, *The National Development Plan for 1976-80* (Ministry of Planning, Baghdad, 1978). Unofficial translation issued by the J. Conway Bureau, Baghdad, 1978, p. 55.

22. Ministry of Planning, *Progress under Planning* (Ministry of Planning, Baghdad, 1975), pp. 89-94.

23. V. Ram, 'Conclusions on Main Problems in Regional Planning and Social Development in Iraq', in *Proceedings of the UNESOB Conference on Regional Planning in Iraq* (Ministry of Planning, Baghdad, 1974), pp. 209-40.

15 THE CHALLENGE OF HUMAN RESOURCES DEVELOPMENT IN IRAQ

J. S. Birks and C. Sinclair

Introduction: Economic and Social Perspective[1]

In comparison with other Arab states Iraq has an unusually favourable endowment of resources. These comprise her land, much of which is cultivable, an abundant (if difficult to control) supply of water, her oil and her people. This almost unique combination gives Iraq a potential for economic development which is of a different scale and type to that enjoyed by most of her neighbours. Comparisons with Saudi Arabia are natural. Saudi Arabia's economic power stems solely from her oil-endowment. Much of Iraq's recent prosperity is also due to her oil, but Iraq enjoys the considerable advantage of a large indigenous population, which Saudi Arabia does not. This chapter is concerned primarily with the development of human resources in Iraq, taking a medium- to long-term view. We begin by providing a perspective on the place of Iraq, in social and economic terms, in the contemporary Middle East.

Iraq has, by Middle Eastern standards, a large population – comprising some 12.2 million in 1977. This represents about 8 per cent of the entire Arab population resident in the Middle East. Egypt, Morocco, Algeria and the Sudan have larger populations. Iraq's indigenous population is double that of Saudi Arabia. As a result of this large population, GNP *per capita* is low by comparison with other oil producers, as Table 15.1 shows.

In 1979 Iraq's oil reserves were estimated at some 33 billion barrels of oil. Table 15.2 enables Iraq's reserves and rate of oil production to be compared with those of a number of other Arab oil-producing states. By this measure Iraq is not quite in the same league as Saudi Arabia but clearly enjoys a prominent place in the second division. At the 1978 rate of extraction Iraq's oil would last approximately thirty-six years. A higher rate of extraction (as occurred in 1979 and 1980), however, would naturally reduce the anticipated duration. At the peak level of production prior to the war with Iran, when Iraq was producing and exporting some 3.5 million barrels per day, Iraqi oil reserves would

Table 15.1: Gross National Product *per capita*, 1978

State	GNP *per capita* (US $)
Kuwait	14,890
United Arab Emirates	14,280
Qatar	12,740
Saudi Arabia	8,040
Libya	6,910
Bahrain	4,100
Oman	2,570
Iraq	1,860
Algeria	1,260

Source: *World Bank Atlas, 1979* (World Bank, Washington, 1980).

last about twenty-six years. Although the war with Iran has, in a technical sense, lengthened the life of Iraq's oil, Iraq will have to produce more in future years in order to repay her present debts. Concern over depletion must obviously constitute a central element in Iraqi development planning: oil reserves will begin to be significantly depleted just when the momentum of expenditure has taken hold.

Table 15.2: Oil Production, Reserves, Revenue and Duration of Oil Reserves in 1978 for Selected Arab States

State	Production (1978) (mbd)	Reserves (1.1.79) (mbd)	Revenues (1978) (US $m)	Anticipated duration of oil at 1978 production levels
Saudi Arabia	8.2	169,500	34,600	57
Iraq	2.6	33,500	10,700	35
Kuwait	2.0	73,800	9,300	101
Libya	1.9	25,000	9,000	36
UAE	1.8	32,400	8,500	49
Algeria	1.2	8,000	6,500	18

Sources: *Naft al-Arab* (Kuwait), February and March 1980; and OAPEC, *News Bulletin*, vol. 5, no. 12 (1980).

Population

Size

The 1977 census constitutes a good basis for establishing the size and composition of the Iraqi population. Table 15.3 shows the reported results in summary, but an inspection of the detailed results permits a more precise estimation to be made. In broad terms the 1977 census seems to have been unusually accurate, despite the difficulties in gathering information on a population distributed widely over sometimes remote regions.

Table 15.3: Population in 1965 and 1977

	1965 Number	%	1977 Number	%	Growth rate per annum
Total population	8,097,320	100.0	12,171,460	100.0	3.4
Citizens abroad	49,800	–	141,700	–	9.1
Urban population	4,112,300	51.1	7,640,670	63.5	5.3
Rural population	3,935,120	48.9	4,389,090	36.5	0.9

Source: Ministry of Planning, *Man: The Object of Revolution* (Ministry of Planning, Baghdad, 1979), p. 12.

The census does, however, suffer from one fault which is common in such censuses carried out in developing countries: certain groups are under-enumerated. This is suggested by the variance of sex-ratios from their expected value, and also by the figures' incompatibility with other information available on population growth. Two groups appear to have been under-represented in the Iraqi census: adult women (to a small extent) and babies and children (to a more significant extent). The former inaccuracy is difficult to correct and we will not attempt to do so here. The latter, which arises from lapses of memory and inaccurate responses on the part of parents (particularly those with large families), can be coped with more easily. The figures presented in Table 15.4, under 'corrected results', upgrade the reported results for babies and children in accordance with current knowledge of demographic variables and past growth rates. The corrected results also take account of age misreporting – a phenomenon which was evident in the adult population.

After correcting the 1977 census for undercounting in this respect, the total national population rises from 12,000,497 to 12,288,797. This is an increase of 2.4 per cent, and so the extent of under-enumeration was comparatively small.

Distribution

In the country as a whole some 63 per cent of the population live in 'urban' areas as defined by the census, the three main cities being

Table 15.4: Reported and Adjusted Population by Age and Sex, 1977

Age	Reported results			Corrected results		
	Male	Female	Total	Male	Female	Total
0-4	1,174,058	1,108,670	2,282,728	1,224,058	1,165,769	2,389,827
5-9	1,063,572	981,387	2,044,959	1,063,572	1,005,294	2,068,866
10-14	814,204	725,755	1,539,959	814,204	775,432	1,589,636
15-19	488,306	521,955	1,010,261	604,660	575,866	1,180,526
20-4	602,362	514,014	1,116,376	539,714	514,014	1,053,728
25-9	422,793	388,146	810,939	422,793	388,146	810,939
30-4	318,043	286,041	604,084	318,043	286,041	604,084
35-9	257,707	237,443	495,150	257,707	237,443	495,510
40-4	186,447	192,590	379,037	217,527	209,857	427,384
45-9	214,064	204,161	418,225	182,984	186,894	369,878
50-4	153,403	167,720	321,123	153,403	167,720	321,123
55-9	121,602	122,776	244,378	121,602	122,776	244,378
60-4	113,053	108,374	221,427	113,053	108,374	221,427
65-9	81,004	74,297	155,301	81,004	74,297	155,301
70-4	59,607	65,036	124,643	59,607	65,036	124,643
75+	112,673	119,234	231,907	112,673	119,234	231,907
Total	6,182,898	5,817,599	12,000,497	6,286,604	6,002,193	12,288,797

Source for reported results: Central Statistical Organisation, *Annual Abstract of Statistics 1978* (Ministry of Planning, Baghdad, 1979), p. 27. The discrepancy between the reported results total given here and the total given in Table 15.3 is accounted for by the inclusion of some marginal categories – mainly Iraqi citizens living abroad – in the former table.

Baghdad, Mosul and Basra. This is a high level of urbanisation for a large country with a sizeable agricultural sector. In Egypt the proportion of the population living in urban areas is 44 per cent (1976 figure).[2] What is yet more surprising is the rate at which the urban population is increasing. Table 15.3 shows this to be, since 1965, 5.3 per cent per annum. By comparison the rural population increased at only 0.9 per cent per annum over the same period. The obvious conclusion is that Iraq has been experiencing a major internal redistribution of population from rural areas to towns, villages and cities. A simple calculation suggests that between 1965 and 1977 some 1.5 million people moved from rural to urban areas, the bulk of whom were single males aged 20 to 35.[3] Partly as a result of this rapid pace of urbanisation the government faces a growing problem in meeting the needs of urban dwellers for social services and, of principal concern here, for employment.

Growth

Iraq has been experiencing a population 'explosion' since around 1965. At present the crude death-rate per annum is believed to be about 11 deaths per thousand population, and life-expectancy is around 55 years. Fertility rates are extremely high, the overall fertility rate being estimated at about 7 – which implies, for the Iraqi population, a crude birth-rate of around 42 births per thousand population. This is a high level of fertility, although not unusually so for the region. The population is increasing at about 3 per cent per annum (exclusive of immigration), a rate which will increase unless fertility levels fall. Iraq's oil wealth is the basic factor which has made this population growth possible – in terms of financing both better health facilities and better living conditions for the population.

Qualitative Considerations

Table 15.5 shows the educational attainment of the Iraqi population aged ten years or more. The overall literacy rate of 44 per cent (for those persons aged 10 years or more) is comparatively high for a country with so large an agricultural sector. There is quite a sharp difference in the level of educational attainment between rural and urban areas. In rural areas the literacy rate falls to 33 per cent. The distinction between rural and urban areas in Iraq is an important one. The relatively low incidence of literacy in rural areas was a major reason for the literacy campaigns which have been mounted in recent years. The government saw low levels of agricultural productivity as the result, in large part, of the poor quality of its agricultural manpower. This is a point to which we will return.

Table 15.5: Educational Attainment by Area of Residence, 1978 (population aged 10 years or more)

Educational attainment	All country	Urban areas	Rural areas
Illiterate	55.9	44.5	77.0
Literate	21.7	25.8	13.9
Primary school certificate	12.9	16.4	6.5
Intermediate school certificate	4.0	5.5	1.3
Secondary school certificate	3.2	4.6	0.7
Higher	2.3	3.2	0.6
Total	100.0	100.0	100.0
Total number	7,555,252	4,923,407	2,631,845

Source: Central Statistical Organisation, *Annual Abstract of Statistics 1978* (Ministry of Planning, Baghdad, 1979), p. 34.

Employment by Economic Sector

The distribution of employment in Iraq in 1968 clearly reflected the dominance of agricultural employment. More than half the total workforce (54 per cent) were employed in the agriculture/fishing sector at that time. By 1977 a dramatic change had occurred in the distribution of employment. Agricultural employment had decreased both in absolute terms and as a proportion of total employment (from 54 per cent to 31 per cent). The construction sector had burgeoned, but the greatest increase was in personal and community services. The latter sector accounted for 40 per cent of all employment in 1977. It is particularly interesting to note that, despite intensive investment in the manufacturing sector, by 1977 manufacturing accounted for only 11.5 per cent of all employment.

The conventional wisdom amongst development economists is that as economies develop there is an employment shift away from agriculture to industry and, subsequently, to services. This paradigm is supported by a wealth of evidence on the evolution of employment patterns throughout the world, as Table 15.7 shows.

A unique aspect of development in oil-rich states like Iraq is their pattern of employment growth. Typically, they have not experienced the 'industrial' phase, where a majority of all employment is in industry. Indeed some (but not Iraq) have barely experienced the supposedly

Table 15.6: Employment by Economic Sector, 1968 and 1977 (000's)

| Economic sector | Total employed | | | |
| | 1968 | | 1977 | |
	Number	%	Number	%
Agriculture	1,254	54.0	943.9	31.5
Industry	174	7.5	344.4	11.5
Construction	66	2.8	321.7	10.7
Distribution	280	12.0	177.8	5.9
Personal and community services	550	23.7	1,213.1	40.4
Total	2,324	100.0	3,000.9	100.0

Source: Ministry of Planning, *Man: The Object of Revolution* (Ministry of Planning, Baghdad, 1978), p. 15.

Table 15.7: Structure of the Labour Force, 1950-70

| | Agriculture | | | Industry | | | Services | | |
	1950	1960	1970	1950	1960	1970	1950	1960	1970
Low-income countries	78	77	75	8	9	10	14	14	15
Middle-income countries	65	59	50	14	17	20	21	24	30
Industrialised countries	25	17	10	36	38	38	39	45	52

Source: World Bank, *World Development Report 1978* (World Bank, Washington, 1978), p. 16.

initial stage of agricultural employment. Instead, they have begun from exactly the opposite extreme, namely having a very large share of all employment in social and personal services. The interesting moment is approaching when we may see these countries experience a declining share of social and personal services in employment and the growth of industrial employment, thus presenting a style of development the exact opposite of the norm.

Before commenting in particular on Iraq's experience in this respect, two points should be noted. First, we can distinguish considerable variance in the level of productivity of those described as working in the 'services sector'. Some types of service sector employment are highly productive, and are even earners of foreign exchange. Examples of these are finance, insurance and banking employment. Some types of service-sector employment obviously support others which are highly productive and which may be foreign-exchange earners – for example car hire companies or computer programming. Typically all civil service employment is included in 'services' as well as all military employment. Productivity in the latter sectors is notoriously difficult to measure, and in countries which use government employment as a form of social security or as a means to 'mop up' unemployment it is usually very low. Somewhere in the middle of the range of possible productivity are those forms of employment which provide useful though not foreign exchange earning services, such as dry cleaning agencies, household service or taxi-driving. At the bottom of the scale of productivity are those who work in the 'informal sector', such as street vendors and petty traders.

The second point to make is that in practice most of the personal and community services employment, so prominent in this region, is not particularly productive. This either results from the lack of other productive employment opportunities or, in the case of the oil-rich countries, from the government's desire to use civil service employment as a means of distributing wealth.

Turning to the Iraqi employment data as shown in Table 15.6 we find an experience consistent with the region but at odds with the rest of the world. It is the view of the authors of this chapter that Iraq enjoys so large a service sector for two main reasons. First, Iraq is a country run along socialist lines with a planned economy. Its government exerts a direct control over the economy and therefore has an unusually large requirement for civil servants. Second, the informal sector in urban areas has proliferated in recent years. An insufficient number of employment opportunities has been created by Iraq's modern development to absorb all the new arrivals in towns and cities. In fact, many of these new arrivals are untrained and illiterate, so are not suitable for employment in Iraq's modern industrial development. It seems likely that a sizeable proportion of Iraq's service sector employment consists of activities which are not particularly productive. Raising productivity, and indeed changing the nature of employment in the service sector, is a major challenge to government.

The Labour Market

Iraq's workforce is a substantial one, having been estimated at about 3.1 million in 1977. In this respect Iraq dominates the Arab oil-exporting countries, as Table 15.8 shows. The crude participation rate was, in 1977, 26.1 per cent—a high rate in comparison with other Middle Eastern countries' rates.

Table 15.8: Major Arab States: National Labour Force and Crude Participation Rates, 1975

State	Population	Labour force	Crude participation rate (%)
Capital-rich			
Iraq	11,727,700	3,060,900	26.1
Saudi Arabia	4,592,500	1,026,500	22.3
Libya	2,223,700	449,200	20.2
Kuwait	472,100	91,800	19.4
United Arab Emirates	200,000	45,000	22.3
Qatar	60,300	12,500	20.7
Total	19,276,300	4,685,900	24.3
Pseudo capital-rich			
Algeria	15,800,000	4,100,000	26.1
Oman	550,000	137,000	24.9
Bahrain	214,000	45,800	21.3
Total	16,564,000	4,282,800	25.9
Capital-poor			
Egypt	37,364,900	12,522,200	33.5
Sudan	15,031,000	3,700,000	24.6
Syria	7,335,000	1,838,900	25.1
Yemen (YAR)	5,037,000	1,425,800	28.1
Jordan (East Bank)	2,616,700	532,800	20.4
Yemen (PDRY)	1,660,000	430,500	25.9
Total	69,044,000	20,450,200	29.6
Grand total	104,885,200	29,418,900	28.0

Source: Based on J.S. Birks and C.A. Sinclair, *Arab Manpower: The Crisis of Development* (London, Croom Helm, 1980), table 1.4, p. 8.

There are two reasons for the high participation rate. One is that Iraq has a large agricultural sector in which many women work. In most parts of the Middle East women's employment tends to be limited to the modern sector and to specific work, mainly teaching, nursing and menial tasks such as cleaning. This observation applies more accurately to the capital-rich states than to the capital-poor. In the latter, as, for example, in Egypt and the People's Democratic Republic of Yemen,

women do participate quite widely in the modern economy. In Iraq the
large number of women employed in the agricultural sector helps to
account for the high participation rate. They actually comprised 17 per
cent of the total workforce in 1977, as Table 15.9 shows. The second
explanation is the prevalence of 'under-age participation'. Economically
active persons aged 10-19 account for 13 per cent of the entire workforce. This is a point to which we will return later.

Table 15.9: Population and Workforce by Sex, 1977

	Males	Females	Total
Population	2,182,898	5,817,599	12,000,497
Workforce	2,589,561	544,378	3,133,939
Crude participation rate	41.9	9.4	26.1

Source: Central Statistical Organisation, *Annual Statistical Abstract 1978*
(Ministry of Planning, Baghdad, 1979), p. 36.

Table 15.10: Economically Active by Economic Sector and Sex, 1977

Economic sector	Employment					
	Total		Men		Women	
	Number	%	Number	%	Number	%
Agriculture, forestry and fishing	943,890	30.0	591,066	22.8	352,824	64.9
Mining and quarrying	36,835	1.2	34,716	1.3	2,119	0.4
Manufacturing	284,395	9.1	235,777	9.1	48,616	8.9
Electricity, gas and water	23,190	0.7	22,241	0.9	949	0.2
Construction	321,696	10.3	316,560	12.2	5,136	0.9
Wholesale and retail trade	224,104	7.1	207,946	8.0	16,155	3.0
Transport, storage and communications	177,799	5.7	172,814	6.7	4,985	0.9
Financing, insurance, real estate and business services	31,089	1.0	26,023	1.0	5,066	0.9
Community, social and personal services	957,979	30.6	871,879	33.7	86,100	15.8
Not adequately defined	58,237	1.9	46,258	1.8	11,979	2.1
Unemployed	74,725	2.4	64,278	2.5	10,447	1.9
Economically active	3,133,939	100.0	2,589,561	100.0	544,378	100.0

Source: Central Statistical Organisation, *Annual Abstract of Statistics 1978*
(Ministry of Planning, Baghdad, 1979), p. 36.

Table 15.10 shows the distribution of employment between economic sectors in 1977. Women's employment is largely concentrated in agriculture, while the largest sector of male employment is community, social and personal services (34 per cent). The withdrawal of males from the agricultural sector, effected through internal migration, has left an odd balance of labour in the agricultural sector. At present women comprise 37 per cent of the total agricultural workforce, and this proportion is growing.

A still more remarkable facet of this dependence on female labour in the agricultural sector is the proportion aged 10-14. More than 18

Table 15.11: Female Employment in Agriculture, by Age in 1977

Age group	Employment in Agriculture (distribution)	% of total	All sectors (distribution)	Representation index
7-9	370 (0.1)	49.0	755 (0.1)	1.0
10-14	65,367 (18.5)	91.5	71,402 (13.1)	1.41
15-19	41,902 (11.9)	73.9	56,706 (10.4)	1.14
20-4	39,315 (11.1)	49.5	79,420 (14.6)	0.76
25-9	33,605 (9.5)	45.6	73,711 (13.5)	0.70
30-4	28,076 (8.0)	47.1	59,622 (10.9)	0.73
35-9	25,326 (7.2)	55.7	45 509 (8.4)	0.86
40-4	24,868 (7.0)	67.1	37,078 (6.8)	1.03
45-9	27,922 (7.9)	73.5	37,970 (7.0)	1.13
50-4	24,260 (6.9)	79.0	30,711 (5.6)	1.23
55-9	16,575 (4.7)	81.9	20,233 (3.7)	1.27
60-4	11,550 (3.4)	82.2	14,044 (2.7)	1.26
65+	13,379 (3.8)	81.0	16,522 (3.1)	1.23
N.S.	309 —	—	695 (0.2)	—
Total	352,824 (100.0)	64.8	544,378 (100.0)	—

Source: Central Statistical Organisation, *Annual Abstract of Statistics 1978* (Ministry of Planning, Baghdad, 1979), p. 36.

per cent of the female agricultural workforce are of this age. This point can be seen from Table 15.11, which also shows that the female

Table 15.12: Employment of Males Aged 10-14 in 1977

Economic sector	Number	%
Agriculture, hunting, forestry and fishing	23,954	26.8
Manufacturing	11,227	12.6
Building and construction	20,876	23.4
Community, social and personal services	6.620	7.4
Other	26,649	29.8
Total	89,326	100.0

Source: Central Statistical Organisation, *Annual Abstract of Statistics 1978* (Ministry of Planning, Baghdad, 1979), p. 36.

agricultural workforce is dominated by two groups, those aged less than 19 (who comprise 30 per cent) and those aged 40 or more. The represent-ation index shown on Table 15.11, moreover, reveals that these two groups work in this sector more frequently than females of other ages even when allowance is made for the fact that there are more working women in the lower-age cohorts. So, even allowing for the larger population of younger women, there is an above-average propensity to work in the agricultural sector at ages below 19 and above 40.

One simple explanation for the above-average participation of women over 40 is that this group has not had the benefit of school education and is both prepared to work on the land and unable to find other work. The under-age participation of young girls is probably explained by the tradition of family participation in farming ventures. The quite sharp difference in the propensity to work on the land between 15-19-year-olds and 20-24-year-olds may be related to marriage. It is not directly related to child-bearing, since we are discussing only those economically active.

Under-age participation is not confined to girls. Some 89,000 boys aged 10-14 (3.4 per cent of the male workforce) are economically active, as Table 15.12 shows. Only 27 per cent of these boys work on the land (as compared with 91 per cent of the 10-14-year-old girls). Manufacturing and construction together employ 32,000 10-14-year-olds, which represents 6 per cent of all employment in those two industries.

As a result of this pattern of dependence on women and under-age participants the agricultural sector is presently relying on a workforce of uncertain permanence and of a low production level. The comparatively poor performance of Iraq's agricultural sector has been noted before, but seldom has manpower been seen as a key factor. Land reforms, inept administration, incorrectly administered prices, over-watering, under-watering, inappropriate crops and inappropriate cropping patterns are the more familiar scapegoats. Here we argue that the exodus of male manpower from rural areas since the mid-1960s, combined with the low level of productivity of the agricultural workforce (which includes a substantial number of children and old women), are critical factors behind Iraq's unimpressive agricultural performance.

It is perhaps surprising that Iraq is now having to import labour. With so large a population and workforce (comparative with other Arab Gulf states), how could she possibly need labour? This is a simple point to answer in respect of highly skilled labour: such labour is required for Iraq's industrial and petrochemical development. The numbers required in this capacity, however, are strictly limited. What is more intriguing is the importation of Egyptian farmers. These farmers from Egypt are reported to number some 100,000 – although no authoritative figures on this subject exist. The justification for bringing in these Egyptians is the vacuum created by the internal migration of labour from rural areas to towns. While the presence of 100,000 Egyptians may help Iraqi agriculture and the individual migrants concerned, it may also create some intractable political problems in the long run.

Future Development and Employment-Creation

In view of the enormous resources and potential in Iraq for development, future commentators may well see the present era as only the beginning of Iraq's modern economic development. Currently, however, the economy is oriented towards a relatively traditional agricultural sector and is highly dependent on oil-extraction and production. Diversification of the economy both into new sources of income and towards a more sophisticated exploitation of resources has yet to be accomplished.

While Iraq's economic potential is immense, the realisation of that potential is by no means assured. Despite the buoyant state of the economy, soaring oil revenues and rapid economic development, not to mention the invaluable asset of a large population and more than sufficient cultivable land area, Iraq lives with a number of deep-rooted problems, some of which are political, some economic. Effecting economic development and avoiding international disagreement or domestic inter-communal strife presents the government with a serious challenge; this is a field where Iraqi governments have not had a record of outstanding success in the past. Indeed, from the perspective of economic development and employment-creation, Iraq's war with Iran is a disaster. The war has slowed down the growth of the productive elements of the economy through the destruction of plant and infrastructure and through the absolute loss to the economy of oil reserves devoted to the war effort which otherwise would have been used for development projects.

It is difficult for any developing countries to create employment opportunities as quickly as the supply of job-seekers increases. Typically, financial capital and foreign exchange are in short supply, while for demographic reasons school leavers and job-seekers are in growing abundance. The modern sector of the economy wherein most job-seekers aspire to work, moreover, tends to be capital-intensive and so uses a relatively small amount of labour. To these quantitative problems can be added the difficulty of matching the qualifications of labour market entrants with the available employment opportunities. Iraq's major advantage over other developing countries in this respect is her oil wealth, and this has been sufficient to provide finance for extensive industrial, petrochemical and infrastructural investment. Yet Iraq has not evaded these problems, despite her comparative wealth. Her population is growing quickly and following the rapid expansion of schools and universities the number of educated school-leavers is also rising. To be added to the demands of this group for employment are those of internal migrants from the rural areas. Both groups focus on the urban areas.

The rate of open unemployment, in 1977, was recorded as 2.4 per cent.[4] Concurrently, though, Iraq has experienced quite acute shortages of skilled labour and in recent years considerable investments have been made in vocational and technical educational facilities, quite apart from the more basic literacy campaigns. The impact of these various training programmes has not yet been sufficient to alter labour market conditions significantly. Iraq currently exports unskilled labour to Kuwait (for example), while still suffering from shortages of skilled labour. The creation of a sufficient number of jobs for labour market entrants in the next decade will not be easy, and we will probably see the emergence of open unemployment and underemployment as key problems. The informal sector, already highly visible in Baghdad, will proliferate.

Notes

1. Views expressed in this chapter represent only those of the authors and are not necessarily shared by any agency or institution with whom the authors have been or are associated.

2. Central Agency for Public Mobilization and Statistics, 'Preliminary Results of the General Population and Housing Census 1976', unpublished mimeograph, Cairo, 1977; for further analysis of demographic aspects of Iraq, see United Nations Economic Commission for Western Asia, *Iraq* (UNECWA, Beirut, 1980).

3. For evidence of this, see Central Statistical Organisation, *Annual Abstract of Statistics 1978* (Ministry of Planning, Baghdad, 1979), pp. 30-3.

4. This seemingly useful statistic is, in fact, rather less informative about labour market conditions than might at first be thought, for the simple and obvious reason that those who are really poor, and therefore presumably potentially unemployed, cannot afford to be so. Unemployment is, therefore, a luxury of the better-qualified. See World Bank, *World Development Report 1980* (World Bank, Washington, 1981), for a discussion of this point.

16 INDUSTRIAL DEVELOPMENT AND THE DECISION-MAKING PROCESS[1]

John Townsend

Introduction

Unlike the countries of the Arabian peninsula, Iraq has a crafts tradition. A day spent in the Iraq Museum shows a range of products both beautiful and useful made by skilled artisans over at least five millennia. Carpets and fine textiles have not survived as have copper, bronze and pottery artifacts, but there is ample evidence of industry being sustained by advanced urban societies. The lands of Akkad and Sumer, of Assyria and Babylon and the cities of Ur, Uruk, Lagash, Ashur, Nimrud and Nineveh, to name but a few, have left much evidence of the skill of their citizens in working with their hands and, by implication, evidence of markets and distribution systems for the products of people's hands. Abbasid Iraq continued this craftsman tradition. Baghdad became a market for a wide range of imported and domestic artisanal products. The city of Mosul produced fine cotton goods and gave its name to the fabric 'muslin'. Under the Ottoman Empire, however, the economy of the land of the two rivers was stifled and Iraq achieved independence in 1932 with a modest industrial sector.

Most of Iraq's major industries were taken into the public sector on 14 July 1964, when the cement, edible oil, asbestos and cigarette-manufacturing industries[2] were nationalised. There were at that time four cement companies, seven textile companies, three cigarette companies, two shoe-manufacturing companies and companies making vegetable oils, jute, asbestos, paper, matches and soaps. The government vested control of these industries in a General Industrial Organisation. Thus for some seventeen years the main thrust of industrial development in Iraq has been inspired, planned and executed by the government, and for thirteen of those years the industrial policies have been those of the Arab Ba'th socialist government. The process of complete governmental control of the industrial sector was not completed until 1972 with the nationalisation of the oil industry.

The difficulties of the early years of public sector control of industry in Iraq were described in a United Nations report, entitled *Review and*

Appraisal of the Process of Decision-Making in the Public Industrial Enterprises in Iraq, which was presented at a conference in Beirut in October 1973. According to Edith and E.F. Penrose this report

. . . showed that industrial enterprises were, in effect, organised as part of the state bureaucracy and were given very little autonomous power of decision. There were several levels of authority over the enterprise, including not only the state organisation to which it belonged but also up to at least four ministries (Industry, Economy, Finance, Planning) and a variety of sub-ministerial agencies. Nearly all decisions had to go through several layers; many of them had to go high up in the relevant ministries. The planning, evaluation and implementation of investment decisions required approval from a number of sources, and even the implementation might be undertaken by an agency outside the enterprise. Pricing decisions were made by the state organisation, and were subject to ministerial approval, giving the enterprise very little flexibility to meet market conditions. Even to sell off obsolete inventories, surplus raw materials, etc., managers of enterprises had to obtain authorization from higher authority and then sell at public auctions according to procedures laid down. Full-cost pricing was common, leading to excess capacity and unwanted stocks. Distribution and marketing were often separated from the productive enterprise; procurement of materials was subject to lengthy procedures and to numerous approvals regardless of the value of the material. In the large enterprises compensation of personnel was regulated and transfers of workers between enterprises had to be approved by the state organisations. (In general resignations from the public sector to transfer to the private sector are not permitted without special authorization; layoffs are illegal.)

The disposal of profits is regulated by law, but enterprises are allowed to retain some of their profits and depreciation reserves for expansion. The forms of finance available to the enterprises are regulated and procedures must be followed with long advanced notice. In practice, there is a reluctance on the part of individuals in the hierarchy to make decisions even if empowered to do so, and in consequence decisions are commonly passed to a level higher than necessary.

Thus, not only are there many levels of decision-making, but the process is highly centralized; delays are long, and are made longer by the reluctance of officials to assume authority. Moreover, there is generally little weight given to the value of time . . .'so that it does not matter how long it would take between the initiation of a decision and its implementation' . . . The cost of capital is largely ignored, and there is no effective provision against the misuse of fixed assets. There are large holdings of inventories because of the time-consuming purchasing system and there is excess involvement of high-level management staff in routine decisions.[3]

It should be emphasised that the above applied to industry in Iraq some ten years ago, at a time when the process of state control was still evolving.

The Period from 1970[4]

The period from 1970 has been marked by unparalleled growth in the industrial sector. This growth stems from the country having acquired more of the essential industrial technology and of the necessary development planning techniques. The process was given added impetus by the oil price-increases between October 1973 and January 1974, when Iraq's oil revenues were multiplied by a factor of over four, thus removing the constraint of shortage of capital from the industrial investment equation. The two development plans covering the period from 1970 to 1980 provided a total allocation of ID 5,199 million for the industrial sector, which came to 15.3 times the allocation of the period 1959-1969 (see Table 16.1).

The figures in Table 16.1 show an enormous upsurge in total plan allocations, as well as a very substantial proportionate increase in the allocation for the industrial sector. Allocations rarely equate exactly to actual expenditure and, given the paucity of available published statistical information on Iraq generally, there is no way of knowing how much money was actually spent over the 1959-80 period, and especially over the period since 1970. Nor is there any way of knowing how much the plan allocation was swallowed up by inflation, or how successful the Iraqi government was in increasing the overall absorptive capacity of the economy to permit maximisation of plan targets.

All that can be done is to trace the patterns of investment in the major industrial projects implemented during this period. At least 50 per cent of actual expenditure over the ten years from 1970 was investment in the extractive industries, specifically crude oil, natural gas, sulphur and phosphates. Projects included a natural-gas collection system in the

Table 16.1: Plan Allocations by Sector, 1959-80 (ID millions)

Sector	Plan 1959-62 Total	%	Plan 1961-5 Total	%	Plan 1965-9 Total	%	Plan 1970-4/5 Total	%	Plan 1976-80 Total	%	Total 1959-80 Total	%
Agriculture	48	12	115	20	174	26	575	19	2,554	18.7	3,466	19
Industry	39	10	167	30	187	28	839	28	4,360	32	5,592	31
Transport and communication	101	26	138	25	110	17	385	13	2,380	17.5	3,114	17
Construction	191	49	143	25	135	20	471	16	2,310	16.9	3,250	18
Other	14	3	–	–	62	9	738	24	2,026	14.9	2,840	16
Total	393	100	563	100	668	100	3,008	100	13,630	100	18,262	100

Source: M. Sader, 'Industrial Development in Iraq', Maghreb-Machrek (Paris), no. 92 (April-May-June 1981), pp. 25-36.

southern oilfields near Basra and the construction of three petrochemical complexes in Basra and Khor al-Zubair. The ethane from the
natural gas provides the feedstock for these plants, the methane a fuel
source for power generation and desalination plants in the region of
Basra, and propane is exported to Japan and Europe. Petrochemical
production includes 60,000 tons a year of low-density polyethylene,
30,000 tons a year of high-density polyethylene and 60,000 tons a year
of polyvinyl chloride (PVC) from one plant, aromatics from a second
and 200,000 tons a year of ethylene from the third. The war with Iran
has delayed the start-up and full operation of these plants. Alongside
the petrochemical plants are fertiliser plants, one with an annual
capacity of 475,000 tons a year of urea and 292,000 tons a year of
ammonium fertiliser, and the second with a planned capacity of 116,000
tons a year of urea, 730,000 tons a year of ammonia and 419,000 tons a
year of carbonic acid. These basic heavy industries are intended to
provide raw materials and feedstocks for smaller-scale downstream
chemical industries.

At the same time as these major petrochemical projects were being
implemented the government of Iraq, aware of the vulnerability of the
country's trade links and oil export links, set about the construction of
new crude-oil export pipelines. The main new pipeline constructed was
the 1,005-kilometre Kirkuk-Dortyol-Ceyhan line through Turkey to the
Mediterranean — now, following the war with Iran, the principal export
link, with a daily capacity of about 650,000 barrels. The latter pipeline
was complemented by a so-called 'strategic' pipeline, linking the northern
oilfields at Kirkuk with the southern fields near Basra. The strategic
pipeline could move crude oil in both directions.

Industrial investment since 1970 has included adding to Iraq's own
refining capacity, with new refineries in Basra and at Baiji. In addition
to a range of refined products, Iraqi refineries now also produce some
220,000 tons of lubricants a year and 630,000 tons of asphalt. Other
heavy-industrial projects launched in the 1970s included sulphur and
phosphate. The sulphur production is of two kinds: at Kirkuk 423,000
tons a year are produced (at peak production) as a by-product of oil
production; at Mishraq sulphur is mined, and from this 450,000 tons a
year of sulphuric acid, 45,000 tons a year of hydrochloric acid, 30,000
tons a year of sodium sulphate and 450,000 tons a year of alum are
made. The phosphate project was constructed at al-Qaim, near the
Syrian border, using phosphate from the mine at Akashat. This project
has a projected annual production capacity of 4.5 million tons of
sulphuric acid, 400,000 tons of phosphoric acid, 600,000 tons of

trisuperphosphate and 250,000 tons a year of monammonium phosphate. These major projects, all either just completed or nearing completion at the end of 1980 when the war with Iran broke out, have the potential to give Iraq a substantial heavy industrial base. The logic of this base is considered in the next section.

The Logic of Industrial Planning in Contemporary Iraq

In spite of its ancient artisan tradition, Iraq is not a land blessed with abundant raw materials. In ancient Iraq, the basic raw material was clay. Modern Iraq has discovered and exploited hydrocarbons, sulphur, phosphates and limestone and is also using the power source provided by its rivers to supply energy for industry. Although this inventory of raw materials is greater than that of many developing countries, it does not represent a well-endowed raw-material resource base for the establishment of industry. Mineral resources known to exist but not yet exploited include iron ore, chromite, copper, lead and zinc, all situated in the north of the country. The extent of these resources is believed to be modest.

In addition to providing crude oil for export, hydrocarbons also give fuel for power generation and feedstocks for petrochemical industries. The abundance, and hence cheapness, of Iraq's energy resources suggest in principle that industries requiring a large volume of cheap concentrated energy to add significant value to raw materials should be economic. It is, therefore, not surprising to find iron ore and aluminium smelters in Iraq's plans for industry—the iron-ore smelter is operating and the aluminium smelter is in the implementation stage. As the basic ores for each industry have to be imported, it is again not surprising to find these basic industries located near Basra and its port facilities. A new port has been constructed at Khor al-Zubair, designed specifically to service these heavy industries.

As a feedstock for petrochemical industries, it is the natural gas element in the hydrocarbon resources which is most significant. Natural gas consists of a mixture of ethane, methane and the natural gas liquids (propane, butane and pentane), plus some sulphur. The sulphur is extracted and, with natural sulphur, forms the basis of an export industry as well as of sulphuric acid manufacture. The natural-gas liquids are used domestically as fuels and are also exported. Methane is used mostly as a fuel for electric-power generation and for the mineral-ore smelters, in addition to constituting a feedstock for nitrogenous fertilisers (ammonia and urea). Ethane is the basic feedstock for the production of ethylene, the building brick of the petrochemical industry. From ethylene, the various polyethylenes are produced.

The large phosphate deposits at al-Qaim are being exploited and will complement the chemical industry based on petrochemicals. Two pan-Arab industrial plants, financed by the Arab Petroleum Investments Corporation (APICORP) are to be built, one near Basra for the production of linear alkylbenzene, and the second near al-Qaim for the production of sodium tripolyphosphate, both these chemical products being key ingredients in detergent manufacture.

On this foundation of basic and intermediate industry a range of industries designed initially to provide for the needs of the Iraqi consumer, to manufacture substitutes for goods which would otherwise have to be imported and ultimately to produce a surplus for export have been established. Further information on the range of these state-owned industries can be found in the appendices to this chapter.

The logic of Iraq's industrial planning is summarised in Figure 16.1. Behind this basic logic there is, of course, the fundamental principle common to all oil-producers: to ensure that the revenues accruing from the nation's depleting hydrocarbon reserves are invested in such a way that the continued prosperity and wellbeing of the community will be guaranteed in the post-oil age. Iraq is in this respect fortunate in that the country's hydrocarbon reserves are substantial, thus giving the government and the people time to develop alternative income-generating projects. Iraqi ministers and officials are fond of quoting the remark attributed to President Saddam Husain, that of the last two barrels of oil produced in the world, one will be Iraqi.

The implication of the extent of Iraq's oil reserves is that investment today in income-generating projects, specifically in industry, does not have to yield a conventional economic return. In any case, Iraq's socialist principles would eschew conventional economic concepts evolved in capitalist societies. It follows that present-day Iraqi industries do not necessarily have to be competitive (in terms of production costs or productivity) with similar industries in Western countries, provided that there is a genuine transfer of technology. Transfer of technology, in this context, has to be measured by the degree to which Iraqi scientists, engineers and technologists have mastered the imported technology, can innovate and adapt this technology to Iraqi conditions and can ultimately develop a technology specific to, and suitable for, Iraq. Until this stage has been reached, and provided that there is genuine and measurable progress towards this goal, conventional

Figure 16.1: Iraq's Industrial Logic

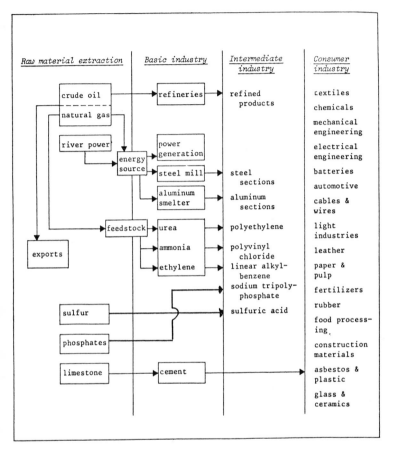

Western-conceived efficiency criteria have dubious applicability. By the same token, the protection of newly launched industries is justified. Such protection is ensured by a system of import licences; import licences are not granted if Iraqi products are available in the volume (and broadly to the quality) required. The question of price-competitiveness is covered by an all-embracing system of price controls.

The Organisation of Public Sector Industry in Iraq

The Iraqi ministries responsible for public sector industry are the Ministry of Oil and the Ministry of Industry and Minerals. In the oil sector, there are four major organisations, the Iraq National Oil Company (INOC), of which the Minister of Oil is president, the State Organisation for Oil Refining and Gas Processing, the State Organisation for the Distribution of Oil Products and Gas and the State Organisation for Oil Projects. The last-named organisation is charged with the design, supervision and construction of new projects in the oil sector.

The Ministry of Industry has broad responsibility for nine state organisations and a number of special departments. The nine state organisations are the State Organisation for Industrial Development (which looks after private sector industry, not officially discouraged but small in size and scope), the State Organisation for Minerals, the State Organisation for Engineering Design and Construction, the State Organisation for Engineering Industries, the State Organisation for Textile Industries, the State Organisation for Chemical Industries, the State Organisation for Construction Industries, the State Organisation for Food Industries and the State Organisation for Electricity. The additional departments include the Directorate-General for Industrial Consultancy, the Directorate-General for the Mixed Sector, the Directorate-General of Industrial Co-operatives, the Directorate-General of the Drug Industry, the Vocational Training Centre for the Electrical and Electronics Industries and the Industrial Bank. Appendix 1 lists the state companies and other production units which come under the control of the various state organisations. This list was compiled in September 1980 and was correct in November 1980. There are, however, frequent organisation changes – some substantial, others being little more than changes of name.

In general, the state organisations can be likened to a Western holding company controlling a number of production units, though this analogy should not be taken too far, given the very different concepts of capital investment current in contemporary Iraq. The role played by the Industrial Bank, which holds the government's share in the equity of so-called mixed sector companies, is of particular interest. The latter companies are an interesting development in that they encourage private sector industrial investment while ensuring an overall government say in policymaking. If ever the government of Iraq should decide to relax its doctrinaire approach to industry and encourage more private sector industrial investment, the mechanisms for so doing exist. If Iraq should emerge from the war with Iran relatively unscathed politically and economically, and should then be invited to become the seventh member of the Gulf Co-operation Council (with Saudi Arabia, Kuwait, Bahrain, Qatar, the United Arab Emirates and Oman), it is not unlikely that some such opening towards the private sector would be made.

The lack of published information on Iraqi industrial output makes a detailed analysis of production difficult. Attempts by foreigners in Iraq to establish even a broad scale of measurement of industrial production have been known to cause the Iraqi authorities to make accusations of industrial espionage; the penalties for people found guilty of such activity tend to be drastic. Published budget information gives a very broad indication of the scale of the various industries (see Appendix 2), but the absence of a detailed breakdown limits the value of these figures.

There is, moreover, no reliable way in which a foreign analyst can obtain even a broad idea of what proportion of local market demand is satisfied by local industry. Broadly, Iraq is self-sufficient in oil products — though some refined products in special categories are imported. The demand for gas for industry and domestic needs is satisfied by the local industry, despite there being some complaints about the quality of the domestic gas distribution services (which is not the responsibility of the manufacturing organisation). Before the outbreak of the war with Iran, the State Organisation for Electricity satisfied all local demand for electric power, and its capital investment plans would have ensured that supply exceeded demand by a comfortable margin for at least the next decade. Apart from these fairly obvious examples, and always taking into account the great difficulties in obtaining any form of statistics for industrial production (especially statistics which can be related to local market requirements), it would seem that Iraqi industry in general satisfies only a small part of domestic demand.

Some evidence of the extent to which Iraqi production fails to cover existing domestic demand is provided by the scale of imports. Table 16.2 sets out the total exports to Iraq from Organisation of Economic Co-operation and Development (OECD) countries in 1977, 1978 and 1979. As an indication of scale, the twenty-four OECD countries supplied 79.2 per cent of Iraqi imports in 1977, 79.2 per cent per cent again in 1978 and 81.5 per cent in 1979. Over the same three-year period, Eastern bloc nations (the Soviet Union, the German Democratic Republic, Hungary, Poland, etc.) supplied, respectively, 8.9 per cent, 7.4 per cent and 5.5 per cent of Iraqi imports.

Table 16.2: OECD Exports to Iraq, 1977, 1978 and 1979 ($US 000's)

Description	1977	1978	1979
Food and live animals	290,691	336,546	594,842
Beverages and tobacco	15,408	23,442	74,873
Raw materials except fuels	43,081	34,788	107,353
Mineral fuels and lubricants	8,802	9,247	16,050
Animal and vegetable oils and fats	5,075	18,581	19,893
Chemicals	179,376	263,198	443,633
Manufactured goods by material	849,414	1,098,970	1,973,130
Machinery and transport equipment	2,121,296	2,440,804	3,563,066
Miscellaneous manufactured	155,567	233,719	408,565
Other	60,847	30,659	46,200
Total OECD exports	3,729,557	4,489,954	7,247,605
Total imports	4,481,000	6,267,000	9,792,000

Sources: Organisation for Economic Co-operation and Development, *Statistics for Foreign Trade* (OECD, Paris, 1977-9), series C; and International Monetary Fund, *Direction of Trade Yearbook* (IMF, Washington, 1981), pp. 211-12.

The desire to produce import substitutes is evidently a key factor in Iraq's industrial strategy and organisation. Of the Iraqi state organisations and state companies producing import substitutes, the State Organisation for Food Industries has three state sugar establishments, a state canning establishment, a state establishment for dairy products, a state establishment for soft and alcoholic drinks, a state establishment for vegetable oils and two tobacco establishments. These establishments manufacture products complementing imports of food, beverages and tobacco, and animal and vegetable oils and fats. The State Organisation for Textile Industries controls twelve state companies producing a range of cotton, woollen and synthetic textiles complementing textile imports. Similarly, the State Organisation for Chemical Industries has companies manufacturing leather goods, pulp and paper, fertilisers, rubber products and petrochemicals.

The State Organisation for Engineering Industries controls state companies making a range of mechanical and electrical products, batteries, trucks, iron and steel products, cables and wires and electrical measuring equipment. One of these engineering units is the State Automotive Industry Company at Iskanderiyah. This factory was originally a foundry set up with Soviet technical assistance to make simple agricultural tools and equipment. The government of Iraq decided early in the 1970s to convert the foundry into a factory assembling motor vehicles from components imported from foreign manufacturers, but using an increasing number of Iraqi-manufactured components. Agreements were concluded with both Swedish and French motor-vehicle manufacturers for the setting up of the necessary manufacturing plants. Both contracts had major training requirements, as well as a provision for about 20 per cent of Iraqi-produced components in the final product. In both cases, the end product was to be trucks. The Company is now producing trucks distributed in Iraq under the brand name Salah al-Din. There have been problems in maintaining the quality of Iraqi-produced components, problems which are being slowly overcome.

The Decision-making Process

It is the contention of this chapter that the central factor which will inhibit the development of Iraq's industrial sector is the process of decision-making. At present, while Iraqi industry is heavily subsidised and protected, the negative aspects of the decision-making process may not be very apparent. Immediately Iraq attempts to market its industrial products internationally, however, the inefficiency and unsuitability of current practice will become apparent. Virtually all industrial decisions in Iraq, from questions of broad industrial strategies to investment questions, priorities, factory locations, choice of technology, contract negotiation for factory building and the licensing of technology, the preparation of raw material specifications, quality control, production planning and production schedules, routine and preventative maintenance, warehousing and storage of components and finished products, product costing and the writing off of scrap are committee decisions. It is extremely rare for an executive in charge of an Iraqi factory or other manufacturing operation to make a decision on any matter of day-to-day routine as well as of major policy without the support of a committee. Documentation, in the form of an authorisation bearing at least two or three signatures, is required for a whole range of decisions which would normally be made in a Western or Japanese factory of similar size and production capacity by a production foreman on his own initiative.

The preference for decision-making by committee stems from four different influences—one coming from within the state, and the remaining three from outside sources: Soviet, Egyptian and East German. The indigenous Iraqi preference for collective decisions seems to spring from a fear that any individual acting on his own will make a decision to favour himself at the expense of his colleagues and, in an industrial environment, at the overall expense of the manufacturing or processing unit. Conversely, collective decisions are favoured because they spread responsibility and avoid any single manager or official risking being accused of making unilateral decisions to suit himself. Overlaying this natural propensity, and, of course, originating from it, is the Arab Ba'th socialist political philosophy of collective leadership. The reasons for this fear of individual responsibility are many and complex and would be a subject for major research over a number of disciplines. For the purpose of this chapter it is only necessary to signal the fact of a natural preference for collective leadership and collective decision-making, without making any value-judgement on the fact.

The close economic links with the Soviet Union from the 1958 revolution until the early 1970s brought to Iraq a very similar decision-making philosophy and also put an additional political element into decision-making. Every major decision, and a significant number of comparatively minor decisions, had to be seen to be taken within an overall political framework. In the simplest terms, a decision which might seem to be a perfectly reasonable *a priori* matter would be wrong if it contradicted, or appeared to contradict, established political dogma. An obvious example concerns Western economic concepts of profit.

The Egyptian influence was introduced into Iraq at the time of the 1964 nationalisation of industry; the Iraqi industrial sector was reorganised at that time along the lines of the Egyptian public sector industries, complete with massive bureaucratic controls. It was charged at the time of the 1964 nationalisation that Iraqi industrial entrepreneurs were inefficient, dishonest and self-seeking, putting their own interests beyond and above those of the nation as a whole. Inadequate accounting records make it impossible to say whether this conception of pre-nationalised industry was correct or not. The significant point is simply that, at the time of nationalisation, government circles believed industry to be completely inefficient and were convinced that an Egyptian-model industrial sector was wholly appropriate to Iraq's needs at that time.

The East German influence is more interesting and more difficult to trace precisely. The links with the Soviet Union, coupled with the inability of the Soviet Union to supply the technology Iraq wanted, caused the Iraqi authorities to look to the German Democratic Republic. The first East German involvement in Iraq, an involvement seen in other Arab and African countries which have followed the

Soviet model, was in intelligence-gathering and internal security matters. The German efficiency in these matters impressed Iraqi policy-makers, and consequently East German overtures to sell industrial technology was taken seriously. East German equipment is now installed in Iraqi textile factories (as well as in the signalling on the Baghdad to Basra railway). Many Iraqi engineers and industrial managers have been trained in East Germany. The result is an interesting marriage of German thoroughness and industrial managerial efficiency with the Iraqi penchant for collective decision-making. The East Germans are probably the only nation in the Soviet sphere of influence which have made Marxist economic doctrines work. The long-term influence of East German management philosophies on Iraqi industry is likely to be a matter of some interest to future economic historians.

In terms of practical industrial decision-making it is necessary to bear in mind the overall Iraqi governmental committee structure. The most senior and most powerful committee in the country is the Revolutionary Command Council (RCC). Both the Council of Ministers and the National Assembly are subservient to the Revolutionary Command Council. More important from the view of economic policy-making are a number of major committees of the RCC, committees whose membership can include officials who are not members of the RCC. These committees include the Higher Committee for Energy, the Trade Regulating Council, the Economic Planning Council and the Foreign Economic Relations Committee, as well as a Budget Committee. All of these can be involved in making decisions on industrial strategies and priorities and in determining major policy issues—such as the projected energy requirement of Iraqi industry, policy on import substitution, factory location, manpower requirements, the countries from which the necessary technology will be sought and how much money should be allocated for industry.

A product of the various committee decisions and recommendations at this stage is the national economic plan. Iraq has had thirty years' experience of economic planning, starting with the independent development board set up in 1950. The Ministry of Planning was set up by the revolutionary government in 1958. The first full five-year plan covered the fiscal years 1965 to 1969 inclusive. This plan was followed in turn by the 1970-5 Development Plan and the 1976-80 Development Plan; a new plan was about to be announced on the eve of the war with Iran. The result of Iraq's lengthy experience in planning is a very high degree of professional competence among senior Iraqi planning officials. The Ministry of Planning developed during the 1970s as one of the more effective and hence more powerful Iraqi ministries, a process which was halted in July 1979 when the then planning minister was arrested and executed for what were alleged to be pro-Syrian sentiments. An announced plan is the basis of industrial decision-making, a process taken a step further by the preparation of annual budgets, in which, of course, the Ministry of Finance has a major role. Once the director-general of a state organisation in the industrial sector has the sanction of a development plan and an annual budget behind him, he can, through appropriate committees, initiate action to implement his plan targets within the framework of his budget allocations.

In the experience of foreign businessmen negotiating with Iraqi committees the salient feature of Iraq's decision-making process is the fear which permeates the system. The penalties for making a wrong decision, and especially a wrong decision involving a foreign company, are severe in Iraq. Iraqi negotiating committees almost always include among their members officials with very great technical and professional competence as well as very great negotiating skill, but these skills do not hide the overriding fear. This fear, and the bureaucracy which gets much of its motivation from fear, permeates throughout the Iraqi industrial decision-making hierarchy. No factory manager dare make a unilateral decision. It is virtually impossible for a factory manager to dismiss a worker. Decisions on relatively minor matters such as routine preventative maintenance, or even ordering a spare part for a machine, involve a complex bureaucratic process involving many signatures. The provision of adequate volumes of spare parts to ensure continuous running is one of the major problem-areas of Iraqi industry. It is not unreasonable that raw material specifications and production schedules be approved by a committee, but for normal efficient industrial management an industrial manager needs to have the authority to resolve minor crises in his factory without elaborate paperwork and without the need to summon a committee.

It can be argued that the complex procedures in Iraq's decision-making process do not matter in the short term, and that as long as Iraq is acquiring technology and operating within a wholly closed economy, untouched by foreign competition on price, the fact of relative inefficiency in certain aspects of the industrial management process does not really matter. There is a certain force in this argument. There is no concept of profit, and in general the quality of Iraqi manufactured products at least compares with that of a broad range of competing imported products. A national policy of price control masks any price-differential. Again, it can be argued with considerable force that the war with Iran demonstrated that the Iraqi system does work, that the lessons learned from the East Germans (basically, how to retain efficiency in a decision-by-committee environment) have been learned, that Iraq has acquired technology and that Iraqi engineers, for example, performed what were almost minor miracles of adaptation and innovation in repairing war-damage in the oilfields and in the electric-power generation and distribution sector.

While in the short run the inefficiencies may be written off as part of the price paid for political stability and the preservation of a political philosophy, however, an efficient use of capital will become essential the moment Iraq tries to export significant production from its factories onto world and regional markets. The competition at that stage will not be from Western industries so much as from the highly capital-efficient industries in countries such as Singapore and Taiwan.

Notes

1. This chapter has been developed from a research project carried out during the last six months in 1980 and concentrating on the business environment of contemporary Iraq seen through the eyes of foreign businessmen and technologists working in Iraq. The main research project was based on fifty detailed questionnaires completed by foreign companies operating in Iraq and was backed up by field-work in Iraq in November 1980. As information was given to the writer in confidence, it will not be possible to provide references for most of the material presented.

Any serious study of contemporary Iraq is hampered by the lack of information, and particularly statistical information, on all aspects of economic development. Much official published material tends to be more of a public relations exercise than an attempt to give precise facts.

2. E. Penrose and E.F. Penrose, *Iraq: International Relations and National Development* (Ernest Benn, London, 1978), p. 470.

3. Ibid., pp. 471-2.

4. This section relies heavily on the article by M. Sader, 'Industrial Development in Iraq', *Maghreb-Machrek* (Paris), no. 92 (April-May-June 1981), pp. 25-36.

Appendix 1

State Organisations in the Industrial Sector (Serial number in parentheses after each organisation designates 1980 budget serial)

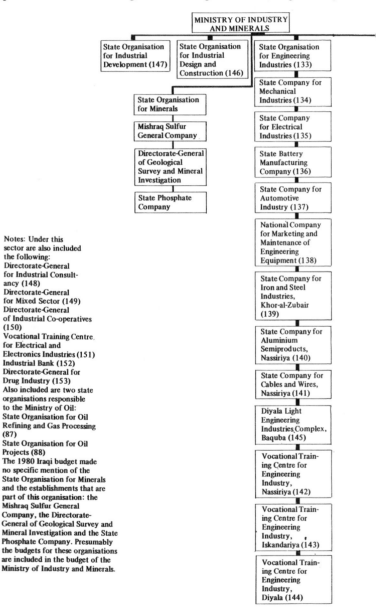

```
                              MINISTRY OF INDUSTRY
                                 AND MINERALS
```

State Organisation for Industrial Development (147)

State Organisation for Industrial Design and Construction (146)

State Organisation for Engineering Industries (133)

State Organisation for Minerals

Mishraq Sulfur General Company

Directorate-General of Geological Survey and Mineral Investigation

State Phosphate Company

State Company for Mechanical Industries (134)

State Company for Electrical Industries (135)

State Battery Manufacturing Company (136)

State Company for Automotive Industry (137)

National Company for Marketing and Maintenance of Engineering Equipment (138)

State Company for Iron and Steel Industries, Khor-al-Zubair (139)

State Company for Aluminium Semiproducts, Nassiriya (140)

State Company for Cables and Wires, Nassiriya (141)

Diyala Light Engineering Industries Complex, Baquba (145)

Vocational Training Centre for Engineering Industry, Nassiriya (142)

Vocational Training Centre for Engineering Industry, Iskandariya (143)

Vocational Training Centre for Engineering Industry, Diyala (144)

Notes: Under this sector are also included the following:
Directorate-General for Industrial Consultancy (148)
Directorate-General for Mixed Sector (149)
Directorate-General of Industrial Co-operatives (150)
Vocational Training Centre for Electrical and Electronics Industries (151)
Industrial Bank (152)
Directorate-General for Drug Industry (153)
Also included are two state organisations responsible to the Ministry of Oil:
State Organisation for Oil Refining and Gas Processing (87)
State Organisation for Oil Projects (88)
The 1980 Iraqi budget made no specific mention of the State Organisation for Minerals and the establishments that are part of this organisation: the Mishraq Sulfur General Company, the Directorate-General of Geological Survey and Mineral Investigation and the State Phosphate Company. Presumably the budgets for these organisations are included in the budget of the Ministry of Industry and Minerals.

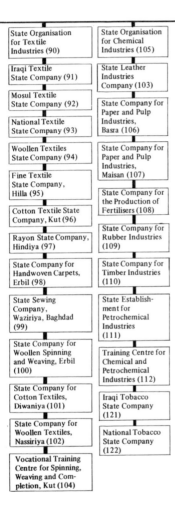

State Organisation for Textile Industries (90)

State Organisation for Chemical Industries (105)

Iraqi Textile State Company (91)

State Leather Industries Company (103)

Mosul Textile State Company (92)

State Company for Paper and Pulp Industries, Basra (106)

National Textile State Company (93)

State Company for Paper and Pulp Industries, Maisan (107)

Woollen Textiles State Company (94)

Fine Textile State Company, Hilla (95)

State Company for the Production of Fertilisers (108)

Cotton Textile State Company, Kut (96)

State Company for Rubber Industries (109)

Rayon State Company, Hindiya (97)

State Company for Timber Industries (110)

State Company for Handwoven Carpets, Erbil (98)

State Sewing Company, Waziriya, Baghdad (99)

State Establishment for Petrochemical Industries (111)

State Company for Woollen Spinning and Weaving, Erbil (100)

Training Centre for Chemical and Petrochemical Industries (112)

State Company for Cotton Textiles, Diwaniya (101)

Iraqi Tobacco State Company (121)

State Company for Woollen Textiles, Nassiriya (102)

National Tobacco State Company (122)

Vocational Training Centre for Spinning, Weaving and Completion, Kut (104)

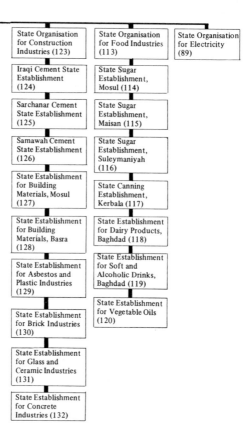

Appendix 2

Revenue and Expenditure of State Organisations in the Industrial Sector, 1980

Budget Serial	State Organisation	Expenditure (Iraqi dinars)	Revenue
	INDUSTRIAL SECTOR		
87	State Organisation for Oil Refining and Gas Processing	142,732,210	113,385,320
88	State Organisation for Oil Projects	11,508,740	5,029,930
89	State Organisation for Electricity	66,147,000	51,347,000
90	State Organisation for Textile Industries	985,880	985,880
91	Iraqi Textile State Company	11,166,096	11,784,195
92	Mosul Textile State Company	7,649,300	7,455,000
93	National Textile State Company	12,005,572	12,649,913
94	Woollen Textiles State Company	14,515,397	13,515,986
95	Fine Textile State Company, Hilla	7,273,138	8,044,636
96	Cotton Textile State Company, Kut	11,837,900	11,864,911
97	Rayon State Company, Hindiya	5,510,818	5,071,520
98	State Company for Handwoven Carpets, Erbil	821,309	457,420
99	State Sewing Company, Waziriya, Baghdad	11,721,040	11,519,887
100	State Company for Woollen Spinning and Weaving, Erbil	2,271,950	2,935,500
101	State Company for Cotton Textiles, Diwaniya	7,009,412	9,235,924
102	State Company for Woollen Textiles, Nassiriya	2,006,550	971,730
103	State Leather Industries Company	22,694,500	23,826,000
104	Vocational Training Centre for Spinning, Weaving and Completion, Kut	310,150	310,150
105	State Organisation for Chemical Industries	897,000	750,000
106	State Company for Paper and Pulp Industries, Basra	16,644,700	17,663,200
107	State Company for Paper and Pulp Industries, Maisan	10,751,098	11,214,325
108	State Company for the Production of Fertilisers	18,959,035	46,339,120
109	State Company for Rubber Industries	4,608,513	4,730,894
110	State Company for Timber Industries	852,000	758,000
111	State Establishment for Petrochemical Industries	8,979,000	10,984,000
112	Training Centre for Chemical and Petro-chemical Industries	1,574,500	2,125,500
113	State Organisation for Food Industries	734,300	719,500
114	State Sugar Establishment, Mosul	29,461,373	24,311,104
115	State Sugar Establishment, Maisan	17,081,026	14,039,274
116	State Sugar Establishment, Suleymaniyah	11,339,368	9,784,155
117	State Canning Establishment, Kerbala	24,510,000	24,462,800
118	State Establishment for Dairy Products, Baghdad	30,450,114	26,889,388

Budget Serial	State Organisation	Expenditure	Revenue
	INDUSTRIAL SECTOR	(Iraqi dinars)	
119	State Establishment for Soft and Alcoholic Drinks	27,153,000	28,452,000
120	State Establishment for Vegetable Oils	65,474,000	64,572,000
121	Iraqi Tobacco State Company	34,307,500	37,879,000
122	National Tobacco State Company	39,216,344	36,521,150
123	State Organisation for Construction Industries	2,152,170	2,019,570
124	Iraqi Cement State Establishment	29,448,370	30,494,886
125	Sarchanar Cement State Establishment	2,339,650	2,438,500
126	Samawa Cement State Establishment	9,552,325	10,514,411
127	State Establishment for Building Materials, Mosul	15,463,375	15,133,200
128	State Establishment for Building Materials, Basra	4,873,290	4,383,190
129	State Establishment for Asbestos and Plastic Industries	18,183,201	18,116,769
130	State Establishment for Brick Industries	6,642,450	9,615,250
131	State Establishment for Glass and Ceramic Industries	6,598,443	6,643,668
132	State Establishment for Concrete Industries	9,429,290	9,704,161
133	State Organisation for Engineering Industries	675,425	684,425
134	State Company for Mechanical Industries	23,006,443	24,824,020
135	State Company for Electrical Industries	11,499,147	12,658,470
136	State Battery Manufacturing Company	6,926,131	8,968,653
137	State Company for Automotive Industry	81,492,420	85,907,272
138	National Company for Marketing and Maintenance of Engineering Equipment	11,734,880	16,775,380
139	State Company for Iron and Steel Industries	46,667,315	50,965,000
140	State Company for Aluminium Semiproducts	16,690,819	16,282,323
141	State company for Cables and Wires, Nassiriya	11,671,719	13,400,951
142	Vocational Training Centre for Engineering Industry, Nassiriya	836,500	1,224,500
143	Vocational Training Centre for Engineering Industry, Iskandariya	674,926	719,926
144	Vocational Training Centre for Electrical Industry, Diyala	905,760	1,053,260
145	Diyala Light Engineering Industries Complex, Baquba	7,214,357	8,207,612
146	State Organisation for Industrial Design and Construction	2,406,000	2,449,000
147	State Organisation for Industrial Development	236,550	224,600
148	Directorate-General for Industrial Consultancy	334,810	334,810
149	Directorate-General for Mixed-Sector Firms' Affairs	127,050	95,100
150	Directorate-General of Industrial Complexes and Co-operatives	272,600	240,650

Budget Serial	State Organisation	Expenditure	Revenue
		(Iraqi dinars)	
	INDUSTRIAL SECTOR		
151	Vocational Training Centre for Electrical and Electronics Industries	228,900	196,950
152	Industrial Bank	29,679,820	3,784,500
153	Directorate-General for Drug Industry	21,500,000	12,000,000
	Total industrial sector	1,060,623,969	1,022,647,169

CONTRIBUTORS

Amal al-Sharqi is Director-General of Children Culture, Baghdad.

H.G. Balfour-Paul is Research Fellow at the Centre for Arab Gulf Studies, University of Exeter.

J.S. Birks, formerly Research Fellow at the Department of Economics, University of Durham, is currently working for the World Bank.

Sa'ad Jawad is Lecturer in Politics at the University of Baghdad.

Peter Mansfield is a freelance journalist and writer on the Middle East.

Tim Niblock is Deputy Director for the Centre for Arab Gulf Studies at the University of Exeter.

Amal Rassam is Associate Professor at the Anthropology Department, City.University, New York.

Barry Rubin is Fellow at Georgetown University's Center for Strategic and International Studies, and a professorial lecturer at Georgetown School of Foreign Service.

Naomi Sakr is Economics Editor of *Arabia* magazine.

C. Sinclair, formerly Research Fellow at the Department of Economics, University of Durham, is currently working for the World Bank.

Alya Sousa is Lecturer in History at the University of Baghdad.

Paul Stevens is Lecturer in Economics at the University of Surrey.

Joe Stork is editor of *MERIP reports.*

Robin Theobald is Senior Lecturer in Sociology at the Polytechnic of Central London.

John Townsend is a former Economic Adviser to the Sultanate of Oman, and currently works for Business International.

Rodney Wilson is Lecturer in Economics at the University of Durham.

INDEX